The Grover E. Murray Studies in the American Southwest

Also in the series

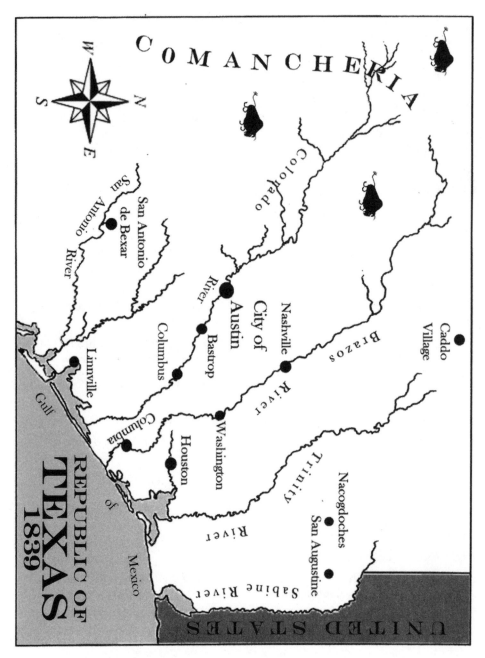

Map of Austin area, 1839. Courtesy of the author.

SEAT OF EMPIRE

THE EMBATTLED BIRTH OF AUSTIN, TEXAS

JEFFREY STUART KERR

TEXAS TECH UNIVERSITY PRESS

This book is typeset in Monotype Amasis. The paper used in this book meets
the minimum requirements of ANSI/NISO Z39.48–1992 (R1997). ∞

Designed by Kasey McBeath

On the cover: (top left) Mirabeau Lamar, courtesy the San Jacinto Museum of
History, Houston, Texas; (top right) Sam Houston, courtesy the George Eastman
House; (center) detail from Austin's original city plan, c. 1839, courtesy the Tex-
as State Archives; (bottom) view of Austin, c. 1860, courtesy the Dolph Briscoe
Center for American History, the University of Texas at Austin, CN12190.

Library of Congress Cataloging-in-Publication Data
Kerr, Jeffrey Stuart, 1957–
Seat of empire : the embattled birth of Austin, Texas / Jeffrey Stuart Kerr.
pages cm. — (The Grover E. Murray Studies in the American Southwest)
Includes bibliographical references and index.
ISBN 978-0-89672-782-3 (hardcover : alk. paper) — ISBN 978-0-89672-783-0
(e-book) 1. Austin (Tex.)—History. 2. Texas—Capital and capitol—History.
I. Title.
F394.A957K475 2013
976.4'31—dc23   2013011214

Printed in the United States of America
13 14 15 16 17 18 19 20 21 / 9 8 7 6 5 4 3 2 1

Texas Tech University Press
Box 41037 | Lubbock, Texas 79409–1037 USA
800.832.4042 | ttup@ttu.edu | www.ttupress.org

In memory of the men, women,
and children forcibly evicted from and carried
to frontier Austin and its territory

CONTENTS

ILLUSTRATIONS

SEAT OF EMPIRE

INTRODUCTION

Want of political unity is the one consistent theme threading its way through the fabric of early Anglo-Texan history. Seemingly no action occurred without bitter squabbling beforehand and angry finger-pointing after the fact. That an independent Texas emerged from those hectic days, given the divided goals and loyalties afflicting the leaders of the Texas Revolution, is nothing short of remarkable.

A split command at the Alamo certainly added little to the effectiveness of its garrison as a fighting unit. Then, after the Alamo disaster, General Sam Houston drew charges of cowardice as he led his army on a tactical retreat toward the east. Realizing that two of his officers had no intention of obeying orders to retreat beyond the Brazos River town of San Felipe, he instead *ordered* them to stay at the Brazos to delay the enemy advance. Bickering continued right through the decisive Battle of San Jacinto. Many officers and men in Houston's army believed strongly that Houston had turned toward Santa Anna's army instead of retreating into Louisiana only because they had forced him to do so at a critical road junction. Mirabeau Lamar, who figures prominently in this book, claimed that the successful charge against the Mexican camp had been launched over Houston's objections. For years after the battle men exchanged heated words over whether Sam Houston's actions had constituted cowardice or heroism. The fact that few minds were changed by these arguments planted the seeds for the growth of two political camps in the nascent republic.

Victory in the revolution did little to quell strife. Santa Anna's life would have ended in front of a Texian firing squad if many, Mirabeau Lamar included, had had their way. When President David Burnet named Lamar Commander-in-Chief of the army, enough soldiers balked that Lamar quickly resigned. Burnet himself resigned not long thereafter due to plausible threats of a military overthrow. One of Sam Houston's initial actions as the first elected President of the Republic, therefore, was to begin furloughing as many soldiers as possible.

The 1836 election that installed Sam Houston as President of the Republic also ushered Mirabeau Lamar onto the national stage as Houston's vice president. A more unfortunate pairing can hardly be imagined. Tall and athletic, outgoing, and at the time still prone to drunkenness, Houston struck Lamar as an overrated demagogue. Short and squat, taciturn, and sober, Lamar impressed Houston as a bumbling fool. Although they may have encountered each other along the march to San Jacinto, the two men first came into more direct contact on the battlefield itself. When Lamar's bold action during a skirmish the day before the battle saved two lives, General Houston offered him command of the artillery. Lamar declined. Later, though, when several cavalrymen and officers insisted that Lamar lead the cavalry in the upcoming battle, he agreed to do so. Houston later expressed puzzlement rather than annoyance at all this, but it was an inauspicious start to the pair's relationship.

Two early issues in Texas politics served to augment the personal enmity between Sam Houston and Mirabeau Lamar. The first concerned the republic's indigenous population. Sam Houston pushed for accommodation, especially with the Cherokee, with whom he had lived on two separate occasions. Mirabeau Lamar believed the Cherokee to be intruders without rights to the Texas land on which they squatted. After succeeding Houston as president in 1838, Lamar implemented policies that resulted in the violent deaths of people that Houston knew and liked. This can only have deepened the personal divide between the two men.

Another contentious issue that brought Houston and Lamar into direct conflict—and the focus of this book—was the location of the republic's capital, which in turn fostered disputes about the pace of western expansion. Caught up in the self-righteous fervor of his age, Mirabeau Lamar envisioned a Texas empire stretching to the Pacific Ocean. As a first step toward realizing his dream, President Lamar pushed hard for moving the seat of government to the western frontier. Taking a more practical approach, Sam Houston fought to keep government back east, preferring to consolidate the republic's hold on the land it had already settled rather than expanding further into Indian and Mexican territory. These antithetical viewpoints helped solidify Texas political factions into something more than personality-based supporter groups.

Many, if not most, Texas cities resulted not from pioneers settling randomly around a convenient water source, but from someone's specific plan. Such had been the case with the city of Houston, created by New York land speculators John and Augustus Allen on the banks of Buffalo Bayou in 1836. Savvy politicking by the Allen brothers gained the new city status as temporary Texas capital, a designation set by law to expire in 1840. The ensuing effort to locate the seat of government thereafter quickly developed into one of the first major political battles of the republic, with President Sam Houston and Vice President Mirabeau Lamar firmly entrenched on opposite sides of the debate. As chief executive, Sam Houston held the initial advantage but Lamar's assumption of the presidency in 1838 transformed the political landscape. Shortly thereafter scores of workmen journeyed from Houston to a remote spot on the upper Colorado River to build a new capital city from scratch. Such were the beginnings of Austin.

Seat of Empire tells the story of Austin's creation against the backdrop of early Texas politics and the extraordinary struggle between two Texas giants, Sam Houston and Mirabeau Lamar. I have aimed the book at general readers of Texas history but have also included numerous annotations and bibliographic references for those wishing for more detail. The tale is entertaining, yet important, for a different outcome would have left us with a much different modern state of Texas. The city of Austin was born in 1839, almost died in the early 1840s, and sprang back to life thereafter. But for a few twists and turns of history, my current hometown would likely not exist, the southern Rockies would be Texas mountains, and we would remember Mirabeau Lamar, rather than Sam Houston, as the political Titan of his age. But it does, and they aren't, and we don't.

The explanation begins with a buffalo hunt.

Chapter 1

MIRABEAU LAMAR'S BUFFALO

I n the fall of 1838, the tiny hamlet of Waterloo, Texas welcomed the most important visitor in its brief history. At the time, the town had not yet even been incorporated, Congress not taking that step until the following January. Lying farther up the Colorado River than any other Anglo settlement, Waterloo presented a humble appearance to the dignitary and his entourage.[1] Only a few log cabins scattered around the mouth of Shoal Creek greeted Willis Avery, James C. Rice, and four other Texas Rangers along as guardians against Indian attack. The Reverend Edward Fontaine, friend of the important man, accompanied the group, and may have had his slave Jacob with him.[2] Commanding the greatest attention, however, was the Georgia native, San Jacinto hero, and highest ranking member of the entourage, Mirabeau B. Lamar, Vice President of the Republic of Texas.

Lamar coveted the presidency. He seemed fated to get it. His most formidable political opponent, President Sam Houston, was constitutionally barred from succeeding himself. Incredibly, two other leading challengers, Peter Grayson and James Collinsworth, had committed suicide within two days of each other. On July 9, while traveling through Tennessee, the unstable Grayson wrote a note begging his landlord to "pardon the frightful scene I have made in your house" and "blew his braines out with a pistol." After Supreme Court Chief Justice James Collinsworth publicly announced his candidacy on June 30, he went on a drinking spree that culminated July 11 in his jumping or falling off a boat into Galveston Bay. Most people believed his drowning death was a suicide.[3]

Lamar thus seemed a guaranteed victor in the coming election. His friends, however, urged him to take nothing for granted. In June Senator Albert C. Horton, a vice-presidential candidate, advised a trip west to court the frontier vote. Judge James Webb also saw political advantage in a western journey:

> It is the opinion of several of your friends with whom I have conversed, that a trip up the Country would be serviceable to you. I think so too— there is no telling what impression may be made on the minds of the

people on the eve of the Election—you know by whom the effort will be made, if made at all, & you therefore know in what section of the Country to expect it—in Houston & all the lower part of the Country, there is no danger.[4]

Lamar evidently saw wisdom in his friends' advice, for he made the risky journey. Once at Bastrop he was well into dangerous frontier territory. After leaving the town and crossing the Colorado River, the vice president and his companions meandered through a lush landscape of tall grass and scattered woods before fording the river again and stopping at Josiah Wilbarger's place on Wilbarger Creek. The party then traversed Webber's Prairie, passed Hornsby's Bend, and paused to rest at Fort Coleman on Walnut Creek. The stockade most likely offered little protection. After its abandonment the preceding April, local residents had quickly begun dismantling its walls and blockhouses to make use of the lumber in other construction projects.[5] Once beyond the remains of the fort, the party waded through several more miles of grassland before reaching Waterloo.

Although Edward Burleson had laid out the town of Waterloo early in 1838, Tennessee native Jacob Harrell was the first Anglo to occupy the site. Harrell and his wife Mary brought their four children to Texas in 1833, settling among Reuben Hornsby's clan at Hornsby's Bend. Two years later Harrell erected a tent several miles upriver on the Colorado's north shore near the mouth of Shoal Creek. Because this spot in the river formed a natural low-water crossing, he likely knew that it lay along an ancient Indian trail long used by travelers heading north and west through the hills.[6]

By 1838 Jacob Harrell had constructed a split-log stockade to replace the tent and moved his family to their new home. Several families followed suit.[7] No Anglo community lay upriver from Harrell and his immediate neighbors; the tiny settlement defined the frontier's extreme edge.

As any good political campaigner must, Mirabeau Lamar quickly joined in local custom upon his arrival in Waterloo. For Jacob Harrell and other frontiersmen, this meant hunting. One morning as Lamar, Harrell, and the others breakfasted in Harrell's cabin, one of Harrell's sons burst into the room with the exciting news that the prairie was "full of buffalo."[8] Quickly astride their mounts, the men rode the short distance to a ravine which intersected the Colorado River. To their delight they encountered great numbers of the mammoth beasts and wasted no time in shooting as many as they could.

With the right weapon a buffalo is easy to kill. Because of its poor vision, it relies primarily on its sense of smell to detect danger. Thus, if a hunter stays upwind and possesses a rifle powerful enough to send a ball through the animal's thick hide, it is possible to pick off large numbers one by one without the surrounding members of the herd sensing danger. When he hunted for food or hides, the Anglo settler preferred this method.[9]

For sport the hunter chose a more thrilling technique. Armed with one or more single-shot pistols, he charged on horseback through the herd while blazing away at the fleeing beasts. At the bottom of the ravine bisecting the prairie near Waterloo, Mirabeau Lamar chased and shot "with his holster pistol" the largest buffalo bull one of his companions had ever seen.[10]

Later, one of the hunters blew a bugle to gather the men atop a hill at the head of the ravine. From the summit stretched a view "which would give delight to every painter and lover of extended landscape." A German traveler later described the scenery as idyllic, while an 1840 immigrant called it "a fairy land." A year after Lamar's visit Thomas Bell wrote home to his brother: "I must consider this the most beautiful country I ever saw what I have yet seen. There is some of the most beautiful lands I ever beheld or ever expect to." James Jones, in an 1839 letter to Lamar, expressed equal enthusiasm: "We are marching through a beautiful country—its face presents a scene of grandeur and magnificence rarely if ever witnessed I imagine in any other part of the American Continent."[11]

Mirabeau Lamar, politician, farmer, adventurer, and military hero, was also a poet. One imagines him regarding with awe the stunning beauty before him as he looked down the hill toward the Colorado River. Perhaps he composed inner verse as he gazed upon the "woodlands and luxuriant Prairies" straddling the waterway. Small hills in the foreground wore crowns of post oak, blackjack, elm, and live oak trees. Thickets of dogwood, hackberry, elm, and live oak blanketed the river bottom. Framing Lamar's view to either side were two "beautiful streams of clear water."[12]

In the short span of three years Mirabeau Lamar had escaped personal despair, obscurity, and political humiliation to attain a position of prestige and power. Barring disaster, he would soon command an embryonic nation destined for greatness. He had just finished a thrilling buffalo hunt in which he had distinguished himself by bringing down an enormous animal, the largest at least one companion had ever seen. He now admired with his poetic eye natural beauty which had consistently stunned far cruder and less imaginative men than himself. Faced with this awe-inspiring vista, Vice President Mirabeau Buonaparte Lamar announced that day an ambitious dream to fellow hunters Jacob Harrell, Willis Avery, Edward Fontaine, James Rice, four Texas Rangers, and maybe the slave Jacob when he cried from the hilltop, "This should be the seat of future empire!"[13]

Austin's hilly topography is evident in this circa 1860 view of the city from the southeast. The Colorado River flows in the foreground, fed by Waller Creek at lower right. The 1853 capitol dominates the town from its position atop the hill from which Mirabeau Lamar became enamored of the region in 1838.
Courtesy of OP1, Austin, Texas, CN12190, the Dolph Briscoe
Center for American History, University of Texas at Austin.

| Chapter 2 |

THE NOMADIC GOVERNMENT

Away with song, and away with charms!
Insulted Freedom's proud avenger,
I bear no love but the love of arms,
And the bride that I woo is DANGER.

From *Give to the Poet His Well-Earned Praise*, Mirabeau B. Lamar

Just three years before his breakfast in Jacob Harrell's Colorado River cabin, Mirabeau Lamar entered the Mexican territory of Texas an unknown. True, he had once occupied a seat in the Georgia state Senate, but his wife's death and two subsequent lost elections had soured the forty-year-old Lamar on life in the Peach State. Thus, the man who followed fellow Georgian James Fannin's footsteps westward across the Sabine River in July 1835 carried dual burdens of wrenching sadness and humbling defeat.[1] No one in Texas knew the name of Lamar, and no one in Texas would have recognized the short, stocky character as he rode through, and fell in love with, the territory's countryside.

Violence loomed in Lamar's new land. American immigrants, never Mexican patriots, chafed under what they perceived as alien and despotic rule. Mexican authorities in turn resented the ingratitude and unruliness of the foreigners in their midst. Lamar quickly sided with the Anglos. He attended a political meeting at the Brazos River town of Washington at which he announced support for Texas independence. He also "contributed [his] mite toward erecting a fort at Velasco" before journeying back to Georgia to close out his life there.[2]

Before completing this business, however, Lamar received word of Santa Anna's invasion of Texas. Desperate to involve himself in the fight to come, he rushed back to join the rebels.[3] Unable to procure a horse after arriving at Velasco, he hurried ahead on foot until, on April 12, he encountered Sam Houston's revolutionary army at Jared Groce's plantation on the Brazos River. Joining the cause as a private soldier, Lamar participated in the retreat to the east that he later derided as "running from an enemy without wasting time to ascertain his numbers."[4]

Private Lamar tasted his first glory in a cavalry skirmish April 20, 1836, the day before the fateful battle at San Jacinto. During this fight, Mexican lancers surrounded Colonel Thomas Rusk, secretary of war in the revolutionary cabinet. Lamar "saw Colonel Rusk's situation, and made a dash at one of the lancers, run against him, knock[ed] down the lancer and his horse, and ma[de] an opening for the escape of Colonel Rusk." This action cost Lamar a painful knee contusion, suffered when his leg collided with the pommel of the Mexican's saddle. Lamar then saved another comrade, nineteen-year-old Walter Lane, who fell from his horse at the charge of one of the Mexicans. Momentarily stunned, a defenseless Lane lay on the ground at the mercy of his assailant. Lamar raced his horse toward the Texan and shot the enemy soldier before he could deliver a death blow to Lane. Company commander Henry Karnes then swooped in to bear Lane away from danger.[5]

Sam Houston offered to reward Mirabeau Lamar's heroism with command of the artillery. Lamar declined because "he did not wish to deprive the officers already belonging to that Corps of the honor which they would certainly win that day." Colonel Rusk next bade Lamar to join his staff as aide-de-camp, to which Lamar agreed. Very shortly thereafter, however, Rusk's new assistant acceded to the calls of several cavalry officers and men to instead lead them in the coming fight.[6] Colonel Mirabeau Lamar thus rode at the head of General Houston's cavalry during the decisive victory of April 21.

No Texian soldier pitied the hundreds of bloated Mexican corpses splayed in the muck of Peggy McCormick's league of land on the San Jacinto River. Fired by the same passion guiding the pen of the anonymous poet previously quoted, these men had surprised and then obliterated the army of the hated tyrant Santa Anna. Mexican resistance dissolved within minutes of the initial Texian charge. Panicked soldiers attempted flight but, hemmed in by water on three sides, presented easy targets for the revenge-minded rebels. The attackers shot, clubbed, and stabbed to death over six hundred men, many of whom died while attempting to surrender. At least one Mexican woman succumbed in the onslaught, run through with a sword by Colonel John Forbes.[7] Eleven Texans perished.

Five days after the rout, Sam Houston caught a furious verbal blast from landowner Peggy McCormick. Complaining that their bodies would haunt her forever, the Irishwoman demanded their immediate removal.

When Houston pointed out the newfound historical significance of her property, Mrs. McCormick cut him off: "To the devil with your glorious history! Take off your stinking Mexicans." That night eleven-year-old Dilue Harris camped with her family in the vicinity and recalled years later, "[we] could hear the wolves howl and bark as they devoured the dead."[8]

Mirabeau Lamar favored adding one more body to the pile. After Santa Anna's capture he composed a letter recommending the Mexican president's execution as a "murderer, tyrant, and enemy to the human race." An anonymous poem in the *Telegraph and Texas Register* vividly summed up the feelings of many Texans:

> Back, back to the covert, thou blood hound of death,
> There is woe in thy footstep, and guilt in thy breath;
> Thou warrest with women, thou curse of the brave,
> Thy pity is blood, and thy mercy the grave.
> But soon the read hour of avenging shall come
> When thy cheek will be bleached and thy utterance dumb.
> When thy arm shall be palsied, encrimsoned with gore,
> And the cold sweat of terror escape from each pore.

Sam Houston and others, however, preferred exploiting a humiliated captive over creating a patriotic martyr, and the Napoleon of the West eventually returned to Mexico to rule again. [9]

Between declaring independence March 2, 1836, and arriving at Houston April 16, 1837, the Texas government occupied no less than six locations.[10] Abandoning San Felipe de Austin because of its vulnerability to Mexican attack, the Texian rebels assembled at Washington March 1, 1836. John Hall, Asa Hoxey, Thomas Gay, and the Miller and Somervell Company had sold Washington's first town lots adjacent to the Brazos River in 1835. The next year, town businessmen rented the largest structure available from owner Noah Byars, and lured the convention by offering it as a cost-free assembly hall.[11]

Visitors to modern Washington-on-the-Brazos State Historic Site find only a single building on the former town site.[12] A sloping meadow of wildflowers and prickly pears fills the landscape between a reconstructed Independence Hall and the old Brazos River ferry crossing. One hundred seventy-seven years ago about fifty houses dotted the grid of streets which crisscrossed this meadow. Arriving members of the Texas provisional government competed for lodging in the town's only inn.[13] On March 1, they gathered in Byars's simple one-room frame construction to debate their future.

Independence Hall
Washington on the Brazos

The Texas Declaration of Independence was signed in this Washington building in 1836. President Sam Houston moved the government from Austin to Washington in 1842. Congress met here until its return to Austin three years later. Courtesy of Prints & Photographs Collection, Texas Capitols-Early, CN03742, the Dolph Briscoe Center for American History, University of Texas at Austin.

"I now think the time has come for Texas to assert her natural rights; and were I in the Convention I would urge an immediate Declaration of Independence." That Stephen F. Austin, the man who had brought so many of the settlers to Texas, could write these words in his January 7, 1836, letter to General Sam Houston carried great weight. Austin had long counseled patience, but now even his had run out. It was therefore no surprise when, shortly after the delegates convened on March 1, George Childress proposed forming a committee to draft a declaration of independence. The following day the convention unanimously approved the committee's declaration, which self-righteously proclaimed, "The necessity of self-preservation, therefore, now decrees our eternal political separation. . . . Our political connection with the Mexican nation has forever ended. . . . The people of Texas do now constitute a free, sovereign, and independent republic."[14]

Over the next fifteen days the delegates wrote a constitution and elected an interim government. The constitution stipulated only that "the presidents and heads of departments shall keep their offices at the seat of government" but did not assign a site. Newly elected President David Burnet selected Harrisburg, a town on the banks of Buffalo Bayou to the east. Burnet insisted that "removal is not the result of any apprehension that the enemy is near us." Addressing Congress, he explained that from Harrisburg his administration "could possess an easier access to foreign countries, from whence our supplies of munitions were to be obtained, and a more direct supervision of its naval and other maritime concerns." General Sam Houston thought otherwise. Responding to Burnet's blast that "the enemy are laughing you to scorn [for retreating]," Houston sneeringly referred to Burnet's removal as "the flight of the wise men."[15]

Headlong flight or strategic withdrawal, Burnet's move put him out of Santa Anna's reach. But not for long. After burning the plantation of William Stafford, Mexican troops reached Harrisburg the night of April 15. Santa Anna had earlier written to General Jose de Urrea, "I have decided to leave for Harrisburg with one section, where the principal leaders of the rebellion are located." Burnet and the Cabinet, however, just did escape. The temporary capital then paid a severe price for hosting the rebel government. One of Santa Anna's officers recorded in his diary on April 19, "Yesterday Castillo Iberry also marched, having stated that the commander-in-chief, greatly annoyed at having failed in the plan he had prepared against the revolutionary heads congregated at Harrisburg . . . ordered him to set fire to this township, and that his Excellency personally lent a hand in its destruction."[16]

Burnet and the Cabinet next met on Galveston Island, which the President called "the last hope of the defense of Texas." On April 26 he received the good news of Sam Houston's stunning victory at San Jacinto five days earlier. The crew of the steamer *Yellow Stone* then required five days to bring aboard enough wood for the journey inland, but on May 1 deposited Burnet and the department heads at the victorious army's camp on Buffalo Bayou. Only a few days later the government was back aboard the *Yellow Stone* for a return trip to Galveston, this time accompanied by Sam Houston, Santa Anna, and most of the captured Mexican officers.[17]

Chosen during a crisis, Galveston Island had no facilities for housing a national government. Burnet later explained, "The entire want of accommodation at the Island rendered it necessary for the government to seek some place where the ordinary office business could be transacted." Shortly after arriving in Galveston, therefore, the nomadic government traveled down the coast to Velasco, and its "delightful sea-breezes, sea-bathing, and the comforts with which [visitors] are everywhere surrounded." Despite the sea-breezes, Velasco served the needs of the government little better than Galveston. A scarcity of oil for lighting at times drove the assembly outdoors. President Burnet, in his first address to Congress, stated the obvious: "Never have they [the government] been in circumstances of comfort and convenience suitable to the orderly conducting of the grave and momentous business committed to their charge."[18]

In search of a more suitable capital, David Burnet next looked to the Brazoria County town of Columbia and its three thousand "intelligent and moral people." On July 23 he issued a proclamation calling Congress to session at the new government seat the first Monday in October 1836.[19] Until then, Velasco would have to suffice.

Meanwhile, Texas citizens overwhelmingly voted for San Jacinto hero Sam Houston in the republic's first presidential election. Houston had feigned indifference when announcing his candidacy,[20] perhaps in deference to the respect most voters felt for his main opponent, Stephen F. Austin. Outdistancing the popular empresario by an almost seven-to-one margin, Houston received the oath of office at Columbia. The inauguration occurred several weeks ahead of schedule. Houston's predecessor and political enemy David Burnet, having already suppressed one attempted military overthrow of his administration, suddenly resigned his interim position October 22 with the request that "the congress will not consider my incumbency as any obstacle to the immediate inauguration of the executive officers elect."[21] Caught by surprise, Houston had only four hours to compose a speech for the ceremony later that same day. Burnet ally Mirabeau Lamar assumed the vice presidency.

At about this time, twenty-one-year-old Frank Lubbock arrived in Columbia from his native South Carolina in search of his brother Tom, who had been sucked into the whirlwind of the Revolution.[22] Lubbock encountered a primitive frontier town in which each house of Congress met in a small frame building and his only available lodging option was to spread his blankets under a live oak tree near the tavern. His experience belied the optimistic sentiment expressed in the *Telegraph and Texas Register*,[23] now operating in Columbia, of September 28, "Yesterday the citizens of this place appointed a committee to prepare the necessary buildings for the accommodation of Congress; and we believe that suitable and convenient rooms will be furnished." President Sam Houston bluntly asserted November 7, "The present position of our Government is one of great inconvenience and absolute embarrassment." Foreshadowing yet

After the Battle of San Jacinto in April 1836, President David Burnet moved the Texas government from Galveston to Velasco and, in July, to this building in Columbia. When Burnet suddenly resigned in October, Sam Houston, first elected President of the Republic, received the oath of office in Columbia. Courtesy of Prints & Photographs Collection, Texas Capitols, Early, CN12189, the Dolph Briscoe Center for American History, University of Texas at Austin

another move, he added that "business cannot profitably proceed, unless Congress will adjourn to some point, where better accommodations and greater conveniences can be speedily obtained or buildings furnished at this place."[24]

Members of Congress, as inconvenienced as the president, responded promptly. A November 2 joint resolution assigned each house the task of appointing a committee of three to recommend the best location. Nine days later the committees reported that they couldn't agree upon a site. The Senate committee recommended Groce's Retreat on the Brazos River while the House committee preferred Nacogdoches. Recognizing the futility of further disagreement, Congress passed "an act locating temporarily the seat of government" November 14, which invited towns to submit proposals to become the republic's capital.[25]

Citizens of Columbia fought to preserve their town's status. They offered to survey and plat 640 acres at their expense and donate one or two square blocks to the government. Proceeds from the sale of town lots would be split between the town and the republic. Members of Congress, however, might have questioned the town's level of commitment in light of a December 12 notice in the *Telegraph and Texas Register*, which implied that local citizens had failed on their promise to reimburse those who had financed construction of the government buildings then in use.

Thomas Gay of Washington, site of the Declaration of Independence, sought to restore his town's former prominence with a less generous proposal. Washington would donate land "for the erection of such public buildings as may be necessary." Gay recognized his offer's weakness: "Your orator would further say, That he is aware that propositions seemingly more liberal have been made by other individuals similarly circumstanced in other Towns; but your orator believing that public convenience rather than *individual interest* to be, the Great end of your deliberations; thus submits, this his proposition to the consideration of your Honorable body." Thomas Borden and the citizens of Fort Bend pinned their hopes on accessibility: "Your memorialist begs to call attention to the fact that a steam navigation is regularly established from the mouth of the [Brazos] river, and not obstructed at any season of the year by any ordinary event. This advantage of navigation is not *prospective*, but in actual operation."[26]

Interestingly, a letter appearing in the November 23 issue of the *Telegraph and Texas Register* proposed a solution that would be adopted by a later Congress:

> I would enquire whether it would not be as well to remain where we are during the present session of congress, and for that body to select and set apart a certain portion of the public domain, in an eligible situation for the capital, lay off the ground in town lots and sell them at auction, reserving such as may be necessary for all the public departments. And whether we would not by this means raise a sufficient fund to erect all the houses required and by so doing put a stop to all petitions on the subject.

Congress opened a joint session November 30 to settle the matter. Fourteen members nominated a total of fifteen locations. Three ballots left Houston and Washington as serious contenders, with Matagorda a distant third. Houston gained two additional votes on the fourth ballot, giving it a majority of twenty-one out of forty votes cast. On December 15, 1836, President Sam Houston signed into law the act moving the capital to his namesake city. "From and after the first day of April next," the new law directed, "the seat of government for the republic of Texas shall be established at the town of Houston, on Buffalo Bayou, until the end of the session of congress which shall assemble in the year one thousand eight hundred and forty."[27]

In May 1837, John James Audubon stepped off the steamer *Yellow Stone*, ascended the west bank of Buffalo Bayou, and caught his first glimpse of the new town of Houston, capital city of the Republic of Texas. He noticed the desolate appearance of the place, the barren landscape surrounding the town, and the "drunk and hallooing" Indians "stumbling about in the mud in every direction." He strode through a collection of half-finished houses, tents, and roofless buildings to approach the "mansion" of President Sam Houston by sloshing through ankle-deep water. A gathering of Cabinet members welcomed the famed naturalist into a log house consisting of two rooms separated by a dog run.[28] Audubon marveled at the filthy, cluttered anteroom. He noted a small table strewn with paper and writing instruments. Several camp beds and trunks lay haphazardly about the room. Upon Houston's arrival, the men removed to the president's private chamber, which was no cleaner than the anteroom. While impressed with Sam Houston, Audubon also recalled, "the place of his abode can never be forgotten."[29]

At the time of Audubon's visit, the town of Houston, capital city of the Republic of Texas, had not yet celebrated its one-year anniversary. New York brothers Augustus and John Allen foresaw great commercial advantage in locating their town at the upper reaches of navigation on Buffalo Bayou.[30] The waterway led directly to Galveston Bay, and thus to Galveston, the largest seaport in Texas. The Allen brothers looked to capture the trade passing from Galveston to the interior: "Situated at the head of navigation on the West bank of Buffalo Bayou . . . [Houston] must ever command the trade of the largest and richest portion of Texas . . . and when the rich lands of this country shall be settled a trade will flow to it, making it, beyond all doubt, the great interior commercial emporium of Texas." In short, according to the brothers, "Nature appears to have designated this place for the future seat of Government."[31]

Despite the optimistic words of the Allen brothers, Congress had taken an enormous leap of faith when it selected Houston as the capital over the established settlements of Washington and Matagorda. Neither congressional selection committee had mentioned the town as a possible capital. John Allen's position in Congress (as representative from Nacogdoches) must have helped. But Congress was full of land speculators at the time, so this alone does not explain the Allen brothers' success.

Assuming that Buffalo Bayou was navigable, Houston's location was indeed attractive. An inland city to which "vessels from New Orleans or New York can sail without obstacles" had a huge advantage in a land without railroads. Mild weather would allow "steamboats of the largest class" to make the eight-hour trip from Galveston year-round. But the important lure for Congress, which had appropriated only fifteen thousand dollars of nonexistent funds for *all* government construction, may have been the Allens' offer to erect and donate to the government a capitol building.[32]

Still, Houston was a meager town even by frontier standards. When young Texas immigrant Granville Rose heard rumors of its founding, he and several friends journeyed from their homes near the Brazos River to see the new metropolis for themselves. They encountered only the hard reality of a speculative dream. Rose's sister recalled that "after being absent some time they said that it was hard work to find the city in the pine woods; and that, when they did, it consisted of one dugout canoe, a bottle gourd of whisky and a surveyor's chain and compass, and was inhabited by four men with an ordinary camping outfit. We had a good joke on the boys at their disappointment. We asked them at what hotel they put up, and whether they went to church and to the theater."[33]

After Frank Lubbock encountered the Allen brothers in Columbia, he moved his general store to Houston aboard the steamship *Laura* in January 1837, about the time of the first sale of lots in the city. It was not a simple journey. From Galveston inland, the steamer enjoyed easy passage as far as Harrisburg.[34] Lubbock's transport then required three days to travel the last twelve miles to Houston.[35] Passengers and crew alike struggled to overcome submerged debris, overhanging tree limbs, and numerous other obstacles to the ship's passage. Impatient at the slow pace of travel, Lubbock and a few others secured a small boat and struck out on their own. Like Granville Rose, they found the national capital only with difficulty: "So little evidence could we see of a landing that we passed by the site and ran into White Oak Bayou, only realizing that we must have passed the city when we stuck in the brush. We then backed down the bayou, and by close observation discovered a road or street laid off from the water's edge. Upon landing we found stakes and footprints, indicating that we were in the town tract."[36]

Two months after Lubbock's arrival an anonymous visitor found a bustling yet primitive town. The entire city consisted of little more than a two-hundred-foot-long one-story frame building, various log cabins, and "a few linen tents which were used for groceries together with three or four shanties made of poles set in the ground, and covered and weath-

1905 photograph of ninety-two-year-old Frank Lubbock (left) and Stephen Sparks, age eighty-nine. Lubbock arrived in Texas shortly after the conclusion of the revolution against Mexico. Lubbock was a passenger on the first steamboat to reach the new city of Houston via Buffalo Bayou. Courtesy of OP1, Austin, Texas, CN12186, the Dolph Briscoe Center for American History, University of Texas at Austin.

er-boarded with rough splint shingles." The grocers, who sold not only food but alcohol, stayed busiest: "It appeared to be the business of the great mass of people, to collect around these centers of vice, and hold their drunken orgies." Texians, noted the traveler, "not only fought, but drank, in platoons." Another visitor, John Dancy, saw great energy in the rough settlement. "This place is improving very rapidly. . . . It is the most animated town I have seen in Texas." Nevertheless, he too found fault: "Houston is now one of the muddiest and most disagreeable places on earth."[37]

Captain Grayson's initial voyage up Buffalo Bayou to Houston on the steamboat *Laura* evidently relieved the anxieties of the new capital city's supporters. Ignoring the exertions of Frank Lubbock and others aboard ship, the *Telegraph and Texas Register* proclaimed under the headline "The Fact Proved" that the boat had progressed upriver "without obstruction." The writer asserted that "thus it is proved that Houston will be a port of entry." But just barely. A later traveler on the bayou remarked, "The Buffalo Bayou is, in many places, just wide enough for the steamboat to pass, brushed by the boughs of trees on both sides."[38]

New *Telegraph* editor and part-owner Francis Moore made the journey himself when he brought his printing press from Columbia to Houston on the steamer *Yellow Stone* April 11. The first Houston edition appeared May 2, the day after Congress reconvened. Government departments were to have moved by April 1 but, as an omen of further trouble, waited until the sixteenth because the new buildings in Houston were not ready on time.[39]

Construction delays affected not only the government. In March the *Telegraph and Texas Register* happily reported that "the offices intended for the reception of the several departments of government will soon be completed; the building also intended for our press is nearly finished." Immediately upon resuming operation in Houston, however, the newspaper complained: "Like others who have confided in *speculative things*, we have been deceived: no building had ever been nearly finished at Houston intended for the press; fortunately, however, we have succeeded in renting a shanty, which, although like the *capitol* in this place, 'Without a roof, and without a floor, Without windows and without a door,' is the only convenient building obtainable." "Without a roof" was no exaggeration. John Audubon's May 4, 1837, diary entry relates, "we amused ourselves by walking in the capitol, which was yet without a roof, and the floors, benches, and tables of both houses of congress were as well saturated with water as our clothes had been in the morning." Six days later "the members [of Congress] assembled . . . but owing to the storm of the preceding night, and the insufficiency of the building, the floor being flooded with water, and the hall unfit for the transaction of business, on motion, adjourned." That same day the Senate also adjourned without conducting any business due to a flooded Senate chamber. Such observations cast suspicion upon a claim in the congressional journal that the House and Senate had convened May 1 in accommodations "fitted up and furnished for business."[40]

Frank Lubbock saw several other drawbacks to Houston: "It was a very muddy place . . . with very poor drainage, so that, with the immense wagon trade, the roads and streets, although very wide and handsome, were almost impassable in wet weather." The country's president, Sam Houston, occupied a rough twelve-by-sixteen-foot log cabin warmed only by a small clay furnace. And, perhaps worst of all, by fall many members of Congress had fallen ill due to, as Lubbock thought, impurities in the water from Buffalo Bayou. Lubbock asked for and received five hundred dollars from Congress to purchase several ten-thousand-gallon

Congress assembled in this building in Houston before Thomas William Ward completed construction. After a heavy rain in May 1837, John Audubon reported that "we amused ourselves by walking in the capitol, which was yet without a roof, and the floors, benches, and tables of both houses of congress were as well saturated with water as our clothes had been in the morning." Courtesy of Bonham (Dora Dieterich) Papers, CN12183, the Dolph Briscoe Center for American History, University of Texas at Austin.

cypress cisterns in New Orleans which, after installation in Houston, "were filled with excellent water, which had a fine effect upon the health of the Members."[41]

Access to better drinking water failed to completely allay fear of contagious diseases. On May 16, 1838, Congressman Oliver Jones of Austin County introduced a resolution in the House authorizing the president and his cabinet to leave the capital for Galveston Island during the "sickly season." After William Menefee successfully moved to strike the words "Galveston Island" from the resolution, House members rejected New

Orleans and the imaginary "City of Austin" as alternatives before agreeing on San Antonio de Bexar as the place of refuge.[42]

Dangers other than disease lurked in and around Buffalo Bayou. When Granville Rose and friends encountered mosquitoes "as large as grasshoppers" on its banks they sought relief by jumping into the water. Granville's sister later recalled, "They thought they would have a nice bath, but in a few minutes the water was alive with alligators." After the ensuing mad scramble left one of the party stranded on the opposite shore, the others found a canoe to ferry him back across. The approaching vessel surprised a large panther, which sprang from the brush and ran away from the waiting man.[43]

Houston did have its optimists. An anonymous report in the May 16, 1837, *Telegraph and Texas Register* expressed astonishment at the rapid pace of building in the city. Houston was a place of constant activity, in which new houses rose to completion in the course of a single day. And the same capitol building that six days earlier had flooded with rainwater "now lifts its towering form above the puny buildings around, like a gigantic live oak amid the prairie bushes." Even the *Telegraph*'s editor, who had complained only days before about the poor facilities housing his printing press, felt moved enough to quote Thomas Moore's poem *Lalla Rookh*:

> Whose are the gilded tents that crowd the way
> Where all was waste and silent yesterday?
> This city of war, which, in a few short hours
> Hath sprung up here, as if the magic powers
> Of Him, who, in the twinkling of a star
> Built the high pillar'd walls of Chilminar,
> Had conjured up, far as the eye can see,
> This world of tents and domes.[44]

Nevertheless, reality continued to dampen such enthusiasm. A newspaper notice appearing October 11, 1837, directed the attention of city officials to the muddy condition of streets throughout town, but especially around the capitol and president's house. Commenting upon the excellent drainage potential of the city, the report urged the digging of furrows in the streets directing stagnant water into the nearby bayou. Even the city's morals seemed inadequate to some. A visitor from the United States complained, "I have said it was Sunday, but you would not have known it, if it had not been *pudding day*. Congress sitting, all sorts of gaming going on so publicly, that you might see the card players thro' the windows as you passed."[45]

Whether their town would remain the seat of government was more than a matter of pride for some Houstonians. The *Telegraph* editor pointed out,

> Most of the citizens who have purchased lots in this city and erected buildings have considered the act "locating temporarily the seat of government" a secure guarantee that their property here would continue valuable at least three years. . . . We trust therefore that this congress will not be so unjust as rashly to deprive these citizens of what they may properly consider vested rights.[46]

But congressmen lacking a financial stake in Houston who had to dodge falling ceiling plaster in the House of Representatives or stand due to an insufficient number of chairs in the capitol might have felt differently. Secretary of the Treasury Henry Smith was one government official definitely displeased with the new capital. He wrote the Speaker of the House October 1 that city officials had promised him a suitable office for his department. He received instead a "temporary shed, as entirely unfit for an office, as it was unsafe for the security of books and papers." Several months later, instead of gaining better space, he was evicted from the shed. When told by President Houston to move the Treasury into the capitol building, Smith found no unoccupied offices. Rather, he discovered that the president lacked the authority to claim space in the building and that department heads would eventually locate in the capitol's unfinished wings. Even President Houston complained in private when he wrote to Anna Raguet, "It is late at night, and I am freezing in a miserable open house."[47]

Muddy streets, unhealthy drinking water, fear of contagion, and inadequate infrastructure combined to sow discontent for Houston throughout the government. Although committed by law to remain on Buffalo Bayou at least until 1840, Congress began mulling over an earlier move. The founding Allen brothers could not have been pleased to read in the October 14, 1837, issue of the *Telegraph and Texas Register*, "Many of the members of congress seem determined to remove the seat of government from this place immediately."

Chapter 3

FALSE START

From recent indications, there can be no doubt that there is a settled purpose among you to act upon this matter at the present session of congress. . . . If a proper regard be had in the selection of a beautiful and eligible site in the upper country, as the permanent seat of government, it can doubtless be made the source of bringing a large revenue into the treasury.

From a letter to the editor written by "A Citizen" appearing in the October 11, 1837, issue of the *Telegraph and Texas Register*

On September 28, 1837, Congressman Thomas Rusk of Nacogdoches rose from his seat in the Texas House of Representatives to offer a proposal. Although he stood in the assembly hall of the national government, his gaze rested not on elegant wall hangings, intricate carpet designs, and the rich sheen of oak desktops, but on crudely assembled chairs, plank flooring, and bare walls. He spoke not to finely dressed aristocrats wearing polished footwear, but to battle-hardened frontiersmen in mud-caked boots. No carriages waited outside to bear their owners home. No cobblestone streets led away from the steps of the capitol. No waiters in fine restaurants polished silverware or laid out expensive china in anticipation of the arrival of distinguished congressmen at the end of the day. Thomas Rusk stood in an inelegant room in a plain wooden building surrounded by the lean-tos, canvas tents, and primitive shacks making up the undistinguished, uncomfortable, and just plain ugly Texas capital city of Houston.

With his proposal Thomas Rusk aimed to take the first step toward the creation of a government seat worthy of the great republic he and his colleagues were certain Texas would become. Members of Congress had gathered in the capital three days earlier at the behest of President Sam Houston, who had ordered a special congressional session intended to yield a new land law, as well as to solve the issue of the republic's eastern boundary with the "United States of the North."[1] But Rusk's resolution ignored these goals. He knew that, while President Houston possessed authority to call this meeting of the people's representatives, the chief executive was powerless to dictate its agenda.

Thomas Rusk wished for Congress to begin the process of establishing a new *permanent* seat of government. He entreated his colleagues to form a committee of three House members "to enquire into the propriety of selecting a site." These three would work in tandem with whatever committee the Senate would appoint toward the same purpose. The House quickly adopted Rusk's proposal and named Edward Burleson and William Menefee to join the resolution's sponsor on the House committee.

Upon receipt of this news from the House, the Senate joined the effort on September 29. Senators James Lester, Emory Rains, and William Wharton agreed to serve alongside their House counterparts. The joint committee's members then chose Congressman Rusk as its chairman.

An anonymous letter writer laid the matter before the public in the October 11, 1837, *Telegraph and Texas Register.* "It will be a very easy matter, as the geographical situation of the country is well known to you all, to settle upon the most fit and eligible site nearest the centre of the republic as the permanent seat of government of the republic. Bastrop is represented as having high claims upon the attention of the government, and perhaps a better location could not be made." The writer poked at the hornet's nest of regional interests by adding: "If commissioners could be appointed at the present session of congress . . . necessary public buildings might be erected so as to be in readiness for the reception of congress at its next session, should they determine not to hold another session here."

Three days later the *Telegraph and Texas Register* reminded its readers that, by law, the city of Houston was to host the government for another three years. Houston property owners would, according to the newspaper, suffer unfairly should the government depart prior to 1840. "We trust therefore that this congress will not be so unjust as rashly to deprive these citizens of what they may properly consider vested rights."[2]

Congress nevertheless pressed on. After Lester and Rusk reported back to their respective bodies around October 11, each house drafted resolutions regarding the site selection process for the other to concur with. On October 14, while debating its own version, the Senate received an approved House resolution on the subject. After interrupting their discussion to examine the statement, the senators quickly laid it aside in favor of adopting their own statement to pass back to the House. Two days later House members gave their consent to the "Joint Resolution locating permanently the Seat of Government." Sam Houston endorsed it October 19, 1837.[3]

Congress planned to jointly elect five commissioners to carry out the directive. Given the slow pace of travel in early nineteenth-century Texas, the commission's November 15 deadline for reporting its decision seems remarkable. Commissioners were to confine their search between the Guadalupe and Trinity Rivers. They could look no farther south than a line connecting the two rivers drawn through Fort Bend County and no farther north than one hundred miles beyond the Old San Antonio Road (which roughly paralleled modern State Highway 21).[4] The stipulated boundaries approximate an enormous triangle with legs measuring 170 and 220 miles.

Rusk kept the process moving when, on October 24, he successfully offered a resolution to invite the senators into the House to elect the five commissioners. Why the task of conveying the invitation required three congressmen is unclear, but Edward Branch, Charlton Thompson, and William Clark crossed the hall to the Senate to carry it out. The Senate matched the House's formality with an official vote of acceptance, at which point the House voted in favor of informing the senators that they could enter their chamber. The two bodies then chose John Greer, John McGehee, and John Bunton on the first ballot, William Scurlock on the second, and Horatio Chriesman on the third.[5]

Meanwhile, the Senate had appointed Isaac Burton, William Wharton, and Henry Augustine on October 23 to study the "expediency" of relocating the capital. The contents of their October 27 report are unknown, but one assumes the three indeed found the idea expedient, for their conclusions sparked no resistance to the ongoing site location effort. The Senate adopted their report with amendment the following day.[6]

Five days beyond the November 15 deadline, commissioners Greer, McGehee, Bunton, Scurlock, and Chriesman appeared before the House of Representatives, apologized for their tardiness, and offered up their recommendations. They declined to commit themselves to one site over others because "your commissioners have no doubt that much more advantageous, certain, and liberal propositions could have been had if a longer time had been given." Commissioners praised Bastrop, Washington, and the Mound leagues as excellent sites, while adding that they had yet to receive a proposal regarding a promising location on the Colorado River about forty miles south of Bastrop. Despite having appropriated sufficient land for government purposes, San Felipe and Gonzales received less consideration due to unfavorable location and lack of timber for construction. Finally, although Tenoxticlan, Nashville, the falls of the

Brazos, and an offer from Henry Austin for a Colorado River site each possessed certain advantages, various drawbacks also meant that they "do not come under the first class."[7]

Laid out by Mexican land commissioner Jose Miguel de Arciniega in 1832, Bastrop had in November 1837 not yet been incorporated by the Republic of Texas. Although renamed Mina by the Texas-Coahuila legislature in 1834, few area residents recognized the change. Town leaders volunteered to donate all unsold land within Bastrop, as well as all of the profits from prior land sales, to the government. Commissioner John Mc-Gehee also pledged two and one-fourth leagues of land. The capital selection commission noted multiple advantages of the town, including plentiful timber, good water, healthy location, and available land. Commissioners approved of the Colorado River as "a navigable stream" and praised the surrounding "fine beautiful country."[8]

Asa Hoxey represented Washington interests in that town's bid for the government seat. His offer included one-half league of land on the east bank of the Brazos River across from the town and another half league adjacent to the western city limit. The government would receive lots free within the town for construction of public buildings. Hoxey stressed the healthfulness of Washington: "It was laid out as a town in the Spring of 1835 and there have been but fifteen persons buried in the Town during all that time not one of whom died with fever." Washington, of course, already had experience as a seat of government for the republic. According to the commissioners, along with the usual advantages of water and timber, it possessed coastal access via the Brazos River. Its "rich and fertile country" augmented its attractions.[9]

The Mound league consisted of three leagues of plantation owner James F. Perry's land and another seven hundred acres owned by Horatio Chriesman, one of the five commissioners. This tract lay twenty miles west of Washington (and thus of the Brazos River) and twenty-two miles east of the Colorado River. Given that twelve thousand acres of unclaimed land sat adjacent to the site, a majority of commissioners believed that the republic stood to make the greatest immediate profit by locating there. Recognizing this, Perry asked $1.50 per acre from the government. Chriesman volunteered to donate his portion.[10]

After thanking the commissioners, the House approved a proposal from Patrick Jack to refer the commission report to a committee of five for further study.[11] Thomas Rusk, fearing that other worthy site applications remained outstanding, moved to table the report. Failing in this, he successfully moved to appoint a committee of three to receive late proposals.[12] Responding to an invitation by the House, the Senate on November 21 appointed five committee members of its own to join the five representatives examining the commission report.[13]

Texas citizens closely monitored the actions of Congress with respect to a proposed government relocation. On November 23, 1837, a letter from "A Western Citizen" appeared in the *Telegraph and Texas Register* objecting to the right of Congress to permanently establish a seat of government *anywhere*. The writer predicted a loss of faith in government "if the seat of government should be located and individuals invest in purchasing property, and a subsequent congress choose to remove the seat of government." Thus, removal would be "unjust" and furthermore, the writer opined, "I do not think that congress has the right [to name a permanent capital]."

Members of Congress recognized that they had allowed the selection commission inadequate time to examine all of the candidate sites. The Senate on December 1 approved a proposal to appoint another commission toward that purpose. Fifteen days later Senators G. W. Barnett and Emory Rains were elected commissioners by their colleagues. Prior to adjourning December 19, the House appointed Patrick Jack, George Sutherland, and Pleiades Lumpkin. The commission's duties included visiting each known site, examining any other proposals that might come in, and reporting back to Congress on the first Monday of the next session.[14]

Chairman Patrick Jack placed an announcement in the February 10, 1838, *Telegraph and Texas Register* directing commissioners to gather at John Moore's plantation on the Colorado River by March 5, 1838. A scant three days after the appointed meeting date, the commission signed a contract with John Eblin for purchase of one league of land bordering Moore's property. The proposed capital would lie on the east bank of the Colorado River near present-day La Grange. As authorized by Congress, the commission then claimed all vacant land within a nine-mile radius of Eblin's league.

Did the commission visit any other sites? If so, no evidence of such trips exists. Members had apparently agreed to divide the workload, as only three showed up to inspect the Eblin league.[15] Certainly there was time between the Eblin contract and the April 14 deadline for other site visits. However the commission occupied itself during that time, its members were in Houston by the appointed day.

Congress reconvened in Houston April 9, 1838. George Sutherland reported the commission's findings and recommendations five days later. He described the Eblin property as commanding a high bluff on the east bank of the Colorado River. A continuous water supply existed in "a

Creek of pure and never failing water" and four permanent springs. Timber and an "inexhaustible stock of building Rock" would serve construction needs, while area farmers enjoyed the benefits of the fertile soil. Interestingly, only Barnett, Lumpkin, and Sutherland signed this portion of the commission's report, implying that the commissioners had indeed split up during their inspection tour.[16]

Legislators found themselves distracted in the days following Sutherland's report. As the Senate adjourned Saturday, April 14, clerk Thomas William Ward, who had built the capitol, and Francis Lubbock, seated in the gallery, began loudly arguing. Something Lubbock said infuriated Ward enough that he charged his antagonist, who responded with a poorly aimed pistol shot in Ward's direction. Among the first items of business Monday morning was a Senate resolution requiring the sergeant-at-arms to arrest both Ward and Lubbock and bring them before the Senate. When Lubbock showed up, senators accepted his explanation of events and dismissed him. Ward, however, "had locked himself up in his house, and refused to be arrested, or seen." A second trip by the sergeant-at-arms proved more successful, and Ward approached the bar to give his side of the story. He must have appeared the aggressor, for the Senate officially reprimanded him once he had finished.[17]

After receiving Sutherland's report regarding a new seat of government, the Senate on April 19 handed it over to a select committee of three for further study. Thomas Rusk once again seized the initiative in the House when, on April 25, he successfully moved to refer the commission report to a special committee for further study. Edward Burleson, Daniel Rowlett, William Menefee, and George Hill joined Rusk on the committee. Working jointly, the two groups had made enough progress by April 28 to request a joint congressional vote two days later to settle the matter. The Senate responded to a House invitation to a vote with the reply that it was not yet ready.[18]

Meanwhile, other site proposals continued to trickle in. Such was the variety of choices that the select joint committee ultimately reported that it would be "improper for them [the committee] to express any opinion to the advantage or disadvantage of any proposition which has come before them." The report then summarized the many options before Congress. These included the town of Comanche (laid out by Edward Burleson on the Colorado River eighteen miles above Bastrop), Groce's Retreat (on the Brazos River), Eblin's league, an offer on the Colorado River from Henry Austin, and the communities of Nashville, Sulphur Springs, Colorado City (near La Grange), Richmond, and Bastrop. Several other offers had arrived after this summary had been prepared. Henry Austin made a second proposal involving land on the Navasota River just above its emptying into the Brazos. Andrew Briscoe and Edward Hall offered land lying between the San Jacinto and Trinity Rivers. James Perry offered up a large tract that included the Mound league, this time for two dollars an acre.[19]

By May 9, 1838, both houses of Congress were ready to make a final decision. This time, the Senate accepted the House's invitation and at three o'clock senators filed across the hall for the joint vote.[20] Selection commission member George Sutherland, as expected, nominated Eblin's league. Nine other locations received nominations. Representative Thomas Gazley of Houston's Harrisburg County might have surprised no one when he placed that city on the ballot.[21] That his colleagues, and perhaps even Gazley himself, did not take the nomination seriously is suggested by the failure of Houston to receive even a single vote. With forty-three members of Congress participating, a majority of twenty-two votes would prevail. On the first ballot, nineteen members opted for George Sutherland's choice of Eblin's league. Nacogdoches and Black's place tied for second with five votes each. Eblin's league picked up seven additional votes on the second ballot, giving it the necessary majority, with Black's place a distant second at ten votes.[22]

All that remained was for each house to put the finishing touches on a final bill to present to President Sam Houston. In the House of Representatives, George Sutherland reported a substitute bill from committee on May 11, 1838. Thomas Hardeman successfully moved that the new capital be named "Austin" in honor of the late empresario. By a 23-to-6 vote, the House passed the bill the next day. The Senate required several days of debate before approving the House bill. Isaac Burton highlighted an issue that would spark vicious debate for years to come when he proposed allowing the general public an opportunity to approve or reject the final bill. Burton's proposal lost. On May 15, 1838, the Senate joined the House in passage of the bill.[23]

Except for Sam Houston's opposition to the idea, Austin, Texas would today lie in Fayette County about sixty miles downstream from its present location on the Colorado River. The Fayette County site itself did not trouble the Texas president. His May 22 veto message to Congress did not even mention it. Instead, the President found fault in the ability of any subsequent Congress to undo the efforts of the present one. Houston noted that, by law, the government would meet in his namesake city until 1840. What would prevent either of the next two congresses from repealing the present bill in favor of some other location? Given the impoverished state of the republic, the president did not feel he could take the chance that the large expenditure called for by the bill would be wasted. Houston closed his message by explaining his own preferred method for locating the capital: "Should the subject be presented to the people, and then their expression ratified by an act of the government, it would be permanently established beyond all ground of doubt or cavil."[24]

Although time was running out on the second Texas Congress, Thomas Rusk did not give up on his attempt to establish a new seat of government. Immediately after the House heard the president's veto message, Rusk moved to refer the message and the bill to a select committee. By a large majority, House members refused.[25] The next day, May 23, Rusk tried again by proposing a different bill entirely. First, however, he needed the House to agree to suspend the rule against addressing new business so late in the session. Unfortunately for Rusk, the 14-to-9 majority favoring the suspension was short of the necessary two-thirds majority. By the same 14-to-9 vote, Rusk did receive permission to have the bill copied into the House journal. His plan should have overcome Sam Houston's objections, in that a number of sites chosen by Congress would have been placed before the voters, who would then make the final choice.[26]

Interestingly, when the House next voted on whether to override Houston's veto, Thomas Rusk voted no. Perhaps he had agreed all along with the president that the voters should have the final say. Or maybe he disliked the choice of Eblin's league enough to allow the bill to die.[27] Congressmen Lumpkin and Sutherland, who had served on the commission that purchased Eblin's league, voted for the bill. In all, a majority of fourteen congressmen favored passage over Houston's objections; twelve were against. Since the constitution required a two-thirds majority to overcome a presidential veto, the bill failed.

Congressman Jones of Brazoria County made one last attempt at salvaging a tangible step by the Second Congress toward establishing a permanent capital. He suggested an act providing for an election "to take the sense of the people on the location of the seat of government at the city of Austin." By "the city of Austin" Jones meant Eblin's league; in essence his proposal amounted to a referendum by the public on the bill that Houston had vetoed. When House members cast their ballots on whether to allow the consideration of this new business, Jones came up one vote short.[28] No one else raised the issue before adjournment. The Second Congress had failed to find the republic a new seat of government.

Chapter 4

THE RAVEN AND THE POET

General Lamar will not pardon a friendly regard in any person for Gen Houston.

October 3, 1838, entry in Ashbel Smith's diary, Ashbel Smith Papers, Dolph Briscoe Center for American Studies, the University of Texas at Austin

He is too base to be respected and too imbecile to be trusted!

Sam Houston, describing Mirabeau Lamar in a December 13, 1841, letter to his wife Margaret, Roberts, *Personal Correspondence of Sam Houston*, vol. 1, 135

Many of those attending the wedding of Eliza Allen and Tennessee governor Sam Houston January 22, 1829, foresaw a presidency in the ambitious groom's future. Houston had long enjoyed the favor of President Andrew Jackson, whose meteoric ascent after the War of 1812 resulted in a position of political preeminence. The president had wielded his rising power to nurture Houston's career ever since the younger man's valor at the Battle of Horseshoe Bend in 1814 caught General Jackson's eye. Following a post-battle promotion to second lieutenant, the young protégé earned praise as subagent to the Cherokee nation, then held a series of appointments and elected positions which culminated in him reaching the Tennessee governor's mansion in 1826. Endorsement and support from Jackson provided crucial assistance each step of the way. As Andrew Jackson's favorite, Sam Houston on his wedding day seemed a strong candidate to become Old Hickory's eventual successor in the White House.

A Virginian by birth, fourteen-year-old Sam Houston moved with his siblings and newly widowed mother to Blount County, Tennessee in 1807. Although he willingly spent long hours devouring *The Iliad* and other classics, Sam was a poor student who attended school only sporadically. He displayed even less enthusiasm working on the family farm alongside his older brothers, who eventually became frustrated enough with their younger sibling that they put him to work in the family store in nearby Maryville. Bored and angry, Sam ran away from home in 1809, finding

Sam Houston lived with the Cherokee during his teens and again after his flight
from Tennessee in 1829. He took a Cherokee name meaning "The Raven,"
but it was his less flattering native nickname of "The Big Drunk" that provided
ammunition for later political enemies. Courtesy of the Library of
Congress, LC-USZ62-92305.

refuge with the Cherokee in Chief Oolooteka's town on an island in the
Hiwassee River[1]. He ingratiated himself so well and so quickly that
Oolooteka adopted the young runaway, soon known among the Chero-
kee as the Raven.

Sam Houston threw himself completely into his new life. He adopted
Cherokee dress and rapidly became fluent in the Cherokee language.
When his older brothers found him after several weeks, he adamantly

refused to return with them to the farm. The brothers left empty-handed to inform their mother that Sam would not be coming home.

Sam remained with Oolooteka and his people for three years. He intermittently visited his mother to chat and beg for money. During this time he also took up drinking, a vice that would plague him for the next three decades. As was common along the porous frontier in that day, he traveled freely between Indian and white society, working occasional jobs as a store clerk and teacher. Frequently finding himself in debt, Houston was in the process of asking another youth named Charles Norwood for a loan in 1813 when his long-time friend instead convinced him to join the army. A year younger than the enlistment minimum age of twenty-one, Sam had to ask his mother's consent to sign up. While granting permission Mrs. Houston presented her son a gold ring with the word "Honor" engraved on the inside curve. Fifty years later Sam Houston's widow would remove this ring from her deceased husband's hand moments after his death.[2]

As had the American Revolution, the War of 1812 forced indigenous nations to choose sides. Indian statesmen agonized over the decision, for they knew that a wrong choice could ruin their people. Many undoubtedly recalled what had happened to the once-mighty Haudenosaunee federation,[3] a British ally destroyed by George Washington in 1779. Weary of the raids made on his forces by the Haudenosaunee, the American commander sent three armies through their country on a devastating rampage of intentional annihilation. Washington's troops torched dozens of Indian villages, destroyed countless acres of crops, and carried off everything else. Scores of Haudenosaunee died in the fighting or in the winter of starvation that followed. Hoping to avoid a similar fate, Sam Houston's Cherokee friends opted for the Americans; the Creek nation, influenced by the great Shawnee leader Tecumseh, sided with the British.

Andrew Jackson in 1814 led an American army to present-day Alabama to challenge the Creeks. His force included the 360 men of the Thirty-Ninth Infantry, a platoon that had as its leader Ensign Sam Houston[4]. The invaders caught up with the Creeks, led by a mixed-blood named Bill Weathersford, at a bend in the Tallapoosa River known as Tohopeka, or the Horseshoe. The Creek force occupied the peninsula formed by the river. It shielded itself in front with a breastwork of logs and felt protected from a rear assault by the water. At midday March 27, 1814, Jackson's infantry charged directly at the breastworks, the Thirty-Ninth Infantry leading the way. The first man to scramble over the logs died instantly.[5] The next man, Sam Houston, dove with slashing sword into the Creek defenders. The men behind rushed to assist their dangerously surrounded leader. During the carnage an arrow pierced Houston's thigh, but he persevered until the enemy fled the area. He then bullied a comrade into pulling the arrow out, after which he limped off to find medical attention.[6] While riding past the surgeon's tent Andrew Jackson spotted Houston lying on the ground and halted to ask about his wound. Observing the ugly gash in the young soldier's thigh, the general ordered his subordinate not to return to the fighting.[7]

Thirsting for greater glory, Sam Houston defied his commander. During mop-up operations at the end of the decisive American victory a group of Creeks fought on from inside a log-covered position in a ravine. Houston responded to a call for volunteers to storm the stronghold. Grabbing a musket, he dared other members of his platoon to follow as he stumbled painfully toward the enemy. A mere five yards from the enclosure two musket balls slammed simultaneously into the reckless youth's body. Houston fell with a shattered right arm and shoulder while continuing to exhort his men to charge. None answered the call. Crippled and alone, the severely wounded ensign crawled out of the ravine to safety. General Jackson subsequently ordered the use of flaming arrows to set the logs ablaze and roast the trapped defenders.

Sam Houston expected to die. Army surgeons indicated agreement by laying him off to the side in favor of treating other, more salvageable men. When Houston survived the night he was placed on a litter and dragged sixty miles to Fort Williams, then on to his mother's home in Tennessee. The local physician at first refused to treat him, wanting to spare the family needless expense in such a hopeless case. But Houston confounded this doctor as well by remaining alive, prompting the man to change his mind two weeks later.

Houston required several years to recover his health. His thigh wound never did fully heal and proved a persistent source of irritation throughout life. Still in the army, he traveled the country on several assignments before accepting the position of subagent to the Cherokee charged with directing their removal west to Indian Territory. With skill and tact, the Raven carried out what must have been the unpleasant task of moving his adoptive father's clan out of its homeland forever. Afterwards he resigned from the military and from his subagent job.

With time on his hands Houston spent six months in 1818 reading law, then opened a practice in Lebanon, Tennessee. Andrew Jackson initiated the future Texas president's political career by endorsing him for an appointment as adjutant general of the state militia. Houston won his first election late that year to become attorney general of the Nashville

United States Congressman Sam Houston posed for this portrait by J. Wood in 1826. The following year, at age thirty-four, Houston was elected governor of Tennessee. Reprinted by permission of the Austin History Center, Austin Public Library, PICB 04210.

district, then won the race for major general of the state militia in 1821. Jackson's endorsement propelled Houston onto the national stage in 1823 with a successful run for Congress. A second two-year term preceded yet another success in his first statewide race, and in 1827 thirty-four-year-old Sam Houston assumed the Tennessee governorship.

Sam and Eliza Houston's marriage lasted eleven weeks. Neither party ever spoke publicly about the reason for their separation, but the jilted bride's family strove to save her reputation by destroying Houston's. The disgraced governor made no attempt to defend himself. He abandoned his race for reelection, quit the governorship, and fled the state. Oolooteka welcomed him into his new town in Indian Territory.[8] Houston resumed Cherokee speech and dress and, except for an occasional letter to Andrew Jackson, cut his ties to white society. He also began drinking heavily, soon earning a new name among the Cherokee, the Big Drunk.

Houston acquired Cherokee citizenship. He involved himself in tribal government, working to maintain peaceful relations between the Cherokee and other indigenous nations dumped into the region by the whites. He took a Cherokee bride, Diana Rogers Gentry, and together the two established a trading post on the Neosho River.

Austin owes its existence to Mirabeau Lamar, who saw the creation of a frontier capital as the key to building a Texan empire. His pursuit of this goal triggered one of the great political battles in republican Texas, which pitted western expansionists like Lamar against the eastern establishment personified by Sam Houston. Although Lamar ultimately failed in his quest for empire, the city he helped create has been the only seat of government the state of Texas has ever had. Courtesy of the San Jacinto Museum of History, Houston, Texas.

Slowly Houston began to reestablish a presence in the United States. He made several trips back east, encountering Alexis de Tocqueville along the way.[9] On a Washington sidewalk in 1832 he attacked and beat with a cane Ohio Congressman William Stanbery over a perceived insult made on the House floor. Defended by Francis Scott Key, Houston appeared before the House of Representatives in a new suit purchased for him by Andrew Jackson. Key's initial efforts seemed lethargic enough that Houston decided to present his own summary at the trial's conclusion. Following a night of excessive drinking, he mesmerized the House the next day with a speech that elicited a rousing ovation. Although officially reprimanded by Congress, Houston felt vindicated enough in the public eye to once again embark on a quest for greatness. His wife Diana stayed behind in Indian Territory. Sam Houston went to Texas.

Like his later enemy Sam Houston, Mirabeau Lamar as a youth in Georgia loved to read. Unlike the restless Houston, however, Lamar found not boredom but fascination in the classroom. He impressed his teachers at academies in Millidgeville and Eatonton while displaying a wide range of academic talents. He enjoyed painting, but found a lifelong passion in poetry composition. He excelled at riding and fencing. Son of a successful plantation owner, Lamar received the comfortable, stable upbringing that eluded Sam Houston.

In 1819 the twenty-one-year-old Lamar acquired a business partner and opened a store in Cahawba, Alabama. Two years later he briefly shared publishing duties at the *Cahawba Press*.[10] Newly elected Georgia governor George Troup enticed the promising young man back to his home state in 1823 when he hired Lamar as his secretary. Lamar stayed on the job for three years, resigning after his 1826 wedding to fellow Georgian Tabitha Jordan. The bride's tuberculosis prompted his resignation, as Lamar deemed his secretarial duties would not allow him to properly care for her.

Two years after the wedding the couple moved themselves and infant daughter Rebecca to Columbus, Georgia, where Mirabeau established the *Columbus Enquirer*. Newspaperman Lamar won a seat in the state Senate in 1829. While he campaigned for reelection in 1830, his beloved wife succumbed to the ravages of tuberculosis. Although, given the nature of her illness, Tabitha's death could not have come as a surprise, it devastated Lamar. He entered a long period of depression, resigning his Senate seat and temporarily abandoning politics. Seeking comfort in travel and poetry, he composed one of his better-known verses, *Written at Evening, on the Banks of the Chattahoochee,* an excerpt of which clearly portrays Lamar's anguish:

> But all the loveliness that played
> Around her once, hath fled;
> She sleepeth in the valley's shade,
> A dweller with the dead;
> And I am here with ruined mind,
> Left lingering on the strand,
> To pour my music to the wind,
> My tears upon the sand.[11]

Until his wife's death, Mirabeau Lamar's star had only been on the rise. Now success abandoned him. He lost a race for Congress in 1832, then lost again two years later. Between the two defeats he helped organize a political party supporting nullification, the right of a state and its citizens to ignore a federal law. Lamar's political beliefs spilled over into his poetry when he penned *Arm For the Southern Land* in 1833. The poem betrays Lamar's penchant for righteous violence against his enemies as well as his inflexible moral certainty:

> ARM for the Southern land,
> All fear of death disdaining;
> Low lay the tyrant hand
> Our sacred rights profaning!

And in the same poem:

> Stand by your injured State,
> And let no feuds divide you;
> On tyrants pour your hate,
> And common vengeance guide you.
> Our foes should feel
> Proud freemen's steel,
> For freemen's rights contending;
> Where'er they die,
> There let them lie,
> To dust in scorn descending.
> Thus may each traitor fall,
> Who dare as foe invade us;
> Eternal fame to all
> Who shall in battle aid us![12]

Sam Houston's wide-brimmed hat, snappy walking stick, and multi-ringed right hand betray his penchant for flamboyance in this undated portrait. Reprinted by permission of the Austin History Center, Austin Public Library, PICB 04207.

After his second humbling election defeat, Lamar gave up on life in Georgia. Leaving his daughter with relatives he traveled to Texas, ostensibly to research a proposed history of the promising Mexican territory. Although he visited his home state many times thereafter, Mirabeau Lamar remained for the rest of his life a Texan.

Sam Houston was the Bill Clinton of frontier Texas. His countrymen adored and reviled him in equal measure, while even his enemies conceded his magnetic appeal and oratorical mastery. He dominated Texas politics for more than two decades. Frank Lubbock later recalled that two factions strove constantly for control of the republic, the "Houston party" and the "anti-Houston party."[13] A politician who defines the name of his *opponents* is a powerful politician indeed.

Mirabeau Lamar's image suffered in comparison. Charming and witty in small gatherings, he often appeared nervous and subdued in public. Whereas Houston's great height and gracefulness lent credibility to his claim of leadership, Lamar's short, stocky build had the opposite effect. Houston's wife Margaret once commented of Lamar, "Returned in time to see Gen. Lamar at Col. Andrew's dinner table. He looks like a great clumsy bear. Poor fellow! . . . I could not suppress a smile as he arose from the table and hobbled along before us to the sitting room." Mary Austin Holley[14] described Lamar as "very taciturn—when he does speak it is in wit or poetry in compliment. He is rather under size—thick set— rosy cheeks—high forehead—hair parted—speaks very slow." Another observer noted, "The Texians call him the dumb President, because of his extraordinary reluctance to speak." Lamar confirmed recognition of his awkward public speech when he told Dr. Ashbel Smith that "after the idea is clear in his mind, he is at great loss for words to express it appropriately."[15]

In a January 1835 speech at a Montgomery County, Alabama public dinner supporting state rights, Mirabeau Lamar foreshadowed his later hatred of Sam Houston with this denunciation of Houston's greatest friend and benefactor:

> Who is Andrew Jackson? Let me not attempt to describe his character; to draw him in his proper colors, the foulest language is too fair. Who can do justice to Calligula and Nero? And who can portray the man who combines all that is revolting in the one with the disgusting ferocity of the other? As an individual, a reprobate; as a military man, a murderer; and as a public functionary, the alternate flatterer and base betrayer of all principles and all parties.

Imagine Lamar's feelings when a scant fifteen months later he caught up with a Texan army commanded by the protégé of the man he had publicly vilified in Alabama. Can it be any surprise that Private Lamar spurned General Houston's battlefield commission as artillery commander after distinguishing himself in the cavalry skirmish the day before the fateful conflict at San Jacinto? A perplexed Houston could only guess at Lamar's motive: "He may have thought as the command was small, only eighteen men all told, that he would have to go on foot, and as he had a fine horse he possibly did not wish to dispense with." If Lamar indeed harbored animosity at that early stage of his relationship with Sam Houston, he felt it grow just before the charge against Santa Anna's troops when, as he later claimed, Houston told him that neither the officers nor the enlisted men favored an attack. Houston denied that such an exchange had ever taken place.[16]

During his vice presidency Lamar's dislike of Sam Houston intensified. President Houston's inner circle did not include the nation's second-in-command. Without much to do, Lamar journeyed back to Georgia to visit family and tie up some loose business ends. Houston complained of Lamar's absence to all who would listen, undoubtedly realizing that word would eventually reach Lamar of his displeasure. In May 1837 Lamar's friend W. D. Redd wrote to the vice president to inform him that "the President makes diurnal inquiries after yourse[l]f at which time he never forgets to express his entire disaprobation of you[r] much lamented absence." At Houston's request, Redd also sent along a note from the president politely asking the vice president to return to Texas. Redd labeled Houston's polite attitude nothing more than political posturing: "I honestly believe [the letter] to be electioneering documents mearly [sic] to subserve his subsequent uses as a testimonial of his kind friendship." Lamar obviously agreed with Redd. He replied to Houston July 7 in an overly obsequious letter laced with sarcasm. After providing assurance that he would hasten back to Texas "with as little delay as possible," he pointed out that he had not yet been able to visit most of his family or attend to any business. But, with duty calling, he would "be pleased at the same time to promote Your Excellency's individual happiness." In case Houston missed the point, he signed the letter "Your friend, Mirabeau Lamar."[17]

Lamar's venom towards Houston spilled over to his friends. In 1841 Jasper County congressman James Armstrong penned a scathing critique of Houston to Lamar, by that time president of the republic: "It seems the big Mingo[18] has been showing himself to his humble servants at San Augustine,[19] who emulate one another in worshiping him. . . . He

This photograph of Sam Houston at around age sixty proves that he never lost his taste for striking attire. Courtesy of the George Eastman House, 78:0758:0001.

says Lamar is a Mussell man and Burnett a hog thief." Another acquaintance, referring to Sam Houston's namesake city, wrote "Before I left Houston (I detest the name)."[20]

Houston ultimately developed similar feelings about Lamar. In private letters he frequently referred contemptuously to his political rival. At the close of Lamar's presidential term in 1841, newly inaugurated President Houston wrote to his wife Margaret, "I must tell you that a Ball was given to Lamar on the 22nd ⋯. I did not attend, but induced my friends to do so lest he might suppose that I thought enough about him to design any thing connected with him. . . . He deserves punishment, but contempt may shield him." In another letter to Margaret, Houston stated, "I met poor Lamar and restrained my contempt so far as to be proudly civil." And, leaving no room for doubt is this statement of Houston's, also to his wife, "He [Lamar] is a bad man, and utterly impure."[21]

Both men strove to maintain public civility. At times each even tried to make peace. In 1838, as Lamar's presidential inauguration approached, outgoing president Sam Houston approached Lamar ally Hugh McLeod, who reported the encounter to Lamar:

> General Houston held a long conversation with me a few days before he left San Augustine—respecting yourself—& requested me to communicate it—He said that officious men, & the enemies of both, had fomented angry feeling between you. . . . He was charged he said with being your enemy, it was false. . . . [Houston would] invoke for you the full confidence & patriotic Support of the Country.

And, at the close of his term in office, Lamar "made several overtures to me [Houston] for friendship . . . or rather an effort at reconciliation."[22]

Sam Houston and Mirabeau Lamar remained personal and political enemies until Lamar's death in 1859. Very few contemporaries were friends to both; an alliance to one indicated opposition to the other. Their tumultuous relationship shaped the most important political issues of the republic's early history. One such question, what to do with the Texas Cherokees, resulted in a quick victory for Lamar and a sustained policy of ethnic cleansing that eventually swept Texas clean of its indigenous people. Another early flashpoint, where to situate the nation's capital, sparked animosities lasting decades. This struggle pitted the Houston crowd against the anti-Houston crowd, easterners against westerners, and believers in Manifest Destiny against everyone else. During the years of the Republic of Texas, which ended in annexation to the United States in 1845, the battle swung back and forth between the two camps, the party in power holding the upper hand. With statehood the advantage swung back to those favoring Lamar's position, although final resolution of the conflict required another twenty-seven years of controversy and compromise. Neither Sam Houston nor Mirabeau Lamar survived to witness the last act, when Texas finally established for itself a *permanent* seat of government.

| Chapter 5 |

SELECTING A SITE

Be it enacted . . . that there shall be and are hereby created five Commissioners . . . whose duty it shall be to select a site for the location of the Seat of Government.

From "An act for the permanent location of the Seat of Government," signed into law by President Mirabeau Lamar January 14, 1839, Gammel, *The Laws of Texas*, vol. 2, 161

Judas betrayed his master, and five commissioners can betray their country.

Congressman Edward Holmes of Matagorda, in a speech to the House of Representatives, *Telegraph and Texas Register*, January 9, 1839

On December 10, 1838, in the ragged town of Houston, Texas, President-elect Mirabeau B. Lamar stood in the portico of his nation's capitol nervously awaiting the biggest moment of his life.[1] An "impressive concourse of spectators," including both houses of Congress and "most of the Elite and Fashion of the Republic" surrounded Lamar in anxious anticipation of the ceremony that would inaugurate his presidency. A copy of the speech Lamar planned to give to mark the occasion filled his pocket. Recognizing his limitations as a public speaker, the eloquent yet shy Lamar preferred the comfort of a prepared text to the risky, freewheeling style of his archrival Sam Houston. Adding to the president-elect's anxiety, the riveting speechmaker Houston lurked nearby in flamboyant dress. Flaunting knee breeches and neatly tied powdered hair, outgoing President Houston, with his elegant appearance, reminded onlookers more of George Washington than of a frontier politician.[2]

Lamar's triumph in the September presidential election over Senator Robert Wilson of Harrisburg brought him an unbelievable 97 percent of the vote.[3] Nobody's first choice, Wilson had joined the race late with a self-nomination after the deaths of Lamar's two chief opponents the previous July.[4] Lamar ally David Burnet found more competition in his vice-presidential race against Albert Horton and Joseph Rowe, but still won decisively with a 55 percent majority.[5] Just two years removed from an ad interim stint as president during and immediately after the successful revolt against Mexico, a contentious term of service which had left him embittered and unpopular, a vindicated Burnet waited to receive his own oath of office alongside Lamar.

At noon Speaker of the House John Hansford of Shelby County quieted the crowd with a call to order before appointing Congressmen John Bunton and Louis Cooke marshals. A special committee of arrangements escorted President Houston, President-elect Lamar, Vice President-elect Burnet, and the various department heads to their places. Speaker Hansford introduced other dignitaries, including the chargé d'affaires from the United States. The nascent republic strove to impress this emissary in particular with its solemnity and adherence to protocol.

Not everyone was happy to have poet Lamar as chief executive. On August 20, 1839, future Texas president Anson Jones confided in his journal, "Gen. Lamar may mean well . . . but his mind is altogether of a dreamy, poetic order . . . wholly unfit by habit or education for the active duties and the everyday realities of his present Station."[6] The editor of the *Brazos Courier* complained shortly after Lamar's election to the presidency that there was "no man who has ever ruled a community . . . so utterly destitute of the qualifications for their station, as this crazy poetaster, whom accident has elevated." And, to hammer the point home, the editor added disgustedly, "The muse of history has bequeathed to us Cromwells and Bonapartes, but Aesop alone has recorded in fable a parallel instance where an ape was made a king."[7]

Most Texans, however, eagerly anticipated a Lamar presidency. The editor of the *Telegraph and Texas Register* noted with satisfaction that "the remarkable degree of confidence and esteem that was everywhere manifested towards President Lamar." Describing the new president as "the pride and ornament of the country," the *Telegraph* gushed that "from his administration, the most fortunate results are expected."[8] All were eager to hear from Lamar his glorious plans for their future.

They would have to wait. Given the chance to provide a farewell address, Sam Houston rose and began regaling the crowd "in a most able and impressive manner." One star-struck correspondent noted, "Almost every soul seemed charmed with his eloquence." The outgoing chief executive spoke humbly of the difficulties of the office, as well as his own shortcomings. He reminded listeners of the sacrifices and suffering a man must endure in the presidency, which to him seemed as nothing less than "a pillow of thorns," adding that he would never hold public office again. Regretting his mistakes, he nevertheless felt obliged to mention the meager means at his disposal during his term. He praised his worthy successor, who by now was engulfed in anxiety and frustration while awaiting his chance to speak. Houston's audience roared its approval. Frequent thunderclaps of applause burst forth from the crowd, but interrupted the speaker only briefly. Finally, after three hours of his "very lengthy and interesting valedictory," Houston "cordially saluted General Lamar and invited him to the chair of state, which he then relinquished, with dignity and complacency."[9]

Having stolen the show, Sam Houston next watched Mirabeau Lamar and David Burnet receive their oaths of office. Speaker Hansford formally greeted the two new officers of the republic, presenting Lamar with a bound copy of the Laws and Burnet with a copy of the Constitution and the rules of the Senate. And now, at last, it was President Lamar's turn to speak. Lamar, however, worn out and irritated, evidently saw the hopelessness of following master orator Sam Houston. He fled the scene, first giving a copy of his speech to his secretary Algernon Thompson. Thompson delivered the unfamiliar text in a listless monotone. The *Telegraph* editor explained the president's actions on the basis of his "delicate health." Witness William Allen saw through this excuse. He also saw mischief in Houston, who, "knowing something of Lamar's nervousness, took occasion to make an exaugural, reviewing at great length his administration, and, by the time he was done, Lamar had become so nervous that he could not read his inaugural, and had to commit it to his private secretary, Algernon Thompson, to be read to an exhausted audience."[10]

Ten days into the Third Congress of the Republic of Texas, twenty-four-year-old Representative Ezekial Cullen of San Augustine County attempted to refocus lawmakers' attention on the task of locating a permanent seat of government. Thomas Rusk, the congressman who initially raised the issue in the Second Congress, no longer held office, but would soon become the nation's chief justice.[11] On November 15, 1838, Cullen introduced a bill in the House defining a process for selecting a site for a new capital. After the clerk's reading, House members agreed to have 250 copies of the bill printed for distribution.[12] Congress then attended to other matters until after Lamar's inauguration. On the day of Lamar's oath of office and Houston's long-winded speech, a seemingly perfunctory proposal in the House by Congressman Mosely Baker highlighted the passions still aroused by the hero of San Jacinto.[13] Baker asked his colleagues to approve a resolution formally thanking outgoing President Houston "for the able manner in which he had discharged his duties."

Although the measure passed, it did so only over the objections of one-third of the members present.[14]

House lawmakers required most of December 1838 to reach agreement on the seat-of-government bill. Cullen brought his bill back up for debate on December 14. Six days later Mosely Baker successfully moved to refer it to committee. When the committee reported a substitute bill the following morning, ensuing debate centered on the boundaries of the territory to be considered by the legislation's mandated site-selection commission. Eastern lawmakers strove to push the eastern boundary to the Trinity River; westerners fought the move.[15]

Controversy also surrounded the concept of employing commissioners to select a site. Members of Congress must have known of Lamar's preference for a frontier capital, for this fight also pitted east against west. Nacogdoches representative David Kaufman in particular objected to the commission's authority to select just one site. On December 21 he proposed that the commissioners choose two sites, one east and one west of the Brazos River. Citizens would make a final choice at the next general election. His amendment lost by a vote of 24 to 9.[16] The *Telegraph and Texas Register* outlined the ongoing struggle for its readers in its December 26 issue:

> Several bills have recently been proposed in congress for the removal of the seat of government from this city. We believe a large majority of the members of congress are in favor of removing it from Houston, but great diversity of opinion exists relative to the point at which it shall be hereafter located. Many of the eastern members are desirous that it should be located upon or near the Brazos, and many of the western members prefer the Colorado for the site. The few who retain the seat of government at Houston thus far appear to hold the balance of power, and unless some compromise shall be effected between the two more powerful parties, the question must necessarily continue vacillating, and the session may close with a farce similar to that of the last session, when all the bright prospects that hovered for a moment over the celebrated Eblin League vanished with a momentary fluttering of a feather. A proposition has been made that a number of commissioners should again be appointed to select the site for the capitol, but we believe this measure finds few advocates.

Matagorda County representative Edward Holmes gave a speech in the House which highlighted many of the salient points of debate. He pushed for a western government seat and favored a Colorado River site in particular. He feared that many immigrants would turn around and go home if the capital remained the "ugly and sickly" city of Houston. Furthermore, those favoring the Brazos River operated from selfish motives related to a proposed railroad running from Galveston through Houston to land which they owned. Conversely, a capital on the Colorado River would benefit all Texans by strengthening the frontier and encouraging immigration to what would one day be the center of population of the republic. Finally, he opposed the idea of allowing commissioners to search along more than one river, feeling that Congress should dictate this choice. Commissioners, after all, could be bribed.[17]

Congressman Kaufman, joined by Mosely Baker, continued to hammer away at the bill with various objections and amendments. William Lawrence of Harrisburg County joined the fray on December 27 by unsuccessfully calling for a popular vote to ratify Congress's choice of location. Each time the boundary issue seemed settled either Kaufman or Baker raised objections until each was eventually ruled out of order. When the House finally voted on whether to engross[18] the bill, only four members (including Lawrence but not Baker or Kaufman) voted against the move.[19] Lawrence was so incensed that he vowed to place an official protest in the House Journal.[20] The next day, December 28, on motion from Cornelius Van Ness, the House heard a final reading of the bill before voting 29 to 3 in its favor.[21]

While waiting for the House to finish its debate on the bill to locate a permanent seat of government, the Senate wrestled with matters large and small. On November 6, 1838, William Wharton of Brazoria County sponsored a successful resolution calling on "all the citizens of Texas . . . to rush to the rescue of the inhabitants of our frontier, who are now experiencing all the horrors of a savage war [against Indians]." Two weeks later senators approved a resolution inviting ladies into their chamber to observe the proceedings and banned all smoking in anticipation of their arrival. On December 21 the Senate voted in favor of legislation banning the residence of free blacks in the republic. And on December 26 George Barnett[22] asked his fellow senators to unseat one of their colleagues. Barnett accused Robert Wilson, still smarting from his humiliating loss to Mirabeau Lamar, of "repeated clamorous oaths . . . and invoking high Heaven to strike dead, in their tracks, all those who voted against him." When called to order, Wilson had refused, "saying he would be God damned if he would." When ordered to sit down, Wilson swore that "no power but God could seat him." Most damaging of all, Wilson stood accused of violating the constitution by disclosing Senate secrets. Barnett's fellow senators were likewise not amused by Wilson's antics; the offender was expelled from the Senate the following January 7.[23]

The House sent its seat-of-government bill to the Senate immediately upon passing it December 28. Senators ordered printed copies for distribution, then heard the bill in its entirety on New Year's Eve. Ironically, westerner Edward Burleson successfully offered a resolution extending the boundary of the territory to be considered eastward to the Trinity River. John Greer of San Augustine County obtained consent to confine the search above the Old San Antonio Road. Senate debate failed to trigger the heated passions evident in the House, and the bill received approval January 4, 1839.[24]

Action now shifted back to the House of Representatives. On January 5, 1839, the House received the Senate's message that it had approved an amended version of the bill to locate a new seat of government. Interestingly, the day before the House had rejected a petition from Edwin Waller to permanently locate the capital at Velasco.[25] Had Waller succeeded with his petition, he would have denied himself a place in Texas history as the man largely responsible for the layout of the present capital city of Austin.

Before the House had a chance to address the Senate's amendments it had to deal with yet another Congressional disturbance. During January 7 proceedings House members were interrupted by loud noises coming from the hallway separating the two chambers. A fistfight had broken out between a Senate member and Dr. Ashbel Smith. Dr. Smith's brother, Senator George Smith, joined the fracas, which ceased only at the intervention of the House sergeant-at-arms. With calm restored, representatives began looking at the Senate's changes to its bill regarding the seat of government. By the end of the day the House had achieved consensus and passed the bill without further tweaking.[26] On January 11 the committee on enrolled bills reported favorably. President Lamar signed the legislation into law three days later.

What exactly had Lamar signed? How would the republic choose its new capital? And, most importantly, would this indeed prove to be a permanent selection? Despite Edward Holmes's objections, Congress would elect a five-member commission to select the most appropriate location within the territory bounded by the Trinity and Colorado Rivers lying above the Old San Antonio Road. Commissioners would swear an oath to perform their duties faithfully. In case this was insufficient, the law also required a one hundred thousand dollar bond from each commissioner. Congress imposed a three-month deadline for the commission to report its findings. The chosen site must contain from one to four leagues of land purchased at a price no greater than three dollars per acre. The power of eminent domain would be applied in the case of a recalcitrant landowner. And, as had the Second Congress, this Congress named Lamar's new seat of empire Austin.[27]

Shortly after receiving word of Lamar's endorsement both houses of Congress moved on to the next step, the election of commissioners. Juan Seguin started things off in the Senate January 15 by successfully offering a resolution to proceed. An immediate point of contention arose when Senator John Dunn asked for a committee of three to explore certain constitutional points with the attorney general. When the request failed, Stephen Everitt clarified Dunn's concerns by proposing to ban any Senate member from the commission. After Everitt's proposal lost a 9-to-3 vote, Senator William Wharton rose in protest, thundering that "great corruption and injury" would result from congressmen serving as commissioners. He quoted the constitution, which banned a member of Congress from holding another office during his term. If this were allowed to stand, what would prevent Congress from forming a fifty-member commission with each member paid a thousand or million dollars per day? Most senators were in no mood for this line of reasoning. Congress had passed a law requiring the Senate to name two commissioners. There was no specific prohibition in that law against choosing a senator. In fact, since the law stipulated that the commission would not begin operating until *after* this session of Congress, most saw no reason *not* to name one or two of their own. Ultimately, Albert C. Horton and Senator Isaac W. Burton garnered the most votes and became the first two members of the capital-selection commission.[28]

House lawmakers addressed the issue January 16, 1839. Five House members, Kindred Muse, William Menefee, George Hill, Louis Cooke, and Isaac Campbell received nominations to serve on the commission. A close vote eliminated Hill and Muse, leaving Louis Cooke of Brazoria County to serve with westerner Menefee (Colorado County) and easterner Campbell (San Augustine County).[29] Thus, of the five men chosen by the two congressional bodies, two lived in the vicinity of the Colorado River, two near the Trinity, and one on the coast about midway between the rivers.

Everyone in Texas seemingly knew that the Lamar administration favored a frontier capital. A reporter in attendance at the House of Representatives wrote to the *Matagorda Bulletin*, "It appears to be the general impression here, at present, that the Colorado will be the favored river whose banks will be honored by the metropolis of Texas." Another correspondent stated, "I am confidently of the opinion that the commissioners will select some point on the Colorado." To forestall criticism of such an exposed position the letter writer added, "It will cause the immediate settlement of one of the most desirable countries on the continent of America. . . . There will be citizens enough around the spot to defend it from the attacks of all the forces which can be brought against it."[30]

Belatedly, some members of Congress realized that, although their legislation provided for site selection, it did not specify what was to be done with the site, nor when the government would actually move there. On the same day that President Lamar signed the selection act into law, Congressman George Hill of Robertson County introduced a supplement stipulating that the president would have twenty thousand dollars at his disposal for constructing government buildings at the new city. Furthermore, the government would move into these buildings by October 1, 1839, allowing it ample time to settle in before the Fourth Congress began the following month. David Kaufman tried to point out that the buildings ought to actually be finished before the mandated move, but his colleagues rejected the notion of qualifying the deadline. Congressman Lawrence, whose district included the city of Houston, by current law the seat of government until 1840, introduced an amendment allowing legal action against the President to recover financial loss incurred by the government's early departure. He suffered an overwhelming defeat when only Mosely Baker joined him in support of the measure. Baker then tried the delaying tactic of indefinitely tabling discussion, but he also found little support. Louis Cooke called the question and the House voted to engross the bill. Three days later, on January 17, representatives voted 21 to 13 in favor of passage. The Senate followed suit the next day.[31]

Modern travelers passing through Bastrop, Texas hardly notice the Colorado River snaking under the Highway 21 bridge on the south edge of town. With favorable stoplights, the driver needn't even slow down while heading east into the area's "lost" pine forest, so-called because of its complete encirclement by more typical rolling Texas prairie. Shortly after entering the woods, the highway turns sharply northeast on its way to College Station seventy-seven miles distant, crossing the muddy Brazos River just before reaching this town. Once through College Station, Highway 21 stretches another sixty miles before spanning the Trinity River twenty miles west of Crockett. In Sam Houston's and Mirabeau Lamar's day Highway 21 was a dirt track, part of the Old San Antonio Road, or El Camino Real, coursing from San Antonio to the Sabine River and the Louisiana border. The law providing for selection of a new seat of government for the Republic of Texas, signed by President Lamar January

14, 1839, confined the search to the region bounded by the Colorado and Trinity Rivers lying north of this road. Congress gave its five-member commission of Isaac Burton, Albert Horton, William Menefee, Isaac Campbell, and Louis Cooke ninety days to inspect this vast territory and return to Houston to report their findings.

Vice President Burnet and Speaker of the House Hansford banged their gavels to close the Third Congress January 24, 1839. Perhaps because Albert Horton of coastal Matagorda County was the only commissioner not clearly identified with the eastern or western factions, his colleagues elected him their chairman.[32] Born in Georgia, Horton moved to Texas in 1835, fought in the revolution, served as a senator in the first two congresses, then lost his 1838 bid for the vice presidency. Fellow Georgian Isaac Burton spent a year at West Point before coming to Texas in 1835. Also a veteran of the revolution, Burton had just completed two terms in the Senate when he joined the commission. Isaac Campbell arrived in Texas two months before the Texas Declaration of Independence and settled in San Augustine County. His seat in the House of Representatives in the Third Congress would prove to be his only public office. At the time of his service on the commission Tennessee native William Menefee had lived in Texas for six years. As a Colorado County delegate to the Convention of 1836, Menefee signed the Texas Declaration of Independence, having just completed a second term in office as the congressional representative of Colorado County. Like Isaac Burton, Kentuckian Louis Cooke also briefly attended West Point. He volunteered for service in 1835 with a New York battalion that traveled to Texas to fight Santa Anna, but arrived after the Battle of San Jacinto. Cooke allied himself politically with Mirabeau Lamar and had represented Brazoria County in the just-completed Third Congress.[33]

On February 10, 1839, several men on horseback set out from Houston in quest of a perfect site for the Texas seat of government. The party included the five members of the capital-selection commission, a cook, a black slave, and others unnamed. Swallowed by the seemingly endless prairie, the group remained completely out of touch for the next two months. Some took this as a sign that, like the Second Congress, this one would also fail to locate a new capital.[34] The commission ignored the Trinity River. Riding along the Old San Antonio Road to the Brazos River, the men turned north and followed its banks as far as the Falls of the Brazos.[35] They then traced the Colorado River from its Old San Antonio Road crossing to the upper falls in modern Burnet County.[36] The commission's return to Houston in April sparked much speculation, but commissioners evidently were tight-lipped about their findings. On April 13 Horton and his co-commissioners gathered at the capitol. Chairman Horton asked each of his colleagues to choose between the Brazos River and the Colorado, known by one early writer as "the noblest river in Texas." Burton and Campbell naturally preferred the more eastern Brazos. Horton's choice of the Colorado swung the commission behind President Lamar's preferred waterway. Horton next pressed his colleagues to select either Bastrop, the most distant upriver settlement of any size on the Colorado, or Waterloo, thirty miles farther upstream. A unanimous vote declared Waterloo the victor.[37]

Why Waterloo? Why an exposed, distant location with so few settlers lying thirty miles beyond the last faint vestige of Anglo civilization at Bastrop? The commission's report stated that, although the Brazos River was "more central perhaps in reference to actual existing population," the Colorado was "more central in respect to Territory." Regarding the defense of a frontier town, "a majority of the Commissioners are of opinion that that object will be as well attained by the location upon one river as upon the other." Furthermore, claimed the report, water and building materials were more plentiful and convenient on the selected river. But the commission's true motive becomes clear in the penultimate paragraph of the report: "The Commissioners confidently anticipate the time when a great thoroughfare shall be established from Santa Fe to our Sea ports, and another from Red River to Matamoras, which two routes must almost of necessity intersect each other at this point." In concluding, the commissioners paid tribute to Lamar's poetic nature:

> The imagination of even the romantic will not be disappointed on viewing the Valley of the Colorado, and the fertile and gracefully undulating woodlands and luxuriant Prairies at a distance from it. . . . The citizens bosom must swell with honest pride when . . . he looks abroad upon a region worthy only of being the home of the brave and free . . . looking with the same glance upon the green romantic Mountains, and the fertile and widely extended plains of his Country, can a feeling of Nationality fail to arise in his bosom or could the fire of patriotism lie dormant under such circumstances.[38]

Mirabeau Lamar would now have his frontier capital. But his sense of victory might have abated a bit had he known of two toasts proposed at a recent San Augustine dinner held in honor of rival Sam Houston. Clearly, the personal animosity between himself and "the Big Drunk" had infected the supporters of each man. Who would triumph in the coming confrontation and how would the results affect Lamar's dream of a western empire? As sated dinner guests pushed back from the table and puffed on cigars, Congressman Ezekial Cullen raised his glass to exclaim, "Mirabeau B. Lamar, the soldier and the statesman. Under his administration Texas has everything to hope and nothing to fear." Foregoing the politeness usually displayed at such gatherings, R. S. Davis rose in counterpoint, "M.B. Lamar, let his days be few, and let another take his office; let his posterity be cut off, and in the generation following let his name be blotted out."[39]

| Chapter 6 |
WATERLOO

I congratulate you, gentlemen, and the country in general, that a question which has
so deeply excited our National Legislature, has thus been put at rest.

President Mirabeau Lamar in a message to Congress November 12, 1839,
Smither, ed., *Journals of the Fourth Congress*, vol. 1, 6

This is an important measure, and should be laid before the people—for whose
benefit laws should be enacted.

Excerpt from a letter in the *Morning Star*, April 18, 1839

Certainly nothing could have been more ridiculous and absurd than fixing the seat
of government here.

Texas traveler Josiah Gregg, Fulton, ed., *Diary and Letters of Josiah Gregg*, 106

In April 1839 Major James Jones and his "little Army of Volunteers" paused in their pursuit of a fleeing band of Texan Indians to camp along the Colorado River near the home of Anglo settler John Webber.[1] On the 14th, in a letter to President Mirabeau Lamar, Jones expressed disappointment at not yet having engaged the enemy, but added that his men "seem delighted with the idea of pursuing them over the mountains." Jones intended to resume the chase on the morrow by heading west toward Waterloo, a small village at the foot of those mountains. There he would remain to protect what he referred to as the "borders of the extreme northern settlements." Local scenery had greatly impressed the major, who extolled the area as "a beautiful country—Its face presents a scene of grandeur and magnificence rarely if ever witnessed I immagine [*sic*] in any other part of the American Continent." Danger, though, lurked in this beautiful land. "Owing to . . . the inroads of the Indians this fair portion of our Republic is but sparsely settled. Many houses are deserted & property rapidly hastening to destruction."[2]

Major Jones unwittingly highlighted both the blessing and the curse of the capital site selection commission's choice. Possessing great natural beauty, the area was also remote and exposed to danger. Many supposed advantages ultimately proved illusory. With its tree-lined streams, expanses of tall prairie grass, abundant springs, and green hills to the west, Waterloo and its environs tricked many early Anglo settlers into viewing the region as one of boundless fertility. Thick woods clustered along the waterways, with those along the Colorado River extending hundreds of feet from either bank. The forest gave way to verdant grassland interspersed with islands of oaks. Refreshing springs dotting the landscape gave the false impression that water would never be in short supply. Where the low undulations leading up to Waterloo from the east encountered the Balcones Escarpment, with its taller, rockier hills, visitors imagined great mineral wealth. The earliest Anglo settlers failed to understand that underlying this apparently rich landscape was a thin layer of soil spread over a rocky limestone base. Also unknown to them was Waterloo's location in a transition zone from a region enjoying annual rainfalls of up to forty-eight inches to one suffering through years with as little as sixteen inches. The most optimistic newcomers therefore mistook a delicately balanced plains environment for an agricultural paradise.

In concluding their report to the president, the five site-selection commissioners had expressed the hope that "we may not have disappointed the expectations of either our Countrymen or your Excellency." Lamar was more on target when he told Congress, "A diversity of opinion upon such subjects, is the unavoidable result . . . in a country so widely extended as ours." Nevertheless, the commission's choice greatly pleased the president. Lamar saw the many advantages claimed in its report as "ample proofs of the judgment and fidelity of the commissioners, and abundant reason to approve their choice."[3]

Others were less convinced. The *Morning Star*[4] complained that the location act itself was faulty, as "the idea of *permanently* locating the seat of government by commissioners appointed by Congress seems to us entirely absurd-the only satisfactory way is to leave it exclusively to the people." Editor John Eldredge added that lack of nearby timber, a relative lack of water, the site's remoteness, and the unproven navigability of the upper Colorado meant that "it possesses none of the advantages of a city." Keeping up the attack, the paper claimed days later that the Senate had stricken the word "permanent" from the bill's title, and that only a clerical error had led to the word's appearance in the final version. The writer therefore saw folly in moving the seat of government prior to the next congress, "for there does not exist the shadow of a doubt that a strong combination of the Eastern and Central delegation will be made, to prevent its permanent establishment at any place west of the Brazos." And in a lengthy April 30 editorial, the newspaper declared that the act itself was unconstitutional. The writer based this claim on the fact that Congress had earlier passed a law placing the seat of government in Houston until 1840. Because many Houstonians had entered into government contracts under this assumption, moving the government prior to 1840 would violate article 16 of the constitution, which prohibited Congress from enacting legislation "impairing the obligation of contracts." Furthermore, argued the writer, the makeup of the commission selecting the site had violated section 23, article 1, which stated that "no member of either house shall be eligible to any office which may be created during his term of service." Four of the five commissioners had been members of the Third Congress creating the commission. And finally, the writer viewed the entire enterprise as "*for the purposes of governmental speculation*. We would like to be shown that article in the Constitution, or anywhere except in the act of which we complain, which authorizes the government to sell any man's land [for such a reason]."[5]

Nor was the editor of the *Telegraph and Texas Register* initially inclined to praise the commission's choice. After conceding the beauty and healthfulness of the location, the author of an April 17 opinion piece decried the sparse frontier population, especially with respect to the very real danger of Indian attack: "Indeed, within a few months past, parties of Indians have ventured many miles below it. As it will not therefore afford them conveniences of life and the security requisite for the purposes intended, we can hardly believe the offices of Government will be removed during the present year." The *Morning Star* cited another reason for doubt that the government would actually move by the mandated date: "It appears to us absurd to suppose that the indispensable accommodations can be prepared for the President and the other officers of Government within the time specified by law—unless, indeed, there should be an 'Aladdin's lamp' at hand, by whose magic spell cities and castles can be reared in a single night." And future president Anson Jones spoke for many when, after the fact of the move, he wrote in his diary, "No policy could possibly have been more unwise than the removal of the seat of Gov[ernmen]t to Austin, and corrupt means were used to place it there."[6]

Everyone venturing up the Colorado River past Bastrop remarked on the region's stunning scenery. William Jones witnessed a resplendent spring in 1839. Writing to President Lamar he marveled at "the most sublime scene I ever saw. . . . I saw it in all the majesty of nature and the verdure of spring. The atmosphere was charged with the most delightful perfume and every shrub and every hill and every flower seemed to extend a welcome to the weary traveler. . . . I never expected to realize your eloquent description of Texas till I saw the lands of the upper Colorado." A. B. Lawrence, author of the travelogue *Texas in 1840*, felt moved enough to write, "Nothing we had ever witnessed of magnificence and beauty, mingled with soft and pleasing imagery, could compare with what is here presented." An anonymous correspondent of the *Telegraph and Texas Register* noted, "The country possesses much romantic beauty, and a more healthy and delightful situation I have never seen."[7] Arriving in time to assist in constructing the new town of Austin, Thomas Bell wrote to his brother on August 7, 1839: "I must consider this the most beautiful country I ever saw what I have yet seen. There is some of the most beautiful lands I ever beheld or ever expect to. . . . The country generally resembles one vast meadow which nature in her playful moments made for the wonder and benefit of man."[8] And settler John Winfield Scott Dancy wrote in his diary on May 27, 1839: "At Austin. Seat of Government. Walked to Capitol Hill. The view was beautiful. The surrounding country is magnificent."[9]

Of course members of the selection commission had not based their choice solely on aesthetics. Their description of the 7,735-acre site praises the 2,000-acre prairie abutting the river "intersected by two beautiful streams of permanent and pure water." Available resources included "stone in inexhaustible quantities," "timber for firewood and ordinary building purposes," and "lime and stone coal." To the west was plentiful cypress and cedar, which could easily be floated downstream for use in construction. Several area streams, including Walnut, Brushy, and Spring Creeks, offered water power. Close by were large iron ore deposits. Commissioners also pointed out the strategic value of the site, occupation of which would deny hostile Indians and Mexicans the most direct route from the Rio Grande to east Texas. And, of course, the commissioners had their eye on the immense profits available from the massive trade sure to develop between the Texas coast and Santa Fe by way of the Texas capital.[10]

Newspaper editors and letter writers continued their squabbling throughout the spring and summer of 1839. One correspondent predicted in the *Telegraph and Texas Register* that, rather than hindering Houston's development, government removal to the new capital would further its progress "as nearly all the trade of the upper valleys of the Colorado as well as the Brazos will eventually be directed to this point." *Morning*

Star editor John Eldredge scoffed, "Austin, as a commercial city, can never come in competition with Houston." Perceiving no advantage to government relocation, Eldredge expressed wonder that President Lamar "seems disposed to act in this instance, so directly in opposition to every thing like reason, common sense, and even propriety." Continuing to chip away at proposed justifications of the removal, Eldredge wrote on June 19, "We cannot imagine . . . that the income to be derived from the sale of lots in the city of Austin will be as enormous as many seem to suppose." Eldredge also predicted that the new city would not be ready in time to receive the Fourth Congress, thus wasting the expenditure of first moving there and then adjourning to another place. He complained that foreign relations would suffer with the capital located so far from the coast. To those who argued that a frontier capital would protect western settlers, he countered that this goal would be better and more efficiently served by erecting a line of forts along the entire frontier. And Eldredge saw folly in placing the vital public archives within reach of the republic's Mexican and indigenous enemies.[11]

Eldredge next shifted his strategy by attacking the supposed advantages of the site. In a July 18, 1839, editorial he addressed the claims of proponents one by one. He first avowed that a man recently returned to Houston from the nascent capital had described unhealthy conditions resulting in several deaths. He stated that, contrary to the commission's report, timber was actually quite scarce in the vicinity, the nearest substantial forest being at Bastrop thirty miles distant. He denied the presence of continuous springs within the town, adding that those currently in use were drained dry daily by the small population. Dry climate and its sandy, gravelly nature rendered the soil relatively infertile. And, of course, the new town would be all but inaccessible except to hardy travelers. Asking his readers why, despite these many drawbacks, commissioners had chosen the site, Eldredge charged them with greedy self-interest: "In that neighborhood alone, could the Commissioners find *vacant land to locate.*"[12]

In response to this diatribe, the *Telegraph and Texas Register* pulled no punches:

> That the removal of the seat of government from Houston, would excite the spleen of *little minds*, and consequently call down the abuse of those whose conceptions never carried them beyond the precincts of their own town, was to have been expected, consequently we are not disappointed in having certain pot-house politicians continually harping

upon this never failing subject, but the following article from the "Morning Star" on the 18th inst goes beyond anything we had conceived the *ignorance* or *impudence* of the enemies of Austin capable of producing.

The *Matagorda Bulletin* registered satisfaction with Lamar's policy: "Thus far without a dissenting voice, all [who have visited the site] agree that it is a most judicious selection, and all speak in favorable terms of the beautiful country which surrounds it." And the *Telegraph and Texas Register* emphasized the beneficial effect upon frontier immigration: "Until the permanent location of the seat of government in that quarter of the frontier, many of the citizens were undetermined about remaining, but the final settlement of that point, together with the assurance that a number of regular forces will be kept up in the country, have removed any remaining doubts upon the subject."[13]

Like many Anglo-Texan pioneers, North Carolina native Edward Burleson yearned to cash in on the republic's vast, available, and cheap land. After the revolution, town after frontier town sprang to life at the hands of speculators, men who searched for and bought large tracts of land, drew a town plan, advertised the fact in newspapers, and then waited for immigrants and other speculators to arrive. Some, like the Allen brothers of Houston, succeeded; many others ended up alone on the prairie, surrounded only by imaginary streets and a few empty shacks. Failed dreams drew the ridicule of a jaded public. One observer wrote, "Texas contains more *cities* than any country in the world. Most of them scarcely contain a house—and many of them never will. But the proprietors give them high-sounding names, and the appellation of *city*, and talk of their future greatness with as much earnestness as if they possessed some of the importance which they *imagine* time would give them."[14]

Edward Burleson arrived in Texas in 1830, secured a land grant the following year, and became a member of the *ayuntamiento* of San Felipe de Austin.[15] He replaced Stephen F. Austin as general of the volunteer Texas army in November 1835, then was named commander in chief in December. When the army disbanded three weeks later, Burleson raised his own company of volunteers. In command of the First Regiment at San Jacinto, Colonel Burleson led his men in the first charge against the Mexican defenses. After the war he served as brigadier general of the militia, as a representative in the Second Congress, and in 1838 as colonel of the First Infantry Regiment in the regular army. The soft-spoken Burleson looked the part of a Texas hero with his blond hair and steel-blue eyes. Acquaintance Josiah Gregg remarked of Burleson, "he is a good, clever, good-humored jovial fellow."[16] He stood just under six feet tall, weighed about 180 pounds, and commanded respect with his bravery and decisiveness. A speech he delivered to his men at the Battle of San Jacinto inspired the battle cry, "Remember the Alamo!"[17]

In the summer of 1838 Burleson turned his focus away from military adventure to land speculation. Realizing the coming popularity of the upper Colorado region, he fixed his gaze on property once claimed by the deceased Stephen Austin.[18] Before his death Austin had acquired a large river tract on the eastern edge of the Edwards Plateau with the aim of settling there. On the fifth of June Burleson wrote to the administrator of Austin's estate, James Perry,[19] to state his intentions: "I have Examined the town Site that I was Speking to you aboute and it appears to meet with almost Universal wish of the people above this place for a town to be laid off." Burleson then did just that, offering riverfront lots at between three and four dollars per acre. He named his town Waterloo. At its inception Waterloo already had at least one resident, Jacob Harrell, who had arrived on the spot in 1835.[20] In 1838 Harrell's house marked the extremity of Anglo settlement on the Colorado River.

In its short life Waterloo never amounted to much. By the time of its selection as the seat-of-government site it housed only four families. Nevertheless, at least one early visitor saw great promise. Noting that "The tide of population appears to be setting that way," the 1838 traveler recorded in his diary many of the same advantages cited by the selection commission a year later. "Romantic beauty," reliable water supply, potential river navigation, fertile land, and the coming Santa Fe trade inspired the diarist to gush, "a more healthy and delightful situation I have never seen." At the moment of his visit, however, which was only a few weeks before Mirabeau Lamar's buffalo hunt, Waterloo offered "nothing in the way of improvement but a name; and I wish it had not *that*, if the proprietors could not give it one without borrowing from a foreign country."[21]

None other than Waterloo founder Edward Burleson provided the visitor a tour of the area. After fording the river below the town, the pair rode two miles west to visit William Barton, whose residence at a "place of peculiar beauty" predated even Jacob Harrell's. Barton, the "Daniel Boone of Texas," feared the same influx of settlers that Burleson dreamed of. "[He] says he cannot bear the idea of being intruded on by settlers, and hopes the mountain at least may protect him from intrusion on one side." The old man entertained his overnight guests with his frontier anecdotes, showed off the clear beautiful springs below his house, and spoke of frequent buffalo sightings.[22] After bidding Barton and Burleson farewell, the visitor rode a bit farther upriver to ascend the highest peak in the area.[23] His account paints a vivid picture of a landscape now drastically altered from former days:

> Arrived at the top, a more beautiful prospect could not be imagined. The Colorado river appeared like an inconsiderable stream of 15 or 20 feet wide. We could see its course 12 or 15 miles, winding among hills; and the broken peaks of the mountains rising one above another, could be seen at the distance of 20 or 25 miles on the north—while the one on which we stood over-topped them all. On the east and west extended the mountain chain to a considerable distance, while on our south, the broad, rich prairie, covered with flowers, and enlivened by its thousand groves of timber, completed the prospect; and made it one of the loveliest of nature's workmanship.[24]

Despite Waterloo's humble appearance, Burleson pushed an optimistic view. Shortly after hosting his anonymous visitor, he wrote to inform James Perry of his efforts: "I have went on to the place that I was Seking [speaking] to you a bout on the Grant at the foot of the Mountains and have Laide out a town which has Commenced Improving considerable." The proprietors of the nearby community of Montopolis had evidently been trying to scare off potential Waterloo settlers by pointing out the unsettled nature of Stephen Austin's original land claim.[25] Burleson asked for Perry's assistance in warding off the attack.

> The proprietors of the lower town [Montopolis] Is know [sic] trying to urge to those that are disposed to Improve in water Loo that you will not Recognize any arrangement that I make with the Setlers Should you hold that Land I have told them that I had a garentee from you Should you hold that you would Secure them and Just a Line from you to me that you would do So would give Intire Sattisfaction and place me from under a pledge to them that you would do so and Confer a favor on your Friend and Servant Ewd Burleson.

Perry backed up Burleson's actions, but his letter didn't arrive until January 1839, five months after Burleson's request.[26] That was the same month that Congress both incorporated Waterloo and passed the act forming the commission to locate a new seat of government. In fact, Mirabeau Lamar sowed the seed of Waterloo's demise by signing the location act into law the day *before* Waterloo's January 15, 1839, incorporation.

| Chapter 7 |
ROAD TO AUSTIN

William Barton was worried. Peering eastward from atop a hill overlooking the Colorado River, he scanned the verdant prairie in vain for any movement that might be his son returning from a trip to Bastrop. As would any prudent Texas frontiersman, "Uncle Billy" carried a hunting rifle, not in the hope of encountering game, but as a precaution against becoming prey himself. Barton had hiked up the incline from his nearby home on the beautiful creek which emptied into the Colorado below him. Multiple gushing springs in the vicinity of his cabin created deep crystal pools of chilled water, which lured a steady stream of visitors to Barton's property. There they swam, fished, and marveled at the two domesticated buffalo calves that Barton kept as pets.[1]

As he squinted into the distance, Barton couldn't help but notice the large patch of mud and bustle which interrupted the landscape. Running from the north riverbank, the brown scar followed a shallow ravine to a dead end at the base of a gentle rise. Crude log structures formed two parallel lines along the ravine, while others randomly dotted the grassland on either side. A much larger structure dominated the western approach to the site, while a gleaming white edifice seemingly guarded the town's eastern aspect. A host of tiny figures scurried among these various buildings. The occasional breeze carried the sound of a pounding hammer to Barton's ears.

Born in South Carolina in 1782, William Barton had accompanied two of his brothers to Mexican Texas in 1828. Feeling crowded when a neighbor settled within ten miles of his Bastrop County home, Barton moved forty-five miles further up the Colorado River in 1837. One therefore suspects that he regarded the construction across the river from his new homestead with no great pleasure.[2]

Barton forgot his anxiety for his son at the crack of a rifle and the whizzing *snap* of a ball smacking his hat brim. In response he raised and fired his own gun at the small cluster of expectant Indians now visible in the distance. One of the attackers fell wounded,[3] but the rest shouted and charged. The elderly Barton turned toward home and raced for his life.

Sprinting down one ridge and up another, Barton whistled frantically for his hunting dogs. Five or six of them bounded toward him but, to Barton's horror, wheeled sharply in pursuit of a deer darting suddenly out of the brush. The winded settler knew his stamina was no match for that of his pursuers. As he crested the next ridge he began waving and yelling desperately to non-existent help. "Here they are boys, come quick!"

To Barton's great relief, the ruse worked. The Indians turned about and ran away from the old man as fast as they had charged after him. Barton didn't waste his opportunity, but fled toward his house as fast as his fatigued legs could carry him. Exhausted upon arrival, he stumbled into Judge Joseph Lee and a group of men who had come out of the house to investigate the sound of the fight. A panting Barton exclaimed to the startled men, "Boys, it's a good thing it wasn't one of you, or you would have been killed shore!"[4]

Even before the selection commission announced Waterloo as the new seat of government, President Lamar began receiving applications for the crucial position of government agent in charge of planning and constructing the new city. The complete slate of applicants is unknown, but one of the unsuccessful candidates was commission chairman Albert Horton. Another, Jackson Smith, a Houston lawyer already disappointed by Lamar when the president passed him over for a job in the Office of Register, wrote Lamar on February 2, 1839, that "if my services as agent for the City of Austin might be acceptable-I will feel myself distinguished by your kindness & favour." Lamar evidently did not find the applicant's services acceptable, for he once again disappointed Smith. Three days later Lamar received a letter from Edwin Waller, who had unsuccessfully proposed his town of Velasco for the new seat of government. Waller indicated that he had forgotten the earlier snub by promising to "become a permanent resident of the place when located," adding that he would "use my best exertions to promote the interest of our Country."[5] His words and reputation impressed the president enough that Waller got the job.

Few men's credentials as a Texas patriot matched those of Edwin Waller. Born in Virginia, Waller arrived in Texas via Missouri in 1831. After settling in Brazoria County he purchased the *Sabine*, a cotton transport ship, and quickly established a reputation with Mexican authorities as a troublemaker by refusing to pay customs duties at Velasco. Waller biographer P. E. Peareson called this "the first 'overt act' of resistance to Mexican authority." The incident led directly to the Battle of Velasco in

Edwin Waller, pictured here late in life, proved an able and scrupulously honest agent for President Mirabeau Lamar. In the space of nine months in 1839, Waller planned and built from scratch the new government seat of Austin. The enormous undertaking involved organizing supplies and a workforce of about two hundred men in Houston, transporting them to Waterloo, laying out the new town of Austin, and constructing the public buildings necessary to house the government. Reprinted by permission of the Austin History Center, Austin Public Library, PICB 10971.

1832, in which Waller and about a hundred other malcontents forced the surrender of the troops under Domingo de Ugartechea manning the port city's fort. A knotted handkerchief saved Waller's life during the fight by deadening the impact of the bullet that struck his head. Waller suffered only a painful bruise and a pair of black eyes.[6]

Despite his subsequent position as Brazoria alcalde,[7] Edwin Waller felt little loyalty to the Mexican government. An early advocate of rebellion, Waller represented Columbia at the San Felipe Consultation in 1835, where delegates elected him a member of the General Council of the Provisional Government of Texas. As the Brazoria representative at the Convention of 1836 in Washington he helped write and then signed the Texas Declaration of Independence. Waller's stance as an "original war man" resonated with another early proponent of Texas independence, Mirabeau Lamar. His later political support of Lamar's presidential campaign helped forge a strong bond of friendship between the two men. Lamar's selection of friend and ally Edwin Waller as agent in charge of the new seat of government could therefore have come as no great surprise. On March 2, 1839, the third anniversary of the Declaration of Independence, the president's secretary J. B. Ransom sent this letter to the new agent: "His Excellency the President has instructed me to inform you that he will confer on you the appointment of Government Agent, for the new City of Austin, the future Capital of the Republic, and that he solicits an interview with you upon the subject as soon as practicable, preparatory to the necessary arrangements, etc."[8]

At its creation, the city of Austin lay within Bastrop County, which had been called the Mina Municipality under Mexican rule.[9] The Mina Municipality's boundaries had been determined through two Mexican government land grants to empresario Stephen F. Austin. In 1840, the Texas Congress lopped off the enormous western chunk of Bastrop County to create Travis County, with Austin as its county seat. Over ensuing decades, as western Anglo settlement progressed, lawmakers whittled away at Travis County, in the process creating eleven other counties.[10]

At ten o'clock the morning of April 3, 1839, when Bastrop County still possessed the massive western portion that included Waterloo, six "disinterested Jurors" gathered before Bastrop County Chief Justice L. C. Cunningham,[11] Sheriff Preston Conlie, and witnesses Robert Gray Green and F. A. Willis to render a decision of vital importance to the few inhabitants of the tiny town. The latter included Waterloo's longest resident, Jacob Harrell, as well as George Neill, Logan Vandeveer,[12] Aaron Burleson,[13] George Duncan Hancock,[14] J. Porter Brown, James Rogers, and Waterloo founder Edward Burleson. Each of these men owned land in or around the town.[15] Each was about to sell that land, willingly or not, to the Republic of Texas. Each was to feel the power of the government to appropriate private property for public benefit.

Empowered by the Third Congress, the five-man selection commission had on March 23 petitioned the Bastrop County court to condemn the land in and around Waterloo for use as the republic's new seat of government. Neill, Vandeveer, Aaron Burleson, Hancock, and Brown now joined the sheriff and justice in the courtroom to hear the outcome of this petition. Cunningham appointed William Pinkney Hill to represent the interests of the absent Edward Burleson and Jacob Harrell. Hill also stood in for James F. Perry, the agent from whom Waterloo residents had purchased their lots. Neill, Vandeveer, Aaron Burleson, and Hancock each received $3.50 per acre. The jury awarded Brown, Rogers, Harrell, and Edward Burleson fifty cents an acre less. Ten days later in Houston, the commissioners notified President Lamar and the Treasury Department that the republic had completed the forced sale to acquire land for its new seat of government. The government owed the former landowners $25,416.[16]

Imagine a young English aristocrat, accustomed to stylish travel along well-manicured British roads, venturing beyond the mud-splattered streets of early Houston, Texas. "Between Houston and Washington there is a certain space of two miles, which . . . was not traversed in less time than four hours, so deep was the mire." No road signs, nor even roads, eased Matilda Houstoun's journey. Instead, as she noted, Houstoun relied on "*plumbing the track,* namely, tracing the path of former travelers." The absence of bridges and causeways meant frequently flooded river valleys. This produced scenes amusing to Mrs. Houstoun, who reported travelers "knee-deep in mud, and looking as though hopeless of rescue, and dying and dead cattle . . . interspersed among bales of cotton." Even exiting the city had been a challenge. "We ascended a hill so steep, as to seem almost impossible for a carriage, however light, to be drawn up it. Stumps of trees were left in the middle of the path."[17]

To build the city of Austin, Edwin Waller would have to haul a mountain of supplies through the same country encountered by Matilda Houstoun. As is still the case, two routes from Houston, where Waller would make most of his purchases, led to the interior.[18] One headed due west through San Felipe to Columbus, from which it followed the Colorado River to La Grange, Bastrop, and Waterloo. The other struck the Brazos River farther north at Washington before heading on to Bastrop and the seat-of-government site.[19] In 1840 A. B. Lawrence took the northern route through Washington, arriving in Austin eleven days after his departure. Lawrence's progress was slower than it could have been had he not chosen, for safety's sake, to accompany a train of ox-drawn wagons making the same journey. His observations paint a detailed picture of the countryside and people between Houston and Austin in the new capital's early days.

While still in the flat plains leading away from Houston, Lawrence delighted in the abundant wildlife: "Among other pleasing views of the day, we saw flocks of deer feeding politely or sporting gaily among the prairies. . . . Their flesh appeared so often upon the tables of our hosts, as proved that their harmlessness afforded them, even here, no protection."[20] Once beyond the prairie Lawrence experienced the same wave of emotion described by others when encountering such beautiful scenery:

> The rolling country appears now fully before us, affording views and
> prospects which are truly delightful—eminence succeeding eminence,

till the low and flat prairie country has entirely disappeared. The extended landscape furnishes such a view as to a yankee would seem the perfection of beauty in hill and dale, and excited in us a propensity to possess some portion of a land destined, at some future day, to rival in wealth and beauty the fairest portions of the world.[21]

After visiting the city of Washington and its six hundred inhabitants, Lawrence met an interesting character, "an eccentrick [sic] individual, who, with no other associates than his dog and chickens, lives in his cabin alone in the border of the forest."[22] This settler startled his guest with his deep animosity toward Indians. Recalling his service in the Texian army, the man casually related an episode in which a camp guard shot and killed an Indian woman pilfering grain from a corn crib. On another occasion a guard fired at a shadowy figure approaching the horses late at night. The following morning the intruder's bloody trail led soldiers to a wounded Indian lying in a hollow:

An officer present then presented his rifle, and asked him where he would be shot, he opened his bosom, pointed to the centre of his breast, and was immediately pierced by a ball at the place indicated. A rope was then attached to his legs, by which the body was dragged some distance and hung upon a tree, as a warning to other Indian depredators, where it remained for several months, and until eaten up piecemeal by the wolves and vultures.[23]

Lawrence's encounter on the road with a teamster from Mississippi will intrigue any modern central Texan who has braved a summer night without mosquito repellant. When asked about these annoying insects, the man stated that "here he was not tormented to death by mosquitoes. . . . He had not seen a dozen since coming to the country." The area's fertility also impressed Lawrence. When he asked a plantation slave his opinion of the soil the man replied, "O a heap better as Alabama, Sir, where we come from. This country make easy work for farmer. Every thing grows here 'out much trouble."[24]

Methodist minister Thomas Asbury Morris saw nothing romantic about travel in early Texas. Commenting that, "The inconveniences and difficulties of extended journeys are not all imaginary," he complained of heat, cold, thirst, dust, swollen streams, mud, and bouncing over "Davy Crocket's railroad, made by laying poles crosswise in the track to prevent the carriage from being entirely swamped." Unpredictable delays were also inevitable. "A freshet may carry off the ferry or bridge, his only dependence for crossing some river, or he may be journeying where there is none to lose, and find himself at a dead halt till the flood subside."[25]

Edwin Waller faced a formidable task. As one observer wrote, "There had not been a tree felled anywhere in the vicinity of the city of Austin prior to the location of the capital there." To build a city from scratch he needed hundreds of workers. Waller himself evidently complained of the difficulty of hiring the needed men, as the *Morning Star* noted: "From letters which we have seen from the agent, we learn that it is impossible to obtain the necessary workmen to erect the buildings which are absolutely indispensable, for the accommodation of the officers of the government." These workers required tools, which would have to either be purchased and hauled to the site or manufactured from material brought along for that purpose. So many men would devour tons of provisions. Not only this food would burden transport wagons; so would the utensils necessary for preparing and serving it. As the *Morning Star* editor observed, "Every comfort and almost the necessaries of life must be sent from Houston in wagons." Moving freight called for innumerable wagons, animals, teamsters, and quantities of fodder. Waller needed men to build and load packing crates in Houston and other men to unload them in Austin. He had to find enough surveyors, mapmakers, and draftsman to lay out a town and enough skilled craftsmen and laborers to construct it. Armed protection against Indian attack might prove crucial. In short, he had to think through thousands of minute details or risk doing without a necessary item after arrival in Austin. And he had to hurry, because President Lamar and the Fourth Congress would show up in only six months expecting everything to be ready.[26]

Waller's authority as government agent carried the potential for great fraud and corruption. A dishonest man in his position stood to make a fortune through kickbacks, graft, and outright theft. Recognizing this, the Third Congress had mandated that the chosen agent post a one hundred thousand dollar bond contingent on faithfully carrying out his duties. Edwin Waller signed this bond April 12, 1839. Twelve of Waller's friends co-signed with him.[27] But of course, Waller would be compensated for his efforts. In addition to a salary of eight dollars per day he would be eligible for a 5 percent commission on lot sales and five dollars per hundred disbursed in construction contracts.[28]

Mirabeau Lamar undoubtedly stood among the spectators watching the departure of Edwin Waller and his impressive convoy from Houston May 2, 1839.[29] The president's dream of westward expansion rode with the train. Given the enormous expense of the endeavor, the republic's financial fortunes also rode with Waller. Each man in the expedition expected eventual payment from the depleted Texas treasury. Every tool, utensil, and scrap of food carried in the multitude of ox-drawn wagons counted against Lamar's one hundred thousand dollar budget.[30] Merely conveying the tons of supplies in these wagons to Waterloo would, at a cost of ten to fifteen dollars per hundredweight, involve a fortune.[31] One contractor's load is reflected in a receipt signed by M. Hemphill for goods provided in Houston by Louis P. Cooke. The varied contents of the wagon indicate the detailed planning required for a successful expedition:

One ham back (sides) 200 barrels
2 boxes of candles
One box of soap
One barrel of beans
One barrel pork
One barrel conf. sugar
One barrel ditto [conf. sugar]
One barrel brown sugar
One sack of salt
One half barrel flour
One half ditto [barrel], biscuits
Two-thirds of a box raisins
Two-thirds of box mustard
One keg of crackers
One sack of coffee
Two ottomans and one half dozen chairs
Two kettles, one brass and the other iron
Two ovens
One griddle
One grill iron[32]

Good weather must have blessed the train, for by May 23 Waller and his men had completed their journey.[33] On the road the hundreds of men and animals would have stretched over several miles. Six to eight yoke of oxen, or twelve to sixteen of the animals, pulled each wagon and its 4,000-pound load.[34] At streams and rivers these loads often proved so heavy that two trips were required for the crossing. After a daily trip of about eight miles drovers bunched the wagons together, removed the yokes, and attached a large bell to each ox. The animals were then turned loose to graze while the men prepared cooking fires and sleeping arrangements.[35]

May 7 found Waller seventy miles up the road in Columbus. There he purchased an additional $415 worth of supplies, including coffee, bread, sugar, salt, blankets, frying pans, a coffee mill, candles, and rope.[36] Two days later Waller remained stuck in Columbus. He explained to Lamar:

Dear Sir

My business progresses as rapidly as I could have expected although one waggon [sic] which I expected to arrive from Houston at Columbia did not come in as I anticipated. I[t] started there from that place yesterday morning, which are now on the way accompanied by a number of workmen. I have found it more difficult than I anticipated to procure workmen but hope to succeed in collecting a sufficient number together before we reach our destination.

William Hunt, who had left Waller at Columbus on the seventh, wrote to Lamar from Houston to vouch for Waller's excuse. He also offered the president some encouragement: "He has been Successful in purchasing tools, provisions &c & will be Enabled to proceed with Expedition in the discharge of his duty."[37]

On May 23 Waller wrote to inform Lamar that he had solved his manpower shortage. He also quoted a colorful citizen's impassioned speech in support of the president, "D—m the people of Houston and Galveston, although they are the Presidents enemies the people of the Colorado, the bone and sinew of the country are his friends." The man behind this statement was frontiersman William Barton. And, as he did in his letter to Lamar, Edwin Waller may have been the first person ever to write these words next to the date on a piece of correspondence: City of Austin.[38]

| Chapter 8 |
BUILDING A CITY

*The city of Austin bids fair to become one of the most refined and
pleasant cities in the western world.*

Early Austin resident Thomas Bell, letter to his brother, November 19, 1839

Thomas Bell had never before seen such beautiful scenery. After crossing the Sabine River to enter Texas he and his companions rode through the Redlands admiring the "rich red soil [that] produces as fine corn and cotton as I ever saw anywhere." Immediately west of the Trinity River the soil seemed poor, but the Brazos River bottomland overwhelmed the young Bell with its lush appearance. The party then traversed seventy miles of trackless wilderness. The men dined on buffalo, turkey, and deer, marveled at vast herds of wild horses, and even caught a few wild mustangs along the way. One herd of a thousand horses regarded the riders "as if their rights were invaded. They seemed to rally and prepare for a charge and dashed directly towards us at full speed until within one hundred yards then made a beautiful curve." On the same idyllic August day in 1839 Bell rejoiced at encountering thick, black soil, abundant springs, and "constant breezes from the mountains which blow a heavy gale throughout the day and night." Having no prior experience with a Texas summer, he also remarked on the lack of rainfall and the "uncommonly low" water level in rivers and streams. Texas heat impressed the newcomer. He and his companions arrived in Austin "all in great health except myself was somewhat unwell last evening produced from riding in the prairies with the hot sun beaming on me."[1]

Austin, Texas in 1839 lured Thomas Bell into an arduous journey of several weeks with its promise, not its present. Nevertheless, Bell liked what he saw: "The location for a city is very fine land rises from the rim in gentle swells and elevations with a fine view of the surrounding country. . . . I think it is probably destined to become a considerable place." He had, unfortunately, arrived five days after the first public sale of city lots, but probably had more of an eye on rural real estate, which he thought cost from fifty cents to a dollar per acre.[2] He wrote home while dining on venison, bread, and coffee at Spicer's Tavern "in the suburbs of Austin," after which he planned to "sleep on the earth and cover with the skies like most of the Texians."[3]

Manuel Flores peered over the steep embankment to glimpse the North San Gabriel River below and knew he was trapped. For the past forty-eight hours the Mexican agent and his thirty followers had eluded pursuit, but now the Texans had caught up to them. Starting out from Matamoros in late April 1839, the party aimed to deliver supplies and communications to Tejano rebel Vicente Cordova as well as to recruit Texas Indians to fight against the Anglo government. On May 14, in the vicinity of San Antonio, Flores and his men surprised and killed four members of a surveying party, then rode north to cross the Guadalupe River at the site of modern New Braunfels. Bad luck intervened the following day near Onion Creek when Lieutenant James O. Rice and ranger B. B. Castleberry crested a hill in pursuit of a deer, spotted the armed group, and raced back to inform their commander, Captain Micah Andrews. Flores and his men had been running ever since.

Neither side knew the strength of the other. Several Texans, including Captain Andrews, had to abandon the effort because of exhausted, lame mounts. On the afternoon of May 17, when Rice and the remaining sixteen rangers rode through a recent Mexican campsite near the South San Gabriel River, the lieutenant counted four campfires and knew that he faced only a small enemy contingent. Manuel Flores, on the other hand, didn't know whether his pursuers numbered ten, twenty, or a hundred men. His last act therefore displayed considerable courage. Rallying about ten of his followers, Flores wheeled his horse away from the cliff and charged the Texans. He evidently hoped this action would allow the rest of his command to find an escape route. Shielded by a grove of live oak trees, Rice and the rangers returned the ineffective Mexican fire with deadly accuracy. Flores and two other attackers tumbled dead from their saddles, Flores with a bullet through the heart. When the fleeing Mexicans left their baggage and about 114 horses and mules behind, the exhausted Texans declared victory. They gathered their booty, rounded up the animals, and started back to an empty spot on the prairie called Austin.[4]

The Flores fight, though but a minor skirmish, imparted lasting effects upon Texas national policy. Among the captured papers were letters from Mexican officials to the chiefs of various Indian nations, including Big Mush and Bowles of the Cherokee, offering inducements to the recipients to take up arms against Anglo-Texans. That the captured saddlebags contained no replies from the Cherokees seemed to matter little to men like President Lamar, who seized on the Mexican letters as further reason to expel the tribe from Texas. With respect to Austin, the incident added roving bands of Mexican raiders to Edwin Waller's list of worries as he commenced building the new Texas capital. It also introduced delay, although Waller reassuringly wrote to Lamar, "I have lost but two days since I arrived at this place which were employed in pursuing a party of Mexicans who were encroaching upon us and who were overtaken and beaten by Capt. Andrews' Company." And while there would be no further significant clashes with Mexican forces during the city's construction, Austin had not yet suffered its last sting from south of the Rio Grande.[5]

Captain Andrews's chase of the Flores party must have drained Edwin Waller's manpower supply, for he gave it as a reason to Lamar to stop work and tour the countryside. Heading west over the mountains he encountered a "fine country" that was "not equal to that on this side which is truly beautiful." As had numerous visitors before him, Waller wrote glowingly of the Austin site:

> An agreeable admixture of hilly and prairie land in just the proper proportion to please the eye and answer the purposes of the farmer together with a rich soil render the country a most desirable one. Numerous clear running streams intersect the country at short distances affording an abundant supply of pure water. . . . The river bank is bluff, from whence a level prairie affording excellent ground for building lots extends back about two thirds of a mile where it rises into hills, most of them covered with timber, which offer desirable situations for the public buildings, private residences &c.[6]

Waller's original conception of the town placed the capitol on a square in the city center. But once at the site he quickly grasped that the topography called for situating the public buildings on high ground to the rear so as to overlook the river. It was from this elevation the previous year that Mirabeau Lamar had dreamed of Texas empire. That Edwin Waller now shared this dream is clear from his prediction to Lamar, "If Congress but meets next session at this place, I am confident this location will remain permanent and another removal not be desired." The optimistic editor of the *Morning Star* obviously concurred, for he boasted, "We may expect soon to see another city reared in the wilderness."[7]

Edwin Waller and his convoy did not travel alone on the road to Aus-

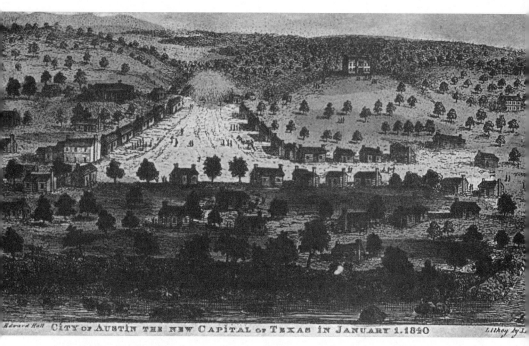

This painting by Edward Hall depicts Austin as it appeared shortly after its construction. The artist is viewing the city from the south bank of the Colorado River looking north along Congress Avenue. Pecan Street runs from left to right. At upper right is the president's house; the capitol is directly opposite on a lower hill at left. The white two-story building on the northwest corner of Congress and Pecan is Bullock's Hotel. Note Waller Creek at far right and the western "mountains" at upper left. Reprinted by permission of the Austin History Center, Austin Public Library, PICA 01082.

tin. As early as May 10, 1839, when Waller was most likely still en route, the *Morning Star* reported, "We have learned by a gentleman direct from the new seat of government, that the road is full of emigrants for that place." Once he had arrived Waller's immediate task was to formulate a town plan. He quickly recognized the advantage of placing the permanent capitol to the rear of the city overlooking the sloping plain leading down to the river. He also shrewdly used the two parallel streams flowing south into the Colorado as the approximate east and west town boundaries. Tradition credits one of Waller's surveyors with naming the eastern stream Waller Creek. The other became known as Shoal Creek for the natural low-water crossing at its mouth.[8]

Waller next superimposed a grid onto the approximate square

Austin's original city plan, as conceived by Edwin Waller and drawn by L. J. Pilie. Shortly after completing this drawing in 1839, Pilie was accused of theft and was flogged and driven from the city. Courtesy of the Texas State Archives, Map Number 0926d.

formed by Shoal Creek, the Colorado River, Waller Creek, and the hill intended for the permanent capitol. Each side of the square was a mile long. The grid consisted of fifteen streets in each direction, yielding 196 blocks.[9] Twenty-one and a half of these blocks were reserved for public use with another two separate half blocks going for churches.[10] City streets would be eighty feet wide except for the major avenues, which would vary between one and two hundred feet. A twenty-foot alley would divide each block in half.

As of July 11 Waller still hadn't named any of the streets. He wrote to Lamar requesting that the president tackle the chore, but did suggest using Texas rivers for the north-south streets and numbers for the cross streets. He also asked Lamar to consider "Colorado Avenue" for the main artery running from the river to Capitol Square.[11] Whoever made the final choice employed only some of these suggestions. The streets bordering the town became North Avenue, East Avenue, Water Street, and West Avenue. North-south streets otherwise took their names from Texas rivers, with the exception of the main artery leading from the capitol, which became Congress Avenue. Rather than numbered cross streets, the plan used the names of Texas trees. The single exception was College Avenue, interrupted by Capitol Square and bisecting the two blocks designated for a university and an academy.[12]

Waller did not wait on street names to put his surveyors to work. As early as May 20 Charles Schoolfield and L. J. Pilie were marking out streets, alleys, and lots according to the agent's plan.[13] People immediately began to squat on desired property. The government had evidently spread the word that improving a lot prior to the first public sale would enable the builder to purchase that lot at the average price paid for similar real estate. Waller disliked this method, as he explained in a letter to the president on May 30: "They [squatters] are selecting the best lots and putting up pole shanties, etc. In this manner all of the most eligible lots upon main street will be taken up."[14] Thus, even before its early identity as a log cabin frontier town, Austin sprang forth as a city of tents.

Prior to pounding the first peg or sawing the first log, early builders faced the formidable task of site preparation. Trees, primarily walnut, pecan, elm, and hackberry, densely covered the area from the river to Cedar Street. Between Cedar and Pecan Streets stood a forest of post oak. From there to Walnut Street blackjack oak predominated, although there were also large numbers of post oak and live oak trees. To the north lay open prairie broken occasionally by clumps of live oaks. A thick carpet of three-foot-high grass blanketed the entire site, with bluebonnets and other wildflowers providing random splashes of color. A large stream divided the town into two equal parts. Named Rio Bravo by early citizens, the creek originated on the hill intended for the permanent capitol, followed Congress Avenue south to Pecan Street, turned east for a block, south on Brazos for two blocks, then east again to join Waller Creek near Cypress Street.[15]

Modern visitors to Republic Square in downtown Austin may relax in the shade provided by a cluster of ancient live oaks.[16] These trees are all that remain of those within the original city limits that greeted Edwin Waller and his two hundred workmen in 1839.[17] As workers cleared lots, streets, and alleys they set aside the valuable timber, such as post oak, for use in construction. Less valuable wood found its way into cooking fires. Protected by the Texas Rangers, woodcutters also operated north of town. A post oak forest several miles away on land now occupied by the Hyde Park neighborhood supplied many of the logs used in 1839.[18] Carpenters hewed post oak trees into rectangular 8-by-10-inch logs for constructing the walls of buildings intended to house various government departments. Waller placed such double log cabins on all four corners of the Congress Avenue crossings of Cedar through Mesquite Streets. A ten-foot-wide hallway separated the two fourteen-foot square rooms, with everything roofed over by post oak clapboards thirty inches long. Bastrop pine served for doors and flooring.[19]

There were no pine trees at the town site, but the Bastrop pine forest thirty-five miles away offered a seemingly endless supply. After felling and trimming a tree, workers placed it on a scaffold for finishing. Two men, one above and one below, operated the handsaw used to cut the tree into usable planks. Teams of oxen then hauled these planks to the emerging capital. One such run in 1839 proved fatal for a slave belonging to Hamilton White. White ordered the man to Austin with a load of lumber, but also gave him three hundred dollars to pay off a debt in town. By nightfall the slave had reached the farm of Reuben Hornsby, eight miles below Austin. Late the next morning Hornsby's wife noticed the man still loitering about the place. When questioned, the man admitted fear of pressing on alone through such sparsely settled country. He declined an offer to wait for company, however, as his master had told him not to delay along the way. A few days later John Wilbarger and a companion found the slave's scalped corpse about six miles from Austin in the vicinity of Walnut Creek. Wilbarger did not find White's three hundred dollars on the body, prompting some to speculate that Anglo robbers had taken the man's scalp to simulate an Indian attack.[20]

Log cabins might suffice for ordinary government office buildings, but not for more prominent public institutions. For these Waller had his men use the sawed pine boards from Bastrop. Thus, the capitol, general land office, treasury, comptroller's department, and president's house, while not exactly majestic, did have a less crude appearance. Even in these buildings, however, Waller used less graceful cedar for floor joists, floor beams, and rafters and post oak saplings for wall studs. Cedar grew in profusion in the hills west of town. Operating on the south side of the river, workers felled hundreds of cedar trees, dragged them to the river's edge across from modern Deep Eddy, and slid them down the bluff into the water. A boom at the mouth of Shoal Creek caught the floating timber. From there workmen dragged it to where it was needed.[21]

Edwin Waller arrived at the undeveloped Austin town site in May 1839 accompanied by at least two hundred men. Waller believed his workforce adequate, for he wrote Lamar, "I do not at all fear a scarcity of hands." Labor remained in demand, though. Arriving shortly after Waller had begun construction, Thomas Bell wrote his brother, "I can get high wages for anything I do here." Waller encountered no facilities, only acres of forest and grassland. Men slept in the open or, if it rained, crowded together under the wagons. They cooked meals over campfires. There was little food except for that which had been carried from Houston, although abundant game in the area provided a steady supply of meat. Water was plentiful, and not just in the river and two main creeks. Springs bubbled to the surface in several places, including two at Congress Avenue and Mulberry Street and another at the intersection of Pecan and Nueces. The previously mentioned Rio Bravo coursed down Congress Avenue while a smaller stream, dubbed Little Shoal Creek, meandered from its source near the modern intersection of Twenty-First and Guadalupe Streets toward Nueces before joining the main creek.[22]

Waller initially set up at least two campsites for his workmen, one along the banks of Waller Creek and the other by the spring at Pecan and Nueces.[23] Livestock spent nights in an enclosed ten-foot-high stockade near the mouth of Shoal Creek. Armed patrols relayed groups of animals to pasture by day. Captains Mark Lewis, James Ownby, and John Garrett each led a ranger company protecting work crews from Indian attack. The men took no holidays. Anxious to have everything ready for the arrival of the Fourth Congress that fall, Waller implemented a seven-day work week. Laborer Thomas Bell seemed content with this schedule: "I pass away the time tolerably agreeably work all day and spend the night at some publick discourse or lecture."[24]

From the moment he first glimpsed the Austin town site, Edwin Waller knew that the nation's permanent capitol building would sit atop the hill at the head of Congress Avenue. Mirabeau Lamar had foreseen a glorious imperial center from its summit and may well have seeded Waller's mind with the notion of placing the statehouse there. Waller also envisioned surrounding Capitol Square with the various departments of government. The Navy and War Departments would flank Congress Avenue, the Justice Department and the General Land Office would face the square from the west, the Treasury and State Departments from the north, and the post office and president's house from the east. Each building would occupy its half block adjoining Capitol Square.

Neither Lamar nor Waller, however, dreamed of an imperial city of crude log blockhouses. And, since the timetable imposed upon government agent Waller allowed for the construction of little else, Capitol Square would have to wait. Waller therefore erected temporary government buildings elsewhere, saving the hill meant for the permanent capitol for later use. All but two of the temporary public buildings were placed along Congress Avenue, primarily between Pine and Ash Streets. The exceptions were the president's house and the capitol. As if attempting to compensate for what he knew would be their pedestrian appearance, Waller placed these two important structures atop the ridges on either side of Congress Avenue, the most imposing locations within the city after Capitol Square.

Waller may have chosen these two sites even before laying out his street grid. As Roxanne Williamson points out in her study of early Austin architecture, the capitol's auxiliary building ended up in the middle of Colorado Street. And, she adds, Waller wrote Lamar on June 2, 1839 to calm the president's fears that something similar would befall the president's house: "The location I have selected does not conflict with the town below as you fear. . . . This selection of mine has been highly approved by all who have seen it and I doubt not will give universal satisfaction." The selection placed the house atop the hill bounded by San Jacinto, Brazos, Bois d'Arc (Seventh) and Hickory (Eighth) Streets. Having decided where to put it, Waller most likely began construction immediately. At the very least, he already had the necessary lumber at hand.[25]

It is no longer possible to experience the majestic panoramic view described by the *Telegraph and Texas Register* as "exceedingly fine" once available to President Lamar from his hilltop residence. Tall buildings long ago obliterated most sight lines. The hill itself was scraped of some of its height to accommodate the modern hotel and office complex that now occupies the entire city block. But a southward glance toward the river while crossing San Jacinto as it runs between this complex and St. David's Episcopal Church affords the pedestrian a small taste of the past. Emerging from the shadows of the enormous Austin Centre, one is surprised to look down upon the rooftops of historic Sixth Street buildings and see San Jacinto Boulevard drop even further to its termination at Cesar Chavez (originally Water Avenue). This perspective clarifies early resident Julia Lee Sinks's observation that "Below, the emerald flat stretched out to the Colorado."[26]

Like most travelers in 1840, A. B. Lawrence approached the nascent city of Austin from the east. Although Lawrence's immediate objective was merely to see the new capital for himself, his ultimate goal involved publishing his observations in a travelogue. But whereas modern travel writers target tourists, Lawrence planned to educate his readers about practical matters pertinent to immigration. After commenting on the beauty of the countryside between Bastrop and Austin, Lawrence recorded his first impression of the new city:

> The first object that attracted our attention was a white house, designated as the residence of the President. "On that spot," said a traveler on horseback by our side, pointing to the President's house, "I for the first time saw a buffalo." . . . It is situated upon the top of a considerably elevated and finely rounded hill, in the front of which is an inclined and level prairie, while in its rear and on the right and left are clusters of oaks of different kinds, all entirely in the state in which they were placed by nature's hand. It commands from its front a fine view of a considerable and beautiful prairie, extending to the Colorado on the south.

Lawrence was not the only newcomer to spot the president's house from afar before gaining any other view of Austin. Julia Lee Sinks mentioned a similar experience. Riding in a wagon on the road from Bastrop, she contemplated the conflicting emotions elicited by her fear of Indian attack and her amazement at the beautiful spring wildflowers when, "'There is the president's house' said the driver, and looking up, we saw perched upon the top of one of the pinnacles of green, a white frame house." And finally, the experience of Presbyterian minister William McCalla illustrates the distance from which travelers saw the house:

> The next morning I rode five miles, guided by the compass, and fell into a promised road which brought me in sight of the president's house in Austin, about the middle of the afternoon. As the river was between

us, I endeavored to find a crossing. In pursuit of this very desirable object I crossed streams, climbed hills, traced paths, breasted ravines and obstructions, and penetrated thickets until dark; when it became necessary to camp out.[27]

To take advantage of the view admired by A. B. Lawrence, Edwin Waller oriented the president's two-story house to face the river. William Walsh recalled a portico the same height as the house in front. By analyzing a painting bill from L. F. Marguaret, architectural historian Roxanne Williamson estimated the building's width at fifty-four feet, length at twenty-four feet, and height at twenty-four feet. The portico measured nine by fifteen feet.[28] The lower floor consisted of two twenty-four-foot-square rooms separated by a fifteen-foot-wide dogtrot. Chimneys flanked the house on either side. A paneled parapet concealed the low-pitched roof, while matching first- and second-story windows encircled the house. An elaborate folding door partially screened the dogtrot, which contained a stairwell connecting the upper and lower floors. This stairway greatly impressed William Walsh, who recalled, "[It] was the first I had ever seen, and I climbed its giddy heights with fear and trembling." As was common in those days, Waller had a free-standing kitchen erected directly behind the main house. L. F. Marguaret painted the mansion's Bastrop pine weatherboarding white. Francis Lubbock, who arrived in Austin shortly after the executive mansion's completion, described it as "the most elegant looking building" in town. William Walsh noted that its "conspicuous" appearance instilled pride in Austin's early citizens. The *Telegraph and Texas Register* informed its readers that "the president's house is the best building in the place. . . . [It] appears almost a palace contrasted with the houses of the frontier hamlets." And years later Julia Lee Sinks lovingly recalled, "The green hill on which it stood was studded with starry daisies and fragrant with lemon balm; its white front, with its upper and lower porticoes, glittered in the sun, the green of the hill lying below, making a soft, shadowy contrast to its brilliancy, and this same sun with its warmth seeming to enter our hearts, made us look up loyally and feel that the house was good enough for a king." [29]

In the three years since the signing of the Declaration of Independence, the Texas government had run the country from a rented hall in Washington, a forgotten Harrisburg structure soon after torched by Santa Anna, a wholly inadequate Galveston Island facility, equally inadequate edifices in Velasco and Columbia, and a rain-soaked, roofless capitol set in the muddy streets of Houston. President Burnet and his cabinet had even

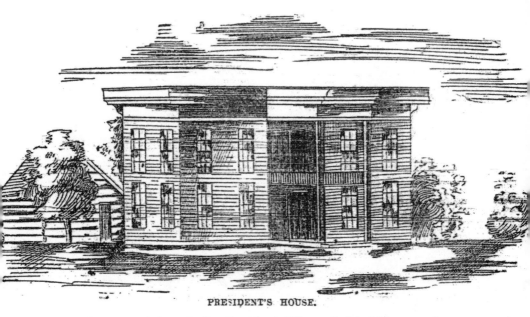

PRESIDENT'S HOUSE.

Mirabeau Lamar's "mansion" on President's Hill occupied the highest spot in town in 1839. Because of severe warping of the green planks with which it was constructed, the building was in such a state of disrepair at Sam Houston's return to the presidency in 1842 that he refused occupancy. Courtesy of the *Galveston News*, February 1896, Center for American History, University of Texas at Austin.

briefly directed the nation's affairs under open sky on the corpse-strewn plain of San Jacinto. Now, for the first time in its history, the young republic was to have a permanent government home, or at least a temporary home in the city of the permanent statehouse of the future. But only if government agent Edwin Waller could build one in the allotted five months.

Waller entrusted actual construction to contractor Benjamin M. Noble. Noble's finished product faced east from the crest of a hill at Colorado and Hickory Streets, or one block west from where Mirabeau Lamar shot his trophy buffalo in 1838. The location complemented that of the president's house; according to A. B. Lawrence, the two structures appeared as symmetrically placed, elevated sentinels on opposite sides of Congress Avenue. While functional, the capitol failed to elicit much pride from citizens or excitement from visitors. Though she provided many details of other early Austin buildings, Julia Lee Sinks made no mention of the statehouse's outward appearance. Newspaperman George Bonnell

OLD CAPITOL OF THE TEXAS REPUBLIC.

The temporary capitol complex constructed by Edwin Waller in 1839 extended into Colorado and Hickory Streets. Note the dog run between the Senate chamber on the building's right and the House of Representatives at left. The short stockade surrounding the complex was derisively known as "Lamar's Folly." Courtesy of the *Galveston News*, February 1896, Center for American History, University of Texas at Austin.

merely called it "commodious and functional," while visitor Edward Stiff complained that "Those [buildings] for public use need no description." German traveler Ferdinand Roemer sniffed, "A more unpretentious building for a law-making body could hardly be found anywhere."[30]

Benjamin Noble employed cedar from the hills for the capitol's frame, which he covered with Bastrop pine planks. Working in partnership with a man named Frazier, L. F. Marguaret painted the exterior white.[31] The building was approximately 60 feet long and 110 feet wide.[32] A dogtrot or central hallway separated the two congressional chambers, with the slightly smaller Senate chamber occupying the north end. Large chimneys stood at either end of the building, and a covered porch spanned the entire front. Seven shed rooms on the west side served for committee meetings. About sixty feet behind the main building was another, smaller structure. Seventy feet wide and twenty feet long, this "retiring room" contained a kitchen and dining room, along with beds, cots, and a room for "refreshments." William Walsh recalled, "I don't know whether these were described as 'contingent expenses' or were sold as articles of commerce, but the business was generally good."[33] Lawmakers drew less intoxicating drink from the two wells located between the retiring room and legislative chambers. If Walsh's memory was accurate, these now lie beneath the pavement of Colorado Street.[34]

One memorable feature of the original capitol building did not appear until later. William Walsh remembered that "surrounding the building there was a stockade of hewn [upright] logs, twelve inches square. . . . A ditch five feet wide and three feet deep surrounded the entire stockade. . . . It must have been about 300 feet square." Julia Lee Sinks wrote of a gravel path ending at "the wooden bridge that led to the gate over the moat or ditch outside of the stockade." The *Telegraph and Texas Register* hinted at this construction in its April 20, 1840, issue: "The good people of Austin are making preparations for defence [*sic*], by fortifying the capitol." A week later the paper reported disagreement about the wisdom of this measure: "The Austin Gazette is striving hard to ridicule the idea of fortifying the Capitol Hill in Austin." A satirical poem in the *Austin City Gazette* did indeed poke fun at the new palisade. The implied German accent of the piece may have been a jab at one Captain Mollhausen,[35] who in June 1840 organized an artillery company to man the guns at the capitol during battle.

How very much I wish I vos
The President of Texas
I'd make the people all shew cause
For rasen such a fracas.
I vonder vot on earth they mean
By makin sich a splutter
About the fort-'t vas meant, 't vould seem
To save their bread and butter.
Its plan and architecture is
Of the true Texian order,
And tho' 'tis rude, I'm sure it forms
The cab'net's *ehef d'ouvre*:
I'm sure Lamar thinks it is right
To save the public archives-
Then tell me, vot's so snug and tight
As rough logs stuck up endvies?
Besides, 't vill answer vondrous vell

For sundry other uses
An amphitheatre vould tell
Or a garden for the muses!
And then it vould be wery nice
If it vos fix'd right handy;
To sit with pretty gals all day,
And suck molasses candy.

That the *Gazette* had company in its attitude toward the "fort" is clear from the actions of contemporary practical jokers: "We understand that some persons have been amusing themselves with filling the big guns in 'Lamar's Folly' with stones."[36]

Finishing touches on the capitol grounds included a variety of martial displays. One visitor from Cincinnati wrote home excitedly of seeing the "Twin Sisters" cannons inside the palisade. These guns originated in Cincinnati and helped carry the day at San Jacinto. The visitor also noted "large piles of muskets, Balls, Bombshells &c., besides a few pieces [of] artillery."[37]

One imagines Mirabeau Lamar, stuck at his presidential post in Houston, dreamily picturing his wondrous new city arising in the wilderness. Friends worked on Lamar's behalf to ensure the city's first father a place in its future. On June 10, 1839, Edward Burleson informed the president, "I have maide an agreement with Capt Sims for a tract that you will be pleased with. . . . I Can only assure you that it is a first Rate tract of Land." After providing further details and signing off, Burleson added a postscript reflecting well on Lamar's choice of government agent: "Judge waller is Getting on finely and I think will be fuly Reddy [*sic*] for the Reception of Congress."[38]

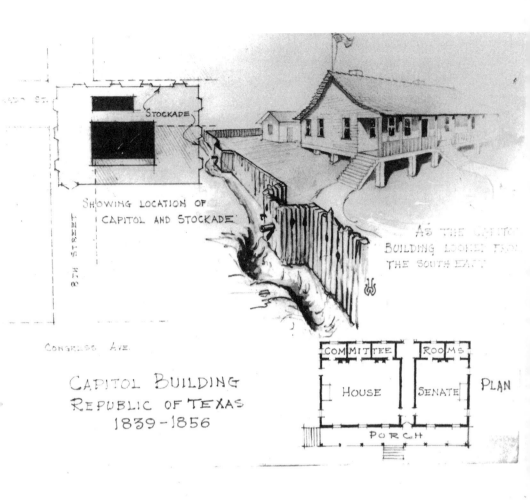

STOCKADE

SHOWING LOCATION OF CAPITOL AND STOCKADE

8TH STREET

CONGRESS AVE.

CAPITOL BUILDING
REPUBLIC OF TEXAS
1839–1856

AS THE CAPITOL
BUILDING LOOKED FROM
THE SOUTH EAST

COMMITTEE ROOMS

HOUSE SENATE

PLAN

PORCH

This drawing of the temporary capitol constructed by Benjamin Noble shows the short stockade known by city residents as "Lamar's Folly." Notice at upper left how the complex extended well into Hickory (Eighth) and Colorado Streets. Courtesy of Capitol Building, Republic of Texas: 1839-1856, Prints & Photographs Collection, Texas Capitols, Early, the Dolph Briscoe Center for American History, University of Texas at Austin, CN03084.

Chapter 9

THERE WILL BE A PUBLIC SALE OF LOTS

The Lots are layd [*sic*], streets & alleys wide, and the several public squares, and lots for the Government Buildings, selected with good taste, by the Agent Judge Waller, who is now engaged in putting up the necessary buildings for Congress.

W. H. Sandusky, Letter to H. J. Jewett, August 1839[1]

The public buildings *shall* be in readiness in time for the next Congress. I have two 16 feet square rooms up now and the rest in progress, therefore entertain no fears upon that score.

Edwin Waller, in a letter to President Lamar, June 2, 1839

Edwin Waller, of course, did not actually build the city of Austin. He organized a mountain of supplies, recruited scores of "mechanics,"[2] procured building materials, arranged armed protection, and planned a city from scratch, but he swung no hammer, sawed no plank, hauled no lumber, shod no horses, nor dug any wells. He hunted no game and cooked no meals. Sweat dripped from his brow as readily as from any man's in the intense summer heat, but the drops fell not on rough cedar joists or post oak logs, but on account sheets, surveyor's notes, and official correspondence. Edwin Waller performed brilliantly as a manager, not a laborer. His contribution lay in organizing and directing the physical work of others.

Who were these others? And what motivated them to risk their lives in hostile territory while toiling ceaselessly under the blazing Texas sun? For those that came willingly the answer was simple: profit. Profit gained either through selling goods or services, or gained through the acquisition of land—land which would surely increase in value in a very short time. Others came because they had no choice. Three years beyond independence from Mexican laws against forced labor, Texans were flooding the republic with slaves. Draftsman William Sandusky reported in August 1839, "The country is settling very fast, and families with their negroes are daily seen on their way to the 'City of Austin', and the surrounding country."[3]

Blacksmith Dennis Walsh came to Austin with the first wagons. He sought employment and a permanent home for his family. According to his son William, the elder Walsh accompanied Edwin Waller from Houston and, upon arrival, assisted in surveying and laying out the town. Dennis Walsh later recalled that all of the animals, wagons, carts, wheelbarrows, axes, drilling tools, and anything else used in public building projects belonged to the government. Waller hired Walsh to maintain this sea of equipment. In addition to repairing tools and vehicles, Walsh kept most of the government horses shod, including a large contingent controlled by Secretary of War Albert Sydney Johnston. On one occasion Waller even directed Walsh to dig a well on "the Old Capitol hill." Despite using explosives to blast through the hard limestone, Walsh failed to reach water. He quit his job November 18, 1839, after a disagreement with Waller, but nevertheless built a two-room cottage in town, to which he brought his family the following January.[4]

Thomas Bell arrived in Austin in August 1839 hungry for any opportunity. In his first letter home he observed, "As to the land generally there is a great deal of the first quality," adding that he imagined it could be had for fifty cents to a dollar per acre. After three months in Austin, Bell explained that although wages were high, prices were even higher, a situation made worse by the low value of Texas currency. Bell briefly contemplated bringing a herd of horses from the United States and selling the animals at the high price they would command in Austin. He could then cheaply purchase mules from Mexican traders in San Antonio and realize further profit back in Mississippi or Louisiana. But he feared that the enormous expense of feeding horses in Austin would limit the number of potential buyers. And the threat posed by Indians and Mexican bandits dampened his enthusiasm for driving valuable animals through dangerous countryside.[5]

Thomas Bell therefore resigned himself to receiving workman's wages. As he explained to his brother, "I have become a considerable carpenter since I came here have built one house and still going ahead as it seems to be the best business that can be followed here at present." Although he detested working for others, he joined a crew building a tavern for Robert Spicer. Bell ridiculed the project with its "log cabins put up round logs switched down covered and lined with pine boards and floors of plank of the same hauled 35 miles," but added that "they keep an excellent house at $4.00 per day." As for his Texas prospects, Bell eventually expressed pessimism: "I do not think this the place for a young man unless he has a capital start upon but the uncertain state of affairs renders investments of capital insecure land titles are so uncertain that people from the States scarcely ever buy land."[6]

Maine native Edward Seiders journeyed south to improve his chance of surviving tuberculosis, then moved to Austin to cash in on the presence of so many immigrants needing supplies. On May 29, 1839, he paid $87.50 in taxes for a license to sell "goods, wares, and merchandize, also distilled spirits" in Bastrop County. Seiders then arranged to have these items shipped from New Orleans to Houston and carried in wagons to Austin. From a tent on Congress Avenue he operated one of the city's first stores. One customer, Captain James Ownby, paid sixty-two dollars on June 9 for knives, bridle bits, and boots. That same month Major William Jefferson Jones purchased horseshoe nails, a saddle, and a pair of boots from Seiders. Seiders's business thrived at first, but when it played out he accepted a job managing Gideon White's plantation on Shoal Creek north of town.[7]

Mr. and Mrs. William Stark stayed busy throughout those early days. William, a skilled carpenter, built tables, chairs, and file boxes. He hung doors on frames he had made himself. He fashioned rails in the capitol, laid a floor in the commissary general's office, and built a desk and bookcase for an unnamed government department. He seemingly accepted any job, large or small, as his surviving claims reflect charges as low as three dollars and as high as four hundred dollars. Mrs. Stark's skills lay with needle and thread. She sewed curtains, table covers, and other cloth articles. Together this duo provided finishing touches to most of Austin's original government buildings.[8]

Examination of the meticulous expense records kept by Edwin Waller yields the names of many others engaged in Austin's construction. James Wall, for example, earned fifty dollars a month assisting with public building construction. In July 1839 subagent R. D. McAnelly assigned him the task of digging a well. Wall excavated eighteen feet of dirt at two dollars per foot and twelve feet of rock at four dollars per foot. Unfortunately for Wall, he was unable to complete the well "[because of] getting my legs broke." Since the injury had occurred on the job, he remained on the payroll and was able to resume work October 26.[9]

Contractor Benjamin Noble submitted an invoice to Edwin Waller in November 1839 that included a charge of $7,754 for lumber and work at the capitol, $4,500 for work and material on other unnamed buildings, $150 for cutting a passage in the treasury building, $425 for hardware, $275 for window shutters, and $100 for the "hire of Negro boy Dick for 2 months." Dick was one of many black slaves leased out by their white owners to the government during Austin's construction. The exact number is unknown, but by January 1840, 145 of Austin's 856 residents were black.[10] The quality of a slave's life in early Texas depended entirely on the disposition and fortunes of his master. Austin's earliest slaves left no first-hand accounts, but if we can compare their experiences to those of the generation that followed them, their lives at times constituted hell. One man by the name of Ben Simpson recalled years later:

> After he [Simpson's owner] comes to Texas, Boss, we never had no home, nor any quarters. When nighttime comes, he have a chain that locks around our necks, then locks it around a tree. Boss, our bed were the ground. Mother, she give out on the way somewhere about the line of Texas. Her feet got raw and bleeding, and her legs swell plum out of shape. Then master, he just take out his gun and shot her. While she was dying, he kick her two or three times and say damn a Negro that couldn't stand anything. He didn't need them anyway, 'cause he could get plenty more. Wouldn't bury mother, just left her laying where he shot her at. He come plum to Austin, Texas.[11]

Josephine Howard was forced by her owner to come to Texas from Alabama as a young child. One morning, without warning, the owner rounded up all of his slaves, put the women and children in wagons, chained the men together to walk, and announced the move. Because Josephine's father belonged to another man he was left behind. His daughter never saw him again.

Born in 1843 on a plantation north of Austin, Andy Anderson remembered relatively benign treatment until his master and master's son both left to fight in the Confederate Army. Then, under a new overseer, "hell stahts to pop." Slashed rations and increased corporal punishment led to numerous escape attempts by some of the slaves. Anderson felt fortunate when sold to a man in Blanco County, but his luck changed when he accidentally damaged a wagon by hitting a stump. After tying Anderson to a stake, the angry overseer administered ten lashes every thirty minutes for four hours. "The last thing I's 'membahs," said the victim, "am that I's wishin' for death."[12]

Rosina Howard, born in Travis County sometime in the 1850s, was more fortunate:

"First thing I 'member is us was bought by Massa Colonel Pratt Washington from Massa Lank Miner. Massa Washington was purty good man. He boys, George and John Henry, was the only overseers. Them boys treat us nice."[13]

Aaron Burleson, who owned a woman named Mary Ann, lived between Bastrop and Austin on a plantation at Rogers Hill. He was a frequent companion of brother Edward in the latter's many campaigns against hostile Indians threatening the new capital. Toward the end of her life Mary Ann told her story:

> I was bawn in Louisiana, but I don' know jes' where. I'se anywhere f'om 97 to 102 years old. I know it was tol' dat I was brought to Texas when I was eighteen months old. A Mr. Turner sold me and mama to Colonel Aaron Burleson. Mawster Burleson bought both of us, 'cause he was a good man and he didn't believe in separatin' a chile f'om its mammy. I do think dat man has gone to hebben. I don' know nothin' about my papa. . . . Sometimes Mawster Burleson would come to de field and weigh cotton fo' us. He was good to us, and he never did lak fo' de wimmen to lift too much. When a woman had a chile and no husband to take care of her, Mawster Burleson would make a man go out and chop wood fo' her and dat slave had better act lak he wanted to. Mawster Burleson was so good to us, dat he never had jes' plain cabins fo' us. He had lumber hauled f'om de Bastrop pineries and he built us slaves good wood dwellin's. . . . We had putty good vittles. I remembah we had so much hog meat dat we'd throw de hogs' head and feet away. Mawster Burleson raised his own hogs. Everythin' dat ole mawster et, we had it too. Sometimes we et deer meat and dah was times when we had bear meat and honey.[14]

Texas slave owners brought their notions of African bondage with them to their new home. Most believed that black slaves inherently withstood prolonged sun exposure and fevers better than the whites. Furthermore, blacks not only tolerated less sanitary conditions, they actually thrived on it. In 1843 English traveler William Bollaert reported the common sentiment among Anglos that "if a Negro child be kept clean and well clothed it will pine and often die; but if allowed to roll and play about in the dirt there is no fear of its thriving."[15]

Bollaert claimed that most Texas slaves had come from Louisiana and Mississippi. He viewed them as inferior to the more docile and efficient slaves of more established slave-holding areas such as Virginia, adding, "But the great secret is to know how to manage them." According to Bollaert Texas slave owners, and by extension those in Austin, treated their human property well. Slaves, believed the Englishman, stopped work at noon on Saturdays and then enjoyed free time until Monday morning. Any that chose to work Saturday afternoon received financial compensation. Masters provided each family with a cabin and half acre of land for a private garden. And all received a week-long Christmas holiday, so that "bedecked out in their best, they visit each other, the evening ending in singing and dancing."[16]

Between April 26 and August 21 Edwin Waller drew a total of $73,000 from the Texas treasury to pay for public building construction. Neri Chamberlain received $650 for erecting a log house and shed. Ervin Holcombe sold nineteen-and-a-half bushels of corn to the government for $87. James Cox supplied several slaves for an unspecified amount of time to earn $460, while Henry Jones took in $254 for the labor of his. Waller gave Henry Blessing a dollar apiece for two empty "flower" barrels, Philip Bowman $8.50 for a day's work, William Fox $54 for sawing lumber, and J. W. Cochran $508 for a house frame. John Foster lost the receipt for his $15 claim while swimming Walnut Creek, but evidently was trustworthy enough to be paid nevertheless. Slaves Mack, Adam, and Ned earned a combined $450 for their white masters while German immigrant Francis Dieterich provided six "gentle stears" for $300. On December 15 Waller distributed wages to thirty-one common laborers. He even settled accounts with a supplier when one contractor came up short of cash. While building the capitol and president's house, Lewis Porter ran out of money to pay his lumberman, Henry Brown. Porter notified Waller of his predicament in a letter reflecting the everyday speech of the Texas frontier: "Sir Owing to my circumstances that I am Placed under Partly in consequence of Some busibody that has more business to attend to of other Peoples than ther own I am at Last compelled to call up on you for a Little more assistance." Brown, "who has acted the gentleman," had sold a quantity of lumber to Porter on credit, which Porter had then used on the two buildings. The contractor needed $461 to pay Brown and he needed it quickly: "a few Dollars wil enable me to complete my Part of job and do me more good than five thousand dollars will when to Late." Waller and Porter evidently were friends, as Porter reminded the agent: "if you cant assist me in acting for the government assist me individually a friend in need is a friend indeed. . . . If you will settle that with him I shall be forever under obligations to you." Although there is no record of Waller's reply, he must have answered favorably because Porter did indeed finish on time.[17]

Herman Ward and his twenty-five-year-old business partner Abner Cook arrived in Austin that summer eagerly anticipating the chance to establish reputations in the construction business. Cook later gained fame as the master builder of many prominent structures in town, including the governor's mansion. His first assignment from Edwin Waller, however, carried a bit less prestige. In October he and Ward received two payments of three hundred dollars each for erecting a "necessary," which, in the delicate language of the times, meant a bathroom.[18]

Mirabeau Lamar's reputation rode into the Texas wilderness with Edwin Waller that summer of 1839. Naysayers abounded; complaints poured in. John Eldredge, editor of the *Morning Star*, grumbled in the May 31, 1839, edition of his newspaper, "We are indeed surprised that the executive should persevere in his determination to remove the seat of government this summer." Furthermore, charged Eldredge, Waller himself had admitted to the impossibility of obtaining an adequate workforce. Anticipating the failure of Waller to complete his task on time, Eldredge prepared the groundwork for blaming the president: "We cannot . . . imagine why he seems disposed to act in this instance, so directly in opposition to everything like reason, common sense, and even propriety." Three weeks later Eldredge expressed further doubt: "The accommodations for the coming year, under the most favorable circumstances, must be few, owing in a great measure to the difficulty in procuring lumber, and workmen, and the impossibility of building stone houses at this time." The editor predicted that Lamar, as mandated by law, would call the Fourth Congress to *assemble* that fall in Austin, then move it back to Houston, thereby wasting a great sum of money. Stuck in Houston, President Lamar must have been cheered by an on-scene report received from supporter Edward Burleson: "Judge waller is Getting on finely and I think will be fuly Reddy for the Reception of Congress." Even the *Morning Star* admitted that Waller "is prosecuting the work with great zeal and dispatch."[19]

In July the *Morning Star* continued its attacks by reporting information about the new capital that it claimed came from recent visitors to the place. One informant questioned Austin's healthfulness by stating, "Very many are complaining, and there have been several deaths." The scarcity of timber in the vicinity was "universally allowed," while local spring water dried up daily. Dry, gravelly soil doomed agriculture. And Austin's remoteness was so self-evident as to require no comment. The editorial writer therefore cautioned would-be Austinites to reflect "before [making] large investments in the lots in this city of—Humbug." The *Morning Star* sarcastically conveyed one piece of good news. Due to the "extreme sagacity" of the government, the republic would realize a financial windfall because the Austin agent (Edwin Waller) now charged those erecting huts twelve-and-a-half cents per tree measuring one foot in diameter. At this rate *only* twenty-eight thousand trees would pay the salary of one Cabinet officer. "Astonishing economy! Most wonderful sagacity!" sneered the writer. The *Telegraph and Texas Register* responded to this critique with contempt:

> That the removal of the seat of government from Houston, would excite the spleen of *little minds*, and consequently call down the abuse of those whose conceptions never carried them beyond the precincts of their own town, was to have been expected, consequently we are not disappointed in having certain pot-house politicians continually harping upon this never failing subject but the following article from the "Morning Star" on the 18th inst goes beyond anything we had conceived the *ignorance* or *impudence* of the enemies of Austin capable of producing.[20]

Information from another anonymous source elicited further sarcasm from the *Morning Star*. Expressing feigned excitement over the prospect of bathing in the "beautiful waters of the Colorado," an editorial writer claimed, "Those who have *seen* the water, tell *us* that it is *nearly* as deep there as a common bathing tub; and a man attempting to swim in it would cut some of the capers of a frog, in a half dried mud puddle." But the editor of the *Telegraph and Texas Register* ridiculed such reports, as well as those who made them, with this story:

> How do you like the new seat of government? Exclaimed an old gentleman to a man who had just arrived from that place. "Oh, it is Horrible, we have got no water there—*we even have to swim our horses across the Colorado river to Barton's Springs to water them!*" Well you don't catch me there, replied the old man, I had rather risk the fevers in the low country, than to live in such a place as that![21]

Edwin Waller's success, and Mirabeau Lamar's reputation, depended not only on the timely completion of government buildings, but also on the willingness of ordinary Texans to invest in and move to the new capital city. Waller therefore began publicizing the public auction of Austin city lots even before he left Houston.[22] As a counterpoint to Waller's newspaper notices of the first sale of public lots, the *Morning Star* ran an article in its July 17, 1839, edition headlined, "Reasons Why Persons Should Not Purchase Lots in the New City of Austin." As mandated by the Seat of Government Act, the initial sale would occur August 1, 1839, at which time no more than half of the town's lots would be auctioned off. Successful bidders would owe one-fourth of the purchase price immediately, with the balance due in equal installments at six, twelve, and eighteen months. Nonpayment ten days beyond the due date would result in forfeiture of the lot and previous payments. The agent would accept only gold, silver, government promissory notes, or audited government drafts.

As it did throughout its history, the Republic of Texas in 1839 teetered on the brink of bankruptcy. The *Morning* Star alluded to this in an editorial disputing Austin's worth to frontier security when it mentioned "our present impoverished state." Recognizing the meager resources at his government's disposal, Mirabeau Lamar hoped to finance his imperial ambition in part from the proceeds of the upcoming auction in Austin. On June 19 John Eldredge of the *Morning Star* labeled such aspiration unrealistic: "We cannot imagine either, much as we have seen and read of speculations in *paper* cities, that the income to be derived from the sale of lots in the city of Austin will be as enormous as many seem to suppose." Later that summer, after the first successful auction, the paper turned accusatory:

> And we believe that the city of Austin will remain the seat of government until it is thought that money enough has been made for the government, and a chosen few, when some great and insuperable objection will be discovered, and a new site will be selected. . . . "Is it right?" is never asked. "Will it be popular?" or "What shall we gain?" are the only questions to be answered. For our part, we are not anxious to see our country powerful or rich, if she is to become so only be intrigue and deception.

President Lamar evidently lost no sleep worrying about such charges. In a letter to the citizens of Velasco declining a public dinner in his honor he exuded self-righteousness: "That I can ever share the confidence and affection of those whose feelings are selfish, and whose purposes are base, is utterly impossible. . . . So far as my own administration is concerned, I feel that I have every reason to invite, rather than avoid such a scrutiny. Conscious of the rectitude of my own intentions . . . I can have no apprehension as to the results."[23]

During his tenure as government agent Edwin Waller stayed out of public debate. His letters to Lamar reflect optimism and complete focus on the task at hand. By July 11, 1839, he had framed the president's house and nearly finished twenty-eight government office buildings. He had assembled all of the necessary timber for construction of the capitol. High wages and the devalued Texas currency had left him short of cash; he needed fifteen thousand dollars from the government as soon as possible.[24] Waller also prepared for the upcoming auction. On July 5 he ordered the printing of 1,200 deeds at twenty cents each and 3,620 notes at ten cents each.[25] While in Houston in late June he promised the post of auctioneer to G. Everrette, contingent upon the president's approval.[26] Lamar apparently did not concur in this selection, as the lucrative position eventually went to a man named J. T. Doswell.[27]

Editor John Eldredge and the *Morning Star* strove to dampen the public's enthusiasm for acquiring Austin real estate. A July 5 editorial pointed out that "the most careful readers of the law locating the seat of government cannot find a sentence in which the permanency of the location is guaranteed."[28] On July 27, five days before the sale, Eldredge offered five reasons for citizens to avoid purchasing Austin property. Two of these dealt with perceived unconstitutionality of the Seat of Government Act.[29] Another reminded readers of Congress's ability to change its mind about the location. A fourth reason avowed that Austin "possess none of the advantages of a city," with its scarce timber, remoteness, poor soil, lack of a navigable river, and relative paucity of drinking water. And finally, Eldredge maintained that *no* congressional mandate was satisfactory "because the *people* alone at the *ballot-box*, can make a permanent location, and it is absurd and idle to speak of such a location, until it is referred to them."[30]

Anger stirred in ninety-year-old John Darlington every time he passed the ancient live-oak trees between Guadalupe and San Antonio Streets. Where he thought he should see a park he saw only weeds and rubble. The majestic trees, to Darlington symbols of frontier vision and courage, stood forlorn and forgotten, drawing hardly a glance from passersby. Fearful that his inevitable passing would sentence these oaks to the lumber mill, the old man in 1911 sat down and wrote a letter to the newspaper: "I am now 90 years old and the only survivor of those who helped to lay off the streets and alleys and build the first houses in Austin in 1839."

Darlington's thoughts while writing this letter might have drifted back to his Virginia origins. His Irish father had accompanied the Lewis and Clark expedition and fought at the Battle of New Orleans. But his early death consigned the son to an unknown apprenticeship. Strife with his master led the seventeen-year-old youth to run away to Texas. Along the way he met and bound himself to John Webster, settling on Gilleland Creek in Bastrop County in 1838. When Webster died in an Indian attack the following year, Darlington found a job in Edwin Waller's workforce, laboring on the capitol and other buildings. And on August 1, 1839, John Darlington waded through knee-high rye grass to stand under the same oaks he now sought to save and witnessed the birth of Austin, Texas.

"The first sale of city lots was made by auction under some live oak trees on the north side of a public square. . . . They still stand there, and I write to suggest that some action should be taken by the city authorities to preserve these trees and protect them. When I am dead no one will remain who can identify the spot."[31]

Why Waller chose this spot for the auction is unknown. Perhaps it was because of its proximity to the workers' camp at Pecan and Nueces Streets, where Waller himself might have had a tent. Maybe he left the choice to his auctioneer J. T. Doswell. Or maybe this was the best open area in the immediate vicinity for hundreds of hopeful bidders and onlookers to gather. Whatever the reason, John Darlington's cherished live oak trees provided the shade for those attending the historic sale on that hot, dry August day.

Waller opened the bidding at 10:00 a.m.[32] Moments later auctioneer Doswell banged his gavel to seal M. H. Beatty's purchase of two lots on block 130 for $590. By day's end Waller had approved winning bids on about three hundred lots, for a total income of $182,585. The purchase price for a lot ranged from $120 to over twenty-three times that amount. Not a bad profit for the republic, which had paid about $25,000 for the entire 7,735-acre site, of which the town composed only a small part. The *Telegraph and Texas Register* crowed, "This is the best sale of town property which has taken place in Texas."[33] Speculators bought up much of the city. Samuel Whiting acquired fourteen lots, Nathaniel Townsend twenty-one, and James Burke six. J. T. Doswell, the auctioneer, bought two lots, both of which he later forfeited. Edwin Waller targeted property in the vicinity of the government buildings he was constructing. He bought three lots facing the president's house across San Jacinto Street, and two lots near the capitol on Colorado Street. His other purchase of the northwest corner lot at Congress and Bois d'Arc (seventh) also suggested an eye toward future profit. Waterloo resident Jacob Harrell successfully bid on four lots, one of which was later donated to him by the government. A modern historic marker at the north end of the Congress Avenue bridge claims this as the site of Harrell's original Waterloo home. Indeed, Harrell did acquire lots 1 and 2 of block 5, which make up the southeast corner at Congress Avenue and Water (First or Cesar Chavez) Avenue. But he also obtained lot 4 in block 26 on the west side of town close to Shoal Creek's drainage into the Colorado River. Since most early accounts of Waterloo situate Harrell's cabin near the mouth of Shoal Creek, either location seems reasonable.

Site selection commissioner Louis P. Cooke bought an Austin lot, as did Waller's subagent R. D. McAnelly. Secretary of War Albert Sydney

Johnston took possession of three lots on the west side of town. Edward Seiders's tent full of merchandise found a home on the east side of Congress Avenue between Cedar and Pine (Fourth and Fifth) Streets. Contractor Lewis Porter, who ran out of government money building the capitol and president's house, fared no better with his personal finances. Porter failed to make the second payment on his corner lot in block 145, thereby forfeiting the property along with his first payment. And finally, someone purchased two lots on the northwest corner of the College Avenue (Twelfth Street) and Lavaca Street intersection on behalf of Mirabeau Lamar. The president later allowed his purchase to revert to the republic by electing not to pay the third installment.[34]

Edwin Waller and J. T. Doswell earned handsome 5 percent commissions from the August 1 lot sale. Waller's $9,129.25 share supplemented his agent's salary of $8 per day and the $5 he was due for each $100 disbursed in construction. Doswell's sudden wealth proved an irresistible target to surveyor L. J. Pilie. Shortly after the auction Pilie was caught with $3,500 of Doswell's money. A jury led by Samuel Whiting sentenced the thief to be tied to the "Liberty Pole," flogged, and expelled from the city.[35]

Three issues stand out among the arguments raised by Sam Houston against transferring Texas government to the Colorado River. Representative Houston stressed the danger of such an exposed frontier position, a risk that would assume greater urgency after he regained the presidency in 1841. He also cried foul at the "fraud" that had been practiced upon the city of Houston, given that Congress would be removing to Austin a year earlier than stipulated by law. This "fraud," he believed, had been urged in large part by land speculators looking to cash in on investment property in a new capital. Finally, Houston objected to the high financial cost of the move, a cost that the cash-strapped republic would have difficulty absorbing. Notwithstanding the expense of the upcoming government move over miles of difficult terrain, the construction costs alone did seem staggering. As noted earlier, Waller spent over $73,000 of government funds in one four-month stretch. And, far from being mollified by the profit from the initial city lot sale, many critics pointed instead to the fact that investors had purchased such a large chunk of the city. In their minds this confirmed Houston's charge of fraud.

One such critic was editor John Eldredge of the *Morning Star.* Despite his mistaken belief that revenue from the sale totaled about $350,000, Eldredge saw no reason for celebration because "a government that will violate one pledge will violate another."[36] The editor predicted that future government duplicity would "make the people wish that the city of Austin had never leaped forth a city in the wilderness." But a correspondent to the *Telegraph and Texas Register* calling himself "Veritas" mocked opponents like Eldredge. He viewed the substantial profit so far gained as proof of public confidence in Lamar's new city and "the best refutation of those malignant snarlers who sit at a distance and retail all the slang they can gather up about the place." A less passionate view came from New Orleans, where the *Picayune* editor observed, "Austin stands a fair chance in our estimation, of being one day, (not far distant) *the St. Louis of Texas.*"[37] Whether John Eldredge, Veritas, or the *New Orleans Picayune* proved most accurate would determine not only the legacy of Mirabeau B. Lamar but the destiny of the Republic of Texas.

| Chapter 10 |

LAMAR'S TRIUMPH

So you are determined the next Congress shall assemble at
Austin—It serves them just right.

Samuel Roberts, letter to President Mirabeau Lamar, 1839

Even without a full load the heavy iron chest would have been too much for one man to handle. But crammed full of navy department papers, office supplies, various kitchen utensils, coffee, salt, and other miscellany, the trunk stubbornly resisted the exertions of several strong men. Four black laborers dripped sweat in the September heat as they dragged the chest outside to the dusty Houston street, then with a triumphant grunt heaved it onto the wagon bed indicated by a nearby white man scribbling in an account book. As directed, the four men next hunted down Alfred Donovan, from whom they asked for and received $1.50 of the republic's money to be divided among them as payment for their efforts.[1]

Texans argued throughout the summer of 1839 about whether Edwin Waller would be ready in time to receive the government in Austin. In July Samuel Roberts[2] pointed out a potential problem to Lamar: "Unless the roads are infinitely better than when I last passed over them, no wagon can be drawn over them. They were then impassable. Not even Jack assable." Nevertheless, on August 12 the *Morning Star* informed its readers that "about the first of September . . . the officers of the government and the public archives will be on their 'winding way' to the new city of Austin." A month later the same newspaper reported, "This is the day designated for the removal of the different departments of the government to the new seat of government; we imagine, however, that they will be delayed a few days." On September 18, the *Colorado Gazette and Advertiser* quoted the [Houston] *Intelligencer*: "Between forty and fifty wagons freighted with the archives of the government, and books, papers, and furniture of the different Departments, have left here for the City of

Austin, the new Seat of Government." And on October 9 readers of the *Telegraph and Texas Register* learned that "all government archives arrived at that city [Austin] in safety . . . all the offices of government [are] open for the transaction of business."[3]

Twenty-five-year-old John Pettit Borden had by 1839 already earned a niche in Texas history. After moving to Texas with his family in 1832, the native New Yorker helped capture Goliad from the Mexican army in October 1835, participated in the successful siege of Bexar two months later, and fought with Sam Houston's victorious troops on the plains of San Jacinto the following spring. Houston trusted the young man enough to name him the republic's first land commissioner in 1837. Borden's able management of the Land Office gained him the respect of the Lamar administration, which in the summer of 1839 charged him with transporting all government archives to the new capital city of Austin. This involved safely moving thousands of pounds of paper, furniture, and supplies over the same primitive roads that had challenged Edwin Waller the previous May. Borden needed dozens of wagons, ox teams, and drivers for the job. He required scores of men on both ends of the journey for loading and unloading cargo. And he had only twenty thousand dollars of the republic's scarce cash to complete the enormous task.[4]

Modern movers arrive at a job equipped with dozens, if not hundreds, of ready-made cardboard packing boxes. John Borden's movers enjoyed no such luxury, instead relying on the skills of carpenters such as Joseph Daniels, who collected forty dollars from Borden on September 13 for making wooden boxes and packing crates.[5] To complete this job Daniels likely dipped into the republic's nail supply, part of which was purchased September 2nd at the Houston House at Main and Franklin Streets.[6] While these preparations were underway Borden's subagent M. H. Beatty scoured the streets of Houston in search of suitable transport wagons for hire.[7] Teamsters signed on to receive eleven dollars per hundredweight of goods delivered safely in Austin. Many of the haulers were probably farmers looking to pick up extra income with their wagons and animals.[8] Once hired, they waited in the street while workmen hauled packed boxes, crates, and trunks outside, where Borden or one of his assistants meticulously recorded each item as it was loaded onto a wagon. The accepting teamster signed a receipt promising to deliver the goods "at the City of Austin, in like order and condition, in a reasonable time."[9]

Thomas Cochrane carried 1,793 pounds of the War Department's property in wagon number 31. The heaviest individual item, a box attributed to paymaster Jacob Snively, weighed 272 pounds. General Albert Sydney Johnston's furniture also traveled in this wagon. Cochrane received $197.23 upon delivering these goods in Austin. John Adkinson earned $330 for transporting three thousand pounds in wagon number 2. Twenty-seven packages of State Department property made up the load, with one box alone weighing 1,200 pounds. Adkinson accepted his cargo September 11 by marking an "X" on the receipt.[10]

Borden did not merely bid farewell to the teamsters in Houston and hope they arrived safely in Austin. He paid men like Joseph Waples six dollars a day to accompany and superintend the train on the road.[11] Borden obviously shared Treasurer Asa Brigham's concern for the safety of the precious archives. Brigham wrote to President Lamar August 25 stating that his duty "produces a considerable anxiety in my mind. . . . The *Books* and valuable *papers* belonging to the office together with all the *receipts & vouchers* (which are quite voluminous) that cannot be packed in the Iron Chest will have to be packed in a Box Water-tight, and placed in charge of a *responsible Teamster*, (which I presume you are aware cannot be found every day)." Ferdinand Roemer's observations on a similar trip leading west from Houston in 1845 prove that Brigham's nervousness about teamsters was well-founded: "Toward noon we came to a stream, the Big Bernard, which was swollen considerably on account of the rain of the previous night. In spite of this the heavier laden wagon was driven recklessly into the stream. When it had reached the middle where the water came higher than the paunch of the horses, two of them refused to go on and threatened to lie down in the water." After separating the animals from the wagon, the driver "plunged into the stream, keeping on only his spectacles. He immediately began to carry the boxes to the opposite shore. . . . The boxes were opened and all the drenched articles, such as shawls, cotton goods, etc., were spread out on the sandy beach to dry."[12]

Borden feared more than careless teamsters when it came to safety of the archives. In 1839 hostile Indians still ranged freely on the frontier, the danger of attack increasing with every step westward. In addition, there was no formal truce yet between Texas and Mexico. Texas politicians, newspaper editors, and ordinary citizens harped constantly on the perceived threat from the south in the form of invading Mexican armies or marauding Mexican bandits. An armed escort therefore accompanied the government wagon train to Austin. In Houston quartermaster Robert Neighbors contracted with S. E. Basset to carry baggage and provisions for a detachment of men of the First Infantry Regiment under Lieutenant Henry Grush. Fourteen miles beyond San Felipe, Basset's team failed.

Reuben Hornsby and his wife Sarah were among the first Anglo settlers around the site that became Austin. Known for their hospitality to travelers, the Hornsbys provided food and shelter for many early immigrants to the city. Their great grandson, Rogers Hornsby, is a member of the Baseball Hall of Fame. Reprinted by permission of the Austin History Center, Austin Public Library, PICB 10836.

Fortunately for Grush and his men, James McGowan was on hand to haul the load the rest of the way to Austin.[13]

On August 24, 1839, someone acting in Houston on behalf of the government purchased three empty boxes from Clarke and Company for three dollars. On October 3 John Borden authorized a one-dollar payment to a recipient known only as Negro Man. In between, the agent in charge of archive transport spent $21,223.41 of the republic's money in successfully moving not only its precious archives, but also its furniture, department files, tools, and other baggage to Austin. Borden received

$392 for his efforts, or $8 per diem for forty-nine days on the job. The biggest expense lay in freight charges, which totaled at least $16,659. This translates into over 151,000 pounds, or seventy-five tons, of cargo. The government spent $2,730 in stipends to forty-two clerks to defray their cost of moving from Houston to Austin. Miscellaneous supplies, carpenters' wages, Borden's salary, and other labor costs accounted for the rest.[14]

Early one morning in October 1839 several wagons rumbled slowly away from Reuben Hornsby's Colorado River farm. The wagons carried John Webster and his wife, their two children, and thirteen other men intent on settling along the San Gabriel River to the north. Until Jacob Harrell planted the seeds of Waterloo in 1835, no Anglo settler lived farther up the Colorado River than Reuben Hornsby. Hornsby, a surveyor by trade, obtained a land grant from Stephen F. Austin in 1830. His property consisted of a bulge of land created by a curve in the river about thirty miles above Bastrop. A family friend later wrote, "A more beautiful tract of land, even now, can nowhere be found. . . . Washed on the west by the Colorado, it stretches over a level valley about three miles wide to the east, and [is] . . . covered with wild rye, and looking like one vast green wheat field."[15] Reuben Hornsby occupied this land with his wife Sarah and their several children in 1832. Known for their hospitality, the couple welcomed travelers such as the Websters throughout those early years.

After saying good-bye to the Hornsbys, John Webster and his traveling companions reached the junction of the north and south forks of the San Gabriel River without incident. From the ridge separating the two forks, however, Webster spotted trouble. Peering into the distance, he could just make out a large Comanche war party heading his way. Alarmed but thinking himself undetected, and therefore safe, Webster turned his group around and headed back toward Hornsby's Bend. They would never make it.

Darkness caught the Webster party on the open prairie. The settlers arranged their wagons in a hollow square for protection and set up camp. But the Comanche did not rest. After following Webster's trail throughout the night they launched a devastating sunrise attack. Caught by surprise, the whites stood little chance. One by one the men fell, pierced by spears, arrows, or bullets, or killed up close by a blow to the head. A man named Reese fired his musket, and then died while swinging the weapon as a club. Others succumbed in similar fashion, as indicated by several smashed guns littering the campsite at its discovery by Dr. D. C. Gilmore. By ten or eleven o'clock all of the men in the Webster party were dead.

The Comanche snatched up Mrs. Webster and her daughter, set the wagons on fire, and melted into the plains.[16]

The attack on the Webster party occurred even as government officials were settling into their new quarters in Austin a scant twenty miles away. In a letter to President Lamar, Judge James Webb had prophetically written, "The Indians are said to be on the road between this [place] & Austin, & it is not considered safe to travel without a party of some strength." An editorial comment in the *Telegraph and Texas Register* that bemoaned the recklessness of settlers such as the Websters also seemed an indictment of the Lamar administration: "When will our people learn to temper their enterprise with prudence? When will they learn to estimate their own individual prowess not superior to that of an *hundred Indians?* We admire the bold and daring spirit of our people; but we cannot discover the wisdom they always display in putting it to the test."[17]

Duty and family tugged from opposite directions at Judge Webb. Having already held two different cabinet positions under President Mirabeau Lamar, Webb most likely assumed there would be a third.[18] In October 1839 he therefore struck out for Austin with his family at his side. Fifteen miles short of Bastrop his son Charles fell ill and could go no further. The wagon train hauling the Webb family possessions did not stop, however, and Judge Webb reluctantly left his family in the care of a Mr. Hills to complete the journey to the new capital on his own. He wrote to friend and confidante Mirabeau Lamar to "beg the favor of you to take them under your charge & protection from that place to Austin." But, perhaps having heard of the attack on the Webster party, Webb warned Lamar to "send word to Austin at what time you will come on, & I will meet you at Barker's five miles above Bastrop with a party of 15 or 20 men to guard you. . . . Don't think of coming through alone, as no one here deems it safe for a family to travel without some efficient protection."[19]

A year after the buffalo hunt at Waterloo that sparked his interest in the region, Mirabeau Lamar anticipated a triumphant return. He certainly must have been glad to leave Houston, or at least the *Morning Star* behind him. With the certainty of the government's impending move from that city, the paper had found a new reason to criticize the chief executive. Thomas Green and other Velasco citizens had the previous August invited Lamar to a public dinner in his honor. Feeling pressed by the demands of his office, Lamar sent Green a lengthy letter declining the offer. While lauding the "good and estimable men . . . the brave, the virtuous and the enlightened portion of my fellow-citizens" who supported him, he also blasted his critics, ascribing their acts to "the malice of the wicked." He professed indifference to the opposition because "that I can ever share the confidence and affection of those whose feelings are selfish, and whose purposes are base, is utterly impossible." Pointing out that "it is not for me to sit in judgment upon those who have gone before," he proceeded to do just that. In an obvious reference to Sam Houston, Lamar claimed that "inordinate vanity has been invested with furtive laurels." While he could excuse the young republic for such folly, "the time has now arrived when it becomes the duty of every genuine patriot to draw the most rigid distinction between virtue and vice. . . . We should speak of men as we know them and things as they are."[20]

Publication of Mirabeau Lamar's letter triggered howls of derision from his political enemies. The *Morning Star* responded viciously.

> Were we to assent to all the charges which malice and hatred could invent against Gen. Houston, so far as *moral character* is concerned, we would quite as soon take his chance of salvation, as that of his equally immoral but less candid successor. . . . He has in the most wanton manner attacked his predecessor; he has most outrageously abused those who were guilty of the *crime* of entertaining opinions at variance with his, as base, treacherous, corrupt, venal, ambitious demagogues.[21]

An even more contemptuous response from the *Brazos Courier* appeared as an October 7 reprint in the *Morning Star.* "But the President's letter; Lamar! Lamar! The Lord deliver us from Mirabeau Lamar! For the credit of the country, we are sorry indeed, sir, that your letter should have placed in such plain colors before the world, the childish egotism of your disposition; we regret that it exposes so much of the malignity of your heart." Addressing Lamar's sideswipes at ex-President Houston, the writer pointed out: "You, sir, ascended the presidential chair at a moment of profound peace, with bright and smiling prospects; you had the advantage of the precedents laid before you by him [Houston] to guide you; and well indeed had it been for the commonwealth, had you followed in his footsteps." And, in a final crescendo of disgust: "Houston made you; with a breath he puffed you into existence. . . . And what has been your return? You have reviled him. . . . Yes, when you shall have been forgotten; when the dim mantle of oblivion shall have thrown its impenetrable shroud over your virtues and your vices, the star of your country shall be the beacon of his fame, and light his name to other times; the Hero of San Jacinto—the President of the Republic."[22]

* * *

At eleven o'clock in the morning of October 17, 1839, every man in Austin, Texas able to procure a horse saddled up and rode east. Following East Pecan Street to Waller Creek, the men urged their mounts through the cool water, up the opposite bank, and across East Avenue. By now the once indistinct trail lay clear, the prairie grass stomped into oblivion over the preceding months by countless wagons, draft animals, and men. At the party's head rode Colonel Edward Burleson and General Albert Sydney Johnston, parade marshals. The standard bearer behind them proudly waved a banner with the words "Hail to our Chief" on one side and "With this we live—Or die defending" on the other. Edwin Waller, town planner and orator of the day, came next, followed by a trumpeter and two-by-two procession of town citizens. Two miles east of Austin this group encountered another, smaller group of riders. Notable among the latter were Louis P. Cooke, one of the five commissioners locating the seat of government; army paymaster Major Benjamin Sturges; and Joseph Moreland, private secretary to the president. But the citizens of Austin had not organized themselves in such grand fashion to greet an ex-commissioner, mid-level army officer, and secretary. Their gaze flew expectantly past those men in search of the morning's prize, the figure bringing legitimacy to their new city, the man validating their months of back-breaking labor. This man was Mirabeau B. Lamar, president of the Republic of Texas, arriving finally to assume control of the nation's government in his new frontier capital.[23]

Upon sighting the president's party Colonel Burleson reversed the order of march, placing himself, Johnston, Waller, and the standard-bearer to the rear. He then formed his men into two parallel lines. As President Lamar passed through these lines from one end, Colonel Burleson and the other town dignitaries approached from the other. Orator of the Day Edwin Waller introduced the chief executive to the excited crowd:

> Having been called upon, by my fellow-citizens, to welcome your Excellency on your arrival at the permanent seat of government for the Republic, I should have declined doing so on account of conscious inability, wholly unused as I am to public speaking, had I not felt that holding the situation here that I do, it was my duty to obey their call. With pleasure I introduce you to the Citizens of Austin; and, at their request, give you cordial welcome to a place which owes its existence as a city, to the policy of your administration.

In Waller's ensuing speech he could not resist a jab at Lamar's political enemies: "Beauty of scenery, centrality of location, and purity of atmosphere, have been nothing in the vision of those whose views were governed by their purses; and whose ideas of fitness were entirely subservient to their desire for profit." Waller closed with a salute to Austin's future: "In the name of the citizens of Austin, I cordially welcome you and your cabinet to the new metropolis; under your fostering care may it flourish; and aided by its salubrity of climate, and its beauty, become famous among the cities of the new world."[24]

President Lamar elicited cheers from the men with "a short but pithy and appropriate speech." At Burleson's order the entourage began the two-mile march back to Austin. As the president neared East Avenue, Thomas William Ward supervised a 6-pounder gun crew's firing of a 21-gun salute. Proceeding west on Pecan Street Lamar acknowledged the cheers of onlookers before halting at Congress Avenue to greet the waiting throng of spectators.[25]

Richard Bullock arrived in Austin with the first wagons in May 1839. Recognizing the immediate need for temporary housing, he accepted a solicitation from Edwin Waller to construct a hotel, selecting lots for that purpose on the northwest corner of what became the intersection of Congress Avenue and Pecan Street. In exchange Waller promised to hold these lots out of the first land sale. Bullock convinced his wife, Mary, despite her delicate health, to assume the role of hostess. Before agreeing to endure the "fatigues, hardships, and privations" inherent to the role, Mary elicited a promise from her husband to place the land titles in her name.[26]

Bullock began construction of his hotel early in the summer of 1839. He had progressed far enough by the August 1 sale that, in his opinion, "a larger number of persons were attracted to said sales & said lots brought higher prices by reason thereof, & that the lots in the vicinity of those improved by himself he feels well assured brought larger prices than they would otherwise have."[27] The result of his efforts, a sprawling complex of mismatched log and frame buildings, appeared to Julia Lee Sinks as a "fort-like mansion."[28] The Bullocks could accommodate sixty or seventy guests. They served meals in a large corner dining room and entertained smaller groups in a parlor of their centrally located residence, where Mrs. Bullock sang and played the piano. A rustic log cabin on the north side of the complex served incongruously as a storage room for French ceramics, a full breakfast service, dinner set, and full tea set, which, according to Julia Sinks, provided "strange contrasts that gave interest to the times." The most striking feature of Bullock's hotel was another log room situated on posts over the dining hall. The awkward structure looked to one

This circa 1870 view of Congress Avenue shows the two-story Bullock's Hotel at far left (immediately behind the tall pole). Situated on the northwest corner of Congress and Pecan, Bullock's was the site of a welcoming dinner for President Mirabeau Lamar upon his October 1839 arrival in Austin. The capitol at the head of Congress Avenue replaced Edwin Waller's temporary building in 1853. Courtesy of Bonham (Dora Dieterich) Papers, 1902-1973, CN02073, the Dolph Briscoe Center for American History, University of Texas at Austin.

observer "like it was frightened and wanted to run away." But, for all its ungainliness, Bullock's hotel created fond memories for its guests. Julia Sinks recalled the place fondly, claiming that "all that sought dignity or assumed dignity in any form found and shared its inviting hospitality. . . . It was the home to all, as I have said before, who came to Austin either for business or curiosity." [29]

At three o'clock in the afternoon of October 17, 1839, Richard and Mary Bullock welcomed President Mirabeau B. Lamar to a public dinner in their hotel. Lamar and scores of guests enjoyed "the delicacies which graced the festive board" prepared by Mrs. Bullock. President-of-the-day

James Burke offered this toast: "Our Guest, Mirabeau B. Lamar, President of the Republic of Texas. His valor in the field of battle signally contributed to the achievement of Texian independence; his wisdom as a statesman has given vigor and firmness to our government, and elevated its character abroad; his lofty patriotism and distinguished public services command the admiration and gratitude of his fellow-citizens." Lamar rose, thanked Burke, then praised Edwin Waller: "The worthy founder of our new seat of government, Judge Waller. By the touch of his industry there has sprung up, like the work of magic, a beautiful city, whose glory is destined, in a few years, to overshadow the ancient magnificence of Mexico." There followed several hours of drinking and toasting. David Burnet, Stephen Austin, Colonel Burleson, and Ben Milam received recognition. Revelers raised glasses to Mexican Federalists, the "Heroes of Texas," the constitution, the press, and the United States. T. G. Forster punned, "The President of Texas: Our skillful MECHANIC. May we never have a worse CABINET-MAKER." One imagines a grim smile on Lamar's face at hearing, "Sam Houston and San Jacinto. They will be remembered as long as Texas possesses a single freeman." The imperial dreamer probably found more to cheer when Dr. M. Johnson proposed, "The Single Star of Texas: It is small but bright, and may it one day be the sun around which the Spanish Provinces will revolve." When the toasts, the alcohol, or both ran out around 8:00 p.m., Lamar rose and excused himself. The crowd gradually dispersed, "highly pleased with the entertainment of the day." [30]

Colonel Edward Burleson played no favorites in welcoming dignitaries to Austin. On the morning of October 28, 1839, he led a cavalry troop three miles east of town to meet the representative of San Augustine County, Sam Houston. The Hero of San Jacinto also received a 21-gun salute and a speech to mark the occasion, this time from Senator Anson Jones.[31] Jones, no Lamar supporter, nevertheless paid tribute to "that progressive improvement by which we have been enabled so far to overcome our national foes and all other obstacles, as to establish the Capital of the Republic itself on what, a few months since, was a wilderness and the very frontier of civilization and settlement." After Jones's speech Houston accepted an invitation to a public dinner in his honor.[32]

November 14 dawned "unusually raw and chilly." Sam Houston's outdoor dinner that day drew a crowd, but, because of the weather, a smaller one than expected. About two hundred guests gathered without shelter for a feast prepared by James H. Hall, after which the usual high-minded toasting followed.[33] Houston answered with "one of the most eloquent speeches we ever remember to have heard; and impressed us with a more favorable opinion of the powerful intellect and generous devotion to his country, than we before entertained. Many passages of his speech were strikingly brilliant." Houston wisely kept private his opinion of Austin's location, which he revealed in a letter to Anna Raguet: "This is the most unfortunate site upon earth for the Seat of Government."[34] He then concluded his oratory by offering his own toast: "Texas: If true to herself, she can be false to no one." But perhaps most notable, at least to any Lamar supporters in the crowd, was this accolade from George M. Collinsworth: "General Sam Houston, Ex-President: The soldier and the statesman; we have tried him once, and we will try him again."[35]

| Chapter 11 |

THE FOURTH CONGRESS

Like many of his fellow citizens, merchant and devout Presbyterian James Burke strove to introduce his own version of civilization to early Austin. Born in South Carolina, the "Sunday School Man" grew up in Tennessee, ran a flourishing business in Natchez, Mississippi, moved to Texas in 1837, and followed Edwin Waller from Houston to Austin in the summer of 1839. He bought six city lots at the first auction in August and a single lot at the second offering November 1, 1839.[1] In the November 12 *Austin City Gazette*[2] Burke announced the opening of a public reading room at Congress Avenue and Bois d'Arc Street.[3] Inviting all—but especially members of Congress—to his business, Burke promised his guests "many of the most valuable Journals from the U. States, in addition to all the Papers printed in the Republic." His room would have "all the facilities and conveniences usually connected with such establishments," and would soon extend borrowing privileges to its patrons.[4]

Burke's reading room lasted less than a week. On November 15, four days after opening, the building caught fire and burned to the ground. The blaze also destroyed Burke's adjacent store. Burke managed to save his merchandise; whether this included his stock of reading material is unclear. The "enterprising proprietor" persisted in the face of this setback and in early December informed his customers that he was back in business.[5] How much business awaited him was the question, however, for, while James Burke battled the effects of Austin's first fire over the fate of "Phoenix Corner," opposing factions in Austin's first congressional session battled over the fate of the city itself.

"[The City of Austin] has many advantages of location not immediately discernible to the traveller [*sic*] who does not look beyond the spot itself," so boasted editor Samuel Whiting in the inaugural edition of the city's first newspaper, the *Austin City Gazette*. Two months later his enthusiasm had not abated, as he boasted, "Our city is still improving; new buildings are daily going up as if by magic. The people are gay, cheerful, and appar-

AUSTIN ABOUT 1839 OR 1841.

Austin viewed from President's Hill in 1839 or 1841. Congress Avenue runs from
right to left. At upper right is the capitol (with flag) at Hickory and Colorado
Streets. The other cross street at left must therefore be Bois d'Arc. Note the dou-
ble log cabin construction of the government office buildings on either side of
Congress Avenue between the two cross streets. The land office building struck
by Angelina Eberly's cannon shot sits just off Congress Avenue at the base of
Hickory Street below the capitol. The painting is by William Sandusky, one of
Edwin Waller's surveyors in 1839. Reprinted by permission. PICA 01079 Austin
History Center, Austin Public Library.

Julia Robertson based her illustrations of early Austin buildings on the recollections of her aunt, Julia Lee Sinks. The drawings accompanied a series of newspaper articles written by Sinks appearing in the *Galveston News* in February 1896. This first sketch views the intersection of Congress Avenue and Pecan Street looking east along Pecan. The Delong house mentioned by Sinks (6) was Alphonse de Saligny's office. Eugene Pluyette sought refuge in this house after being attacked in the street by Richard Bullock. Courtesy of the *Galveston News*, February 1896, Center for American History, University of Texas at Austin.

ently prosperous and happy. Strangers crowd upon us from all parts of the country, and from the United States; and all appear delighted. The weather is fine, streets clean, provisions plenty, and nothing to mar or disturb our enjoyments." Hundreds of Texans evidently agreed with Whiting, as a January 1840 census counted 856 residents.[6] One hundred of the total were children. Men outnumbered women by a nine to one margin. Drinkers and gamblers enjoyed greater variety than shoppers, choosing from a total of thirteen taverns, billiard rooms, and faro banks[7] compared to only nine general stores. Sinners and citizens alike patronized the nine groceries. These establishments sold both food and liquor.

Much of Edwin Waller's street grid in the fall of 1839 remained to the imagination. Only Congress Avenue and Pecan Street spanned the entire city, forming a symmetrical cross neatly dividing the town into four rectangular sections. Newcomers beheld a line of government buildings along Congress Avenue, the capitol, the president's house, and "here and there . . . small houses scattered on lots, bordering on streets that were to be." Most of the government offices were along Congress Avenue between Pine and Hickory Streets. Proceeding south on the west side of Congress from Hickory, one encountered the double-log houses of the State Department, Secretary of State, and Navy Department. Just behind the latter building were the president's office and the home of Judge Webb. Across Bois d'Arc sat the corner store and reading room of James Burke, Samuel Whiting's printing office, and Bullock's hotel. Locals often gathered in front of the hotel, seating themselves on "Bullock's Logs" to enjoy drink and debate. In the early 1840s an anonymous author regularly left copies of what came to be known as the *Austin Spy* on these logs. The discoverer of the circular would read it aloud to the assembly, which delighted in its "pungent" wit and humor.[8] South of Pecan Street were a two-story store building belonging to Alexander Russell[9], an anonymous log cabin,[10] and the Treasury Department. The General Land Office in 1839 lay at Pine and Colorado Streets just west of Congress, while the postmaster general occupied a lonely position on the southwest corner of Congress and Cypress. Turning around to walk north along the avenue from the river took one past the commissary general's office on Brazos between Pine and Pecan. A two-story hotel occupied the southeast corner of Congress and Pecan, placing it catty-corner from Bullock's. Just past Bois d'Arc came the double-log houses of the auditor, War Department, and adjutant general. Across Hickory Street were the quartermaster and Executive Business offices. And finally, somewhere above Pecan Street "stood the little house known in the dark days as the dead house. There many victims of Indian cruelty were laid before burial."[11]

Congress Avenue itself remained nothing more than a dusty, beaten-down roadway. There were yet no sidewalks. Stumps and trees still obstructed not only Austin's main avenue, but every street in town. Julia Lee Sinks, whose home was the last on West Pecan Street, recalled, "The knolls beyond the quarry branch were interspersed with timber, and sometimes though not often, we would see galloping past the open spaces beyond the blanketed Indian."[12]

One month into the Fourth Congress of the Republic of Texas, Representative Sam Houston of San Augustine picked up his pen to compose a letter to his friend Anna Raguet. The ex-president wrote while shivering from fever and "the dumb Ague." He feared his illness might limit his attendance in the House where "there has been some warmth [to the debate] this session." Outside of such warmth, however, Houston found only "cold and open houses" in his nation's new capital. He complained of the plain food and lack of society, adding that he did not visit "court."

Government office buildings on the west side of Congress Avenue between Bois d'Arc and Hickory Streets. The capitol is at upper right. Courtesy of the *Galveston News*, February 1896, Center for American History, University of Texas at Austin.

This 1860s northwest view of Congress Avenue at Pecan Street shows two of Austin's original buildings. The structure on the southwest corner of the intersection is Russell's store, later occupied by Francis Dieterich. Bullock's Hotel is partially visible directly across Pecan. Courtesy of Bonham (Dora Dieterich) Papers, CN12185, the Dolph Briscoe Center for American History, University of Texas at Austin.

THE DEAD HOUSE.

The precise Congress Avenue location of the building described by Julia Lee Sinks as "the Dead House" is unknown. Courtesy of the *Galveston News* February 1896, Center for American History, University of Texas at Austin.

Noting the heavy expense of moving the government to Austin, Houston predicted that, unless something changed, government operations would cease due to lack of funds. "I might have been happy in ignorance at home," wrote the frustrated congressman, "had I known the full extent of Lamar's stupidity."[13]

Vice President David Burnet opened the Senate session of the Fourth Congress November 11, 1839, by commenting on the "new scenes which surround us." Praising the natural beauty of these new surroundings, Burnet conceded that, because of the inherent difficulty in choosing among so many eligible spots to locate the capital, *some* dissatisfaction was inevitable. He described himself as indifferent to the issue, but added that there could be no question regarding the chosen site's qualifications. Burnet called for acceptance of Austin as the permanent capital by remarking, "Frequent removals of the seat of government are not only costly, and otherwise injurious in our domestic concerns, but are apt to excite suspicions abroad, of instability in the government itself."[14]

One day after David Burnet addressed the Senate, President Lamar in his message to Congress adopted the attitude that the issue had indeed been permanently settled. He claimed to have acted with such alacrity in removing the government because "the act of the last Congress directing the removal . . . was an expression of legislative will too decisive to permit me one moment to falter in carrying it out." Lamar praised Edwin Waller's successful and energetic efforts, pointing out that government officials had been able to resume their duties in Austin at the appointed time "with very little inconvenience to themselves." As had Vice President Burnet, the president admitted that universal satisfaction was an impossible goal. Nevertheless, the many advantages of Austin provided "ample proofs of the judgment and fidelity of the commissioners, and abundant reason to approve their choice." And, in case anyone felt inclined to complain about Austin's primitive facilities, Lamar added, "I cannot believe that a people who have voluntarily exchanged the ease & luxuries of plentiful houses, for the toils & privations of a wilderness will repine at the sacrifice of a few personal comforts which the good of the nation may require of them."[15]

William Lawrence most decidedly did *not* consider the seat-of-government location a closed issue. As the representative from Harrisburg, Lawrence spoke for those in Houston who felt cheated by the government's removal prior to the year 1840. He also gave voice to eastern concerns regarding Austin's remoteness and to countrywide advocacy of a national referendum to decide the question. It had been Lawrence who, in the Third Congress, had tried repeatedly to forestall passage of the act removing the government from Houston. Failing that, he had unsuccessfully introduced legislation allowing Houstonians injured financially by the early move to sue the government for compensation. Lawrence therefore surprised no one when, on November 15, he informed the House of his intention to introduce a resolution six days hence regarding the *temporary* location of the seat of government.[16]

Lawrence's bill, introduced a bit tardily on November 25, dripped with righteous indignation. The preamble solemnly intoned:

Whereas much clamor, and excitement prevails [throughout] the body politic, in relation to the location of the Seat of Government, and
Whereas believing it to be a duty incumbent upon us, as the Representatives of the people, to consult their views and subserve their interests with a due regard to those principles of economy, which should ever characterize the Legislation of a free people, and

Whereas being impressed with a solemn conviction of the evils which have arisen, and which must inevitably arise from the present unsettled state of this perplexing and all-absorbing question, for remedy where-of.[17]

The legislation mandated that an election be scheduled May 25, 1840, for voters to place the seat of government either at Austin or at a previously rejected site on the falls of the Brazos River. Placement would be *temporary*, committing the government for twenty-five years only. And, if voters opted for the Brazos River site, the city of Austin would keep its name, because the new capital would be known as the City of Texas.

William Menefee of Colorado County called the bill up on November 28. The House scheduled debate for December 2. On the appointed day Representative Sam Houston's booming voice echoed throughout the House chamber. "Fraud!" charged the congressman. Easterners in general, and Houstonians in particular, had been defrauded by congressional placement of the national capital in such a remote place! Houston recalled the words of a visitor from Alabama who described Austin as lying forty miles beyond civilization where "he had never heard the sweet voice of a woman, nor the prattling of children." He admitted to the wealth and beauty of the Colorado valley, but predicted that any potential wealth would be offset by the cost of operating on the frontier. He again stated his fervent belief that only the people could decide on a permanent seat-of-government site. Returning to the theme of fraud upon the east, Houston thundered, "The day of retribution [will] come; and they [easterners] will assert their rights—aye, even if they have to separate from a people who have cheated them out of their rights." But a national vote would "let their voice be heard, and they will be satisfied."[18]

William Jack of Brazoria County rose the next day in rebuttal to Houston. Jack took issue with a crack Houston had made regarding the "too precipitate" government withdrawal from Washington in 1836.[19] He reminded his colleagues that Houston himself had triggered this movement by retreating eastward with the army, then added, "The army did not stay behind to listen to the 'voice of woman or the prattling of children,' but left them behind to the tender mercy of a barbarous enemy." Jack saw no breach of public faith in removal to Austin because the city had been placed on government-owned land; hence all profit from lot sales went into the public treasury. Nor did Jack agree that a national referendum would permanently settle the question. No, a vote by the people "would be just as liable to opposition as a vote by their representatives in congress." Jack charged hypocrisy in those pushing for yet another expensive removal while at the same time calling for economic retrenchment. And he professed astonishment at Houston's prediction of sectional strife if the capital remained at Austin by exclaiming that he "hoped the gentleman could not have been sincere in the remark, but if he was, he would assure him that we had not yet become sufficiently corrupt to carry local matters to such a pitch." In summarizing, Jack contended that Texas was too large a territory for the average citizen to cast a knowledgeable vote regarding seat-of-government placement. Rather, "the power were much better left to their Representatives in Congress, who would appoint Commissioners as they did in this selection, to choose the most suitable place."[20]

William Lawrence next offered a lengthy speech in support of his legislation. In reminding his colleagues that easterners indeed had been defrauded, he blasted the five selection commissioners by claiming that "eastern members [of the commission] had been bought up, and the west saw they had the power, and determined to use it." Lawrence cited many of the same arguments in favor of the bill used earlier by Sam Houston. His central theme also mirrored Houston's, namely: "The question will never be settled, until it is fixed by the people, and the quicker it [is] done, the better for the country."[21]

William Gant of Washington County observed futility in the current debate, as he felt that each member had made up his mind long before. He also decried a push for an election in which voters would name their own preference, rather than selecting from a slate provided by Congress. Such a course would place the people at the mercy of demagogues interested only in using the issue to further their own careers. "The liberties of a people in a free government were never in any danger until they destroyed their rights themselves," warned Gant. Rather than a popular vote, Gant proposed a people's convention aimed at passing a constitutional amendment naming a permanent capital.[22]

Kindred Muse of Nacogdoches followed with lukewarm support of Gant's proposal, stating that he favored it only as a fallback position if the bill under consideration failed.[23]

Brazoria County representative John Harris closed the December 3 debate with the following argument against the bill:

> Remove the seat of government now, and all confidence will be lost to every future location; and there could be realized but a very limited amount from the sales of lots at any newly selected site. The seat of

government would be in a state of continual motion, and without the slightest regard to the public interest, would perpetually oscillate between river and river, and its motion would be so directed as to touch those points best calculated to advance private and sectional interests.[24]

Austin citizens watched with fascination the ongoing congressional debate over the fate of their city. The *Austin City Gazette* noted, "That the subject is an exciting one, is shown by the crowded galleries, and the large number of ladies which have attended the debate, from its commencement up to the present time." Gallery visitors praised the "fine specimens of eloquence, and much solid argument and logical reasoning"[25] produced by debate participants. William Menefee, one of the five commissioners locating Austin, unexpectedly and anticlimactically ended the spectacle on December 4 by moving to strike the enacting clause from Lawrence's bill. The ensuing 21-to-16 favorable vote effectively killed the legislation, thereby ensuring that, for the foreseeable future, the seat of government would remain at Austin.[26] William Lawrence choked while swallowing this defeat. According to the *Austin City Gazette*, "Intimation induces us to believe that Col. Lawrence is not yet satisfied with the location of the Seat of Government. In justice to Col. Lawrence, (though differing in opinion) we must say that he is entitled to much credit for his talent and unremitting zeal in support of his bill for the temporary location of the seat of Government. We only regret that he was not engaged in a better cause."[27]

Members of the Senate seemed more inclined to accept Austin as the national capital. No senator in the Fourth Congress proposed legislation threatening the city's status as government seat. Instead, the Senate ignored that particular issue, focusing on crafting an act of incorporation. Anson Jones got the ball rolling November 13 by successfully calling for a suspension of Senate business so that he could introduce the necessary legislation.[28] After modifications by the judiciary committee, the Senate quickly passed the bill and referred it to the House. On December 21, again on motion by Anson Jones, senators accepted House modifications, and six days later President Lamar signed into law the act officially creating the city of Austin.[29]

According to the Incorporation Act, Austin voters would soon elect a mayor and eight aldermen to form a nine-member city council directing city affairs. Voters would also select a treasurer, recorder, and city marshal. The city council would create and fill any required subordinate positions. Congress spelled out each officer's duties, powers, and restrictions on powers in the act's details.[30]

As Austin headed into the year 1840 its future seemed secure. Edwin Waller had accomplished what many thought impossible by constructing a frontier city from scratch in just five months. John Borden had accomplished the difficult task of moving tons of government archives and supplies from Houston without a hitch. President Lamar, members of Congress, and scores of public servants had arrived triumphantly in Austin to smoothly resume government operations. City supporters in Congress had successfully stymied a challenge from the opposition to seemingly preserve Austin's status as permanent government seat. And now, with a congressionally bestowed charter as proof, Austin had improved its status from *planned* city to *existing* city. Events of the preceding months therefore lent credibility to Congressman William Jack's claim that "even many who came here, prejudiced against this place, are now pleased."[31]

| Chapter 12 |
FRONTIER CAPITAL

The people are very intelligent and polite—I have not lived in better
society in 25 years.

Brewster H. Jayne, writing from Austin to Juliet Jayne, June 7, 1840

As we lay in bed yesterday morning thinking of the joyful era, there crept into our
mind a remembrance of our last Christmas in Austin in 1841, then socially the
pleasantest place we have ever known.

From an article in the Clarksville *Standard*, December 24, 1885

At Austin, mid every discomfort and privation no room nor bed
to be had for love or money.

Anson Jones, Brazoria County senator in the Fourth Congress, part of diary
entry from October 31, 1839

A strange fact for a place of which so many hard things are said.

Presbyterian minister William McCalla, referring to his surprisingly pleasant
experiences during an 1840 visit to Austin, *Adventures in Texas*, 32

One winter day in 1839 two men rode west out of Austin, Texas. One rider loomed tall and imposing in the saddle, sitting comfortably atop his mount while admiring the scenery with curiosity. This was Sam Houston. The other carried himself with equal confidence, but presented a less dashing appearance due to his unusual right leg. A childhood illness had crippled the extremity, leaving it strangely atrophic and contracted at the knee. To compensate for this disability, the man had attached a wooden peg to his right knee, thereby enabling contact with the ground. From a distance this produced the illusion of an extra leg. Friends thus knew Robert Williamson as "Three-Legged Willie."[1]

Houston and Williamson forded Shoal Creek and followed Pecan Street to its western terminus. Turning northwest, the pair rode through a patchwork of woodland and open prairie before ascending the gentle slope of the tallest peak in the hills west of Austin.[2] The spectacular view from the summit moved both men to dismount and stare appreciatively into the distance. Houston finally broke the silence by slapping his companion on the shoulder and trumpeting, "Upon my soul, Williamson, this must be the very spot where Satan took our Savior to show and tempt Him with the riches and beauties of the world!" Three-Legged Willie's reply reflected his equally awestruck mood, "Yes, General, and if Jesus Christ had been fallible, He would have accepted his Satanic majesty's proposition."[3]

Pedestrians strolling up Congress Avenue early in 1840 might have noticed larger than usual crowds in front of Bullock's hotel. A jumble of logs left in front of the hotel during city construction offered seats to those with a few spare moments. These "Loafer's Logs" now constituted an informal arena for joke-telling, story-swapping, and political squabbling.[4] Cheap and readily available liquor fueled the proceedings, lending a clubhouse atmosphere to the popular gathering spot. Regulars included Hugh McLeod, Richard Brenham, T. G. Forster, Ira Munson, James M. Ogden, and others "who kept the company in a roar by their witty sallies and bon mots."[5]

Crowds might have also been larger than usual in front of the Treasury building just down the avenue from Bullock's. This one-story frame structure sat about fifteen feet from the street. A steady stream of mechanics, rangers, clerks, and others receiving government pay kept the front yard filled with waiting and gossiping men.[6]

Asa Brigham organized the city election—Austin's first—that was responsible for the increased activity at Bullock's and the Treasury office.[7] City residents, never at a loss for controversial issues, now had a particularly juicy one to trigger argument. Who among them would direct city affairs? Who would set rules, impose taxes, and prioritize public projects? Who would organize defense, settle disputes, and control city revenue? And who would expose themselves to public blame and humiliation should events take a sour turn?

Edwin Waller figured he was up to the task and announced he was running for mayor. Like many others who helped build Austin in 1839, Waller stayed to make the city his home. His house on the northeast corner of Mulberry Street and Congress Avenue hosted the first Masonic meeting in Austin on October 11, 1839. Other aspirants must have realized the futility of running against the man credited with constructing the city, for Waller easily won an uncontested election. Years later William Walsh recalled that Waller, "a thorough gentleman, courteous and refined but of iron firmness, was a fortunate selection for the troubled times."[8]

On January 13, 1840, 187 men stopped by Spicer's Tavern throughout the day to have a drink and cast a vote in that first election. Former Waterloo resident Jacob Harrell won a seat on the council. Samuel Whiting of the *Austin City Gazette* also gained a spot. Other notable victors included Charles Schoolfield, who had helped with the original town survey, and Moses Johnson, a future mayor.[9]

Within a month of its formation Austin's city council passed a number of ordinances reflecting contemporary Anglo-Texan attitudes and fears. Any landowner starting a fire on his property which endangered neighboring property faced a twenty dollar fine. The cutting of trees in city streets or alleys without permission from the mayor or three aldermen was prohibited. Indians could henceforth no longer camp within the city. Selling liquor to slaves or Indians brought fines of ten dollars and twenty-five dollars, respectively. A slave caught out after 10:00 p.m. without a pass would receive ten lashes. And prison, a fifty-dollar fine, or both awaited any white or Mexican caught associating with black slaves.[10]

Texas in the 1830s and 1840s offered ambitious preachers a seemingly unlimited supply of errant souls. Writing about his visit to Austin, Presbyterian minister William McCalla wrote, "I prayed for murderers, adulterers, swearers, liars, Sabbath-breakers, gamblers, and drunkards; and testified against such characters; but invited them to come, and take of the water of life freely." Men of the cloth in search of souls to save flocked to the new republic, which everyone in the United States "knew" was home to countless thieves, murderers, swindlers, and fugitive husbands. The biggest names in the young nation's history seemed to fit one or more of these descriptors. Jim Bowie had smuggled slaves and sold fraudulent land titles in Louisiana while William Travis had left a pregnant wife and son behind in Alabama. Even Sam Houston, the Hero of San Jacinto, was a drunkard who had humiliated his first wife, taken a second *Indian* wife, then left her to go to Texas. Joseph M. White of St. Louis summarized this pervasive attitude about Texas residents in a letter to Mirabeau Lamar: "The idea too generally, & most erroneously circulated that Texas is the rendezvous of absconding debtors, & fugitive fellows must be checked, arrested, & put down—By some such act as this the country will acquire moral influence, & be associated with immigrants of another Class."[11]

Reverend Amos Roark answered this call. At the direction of the Presbyterian Church he accompanied missionary Samuel Frazier on a trip to Texas in 1838, winding up in Austin the following year. During the horseback journey from the United States Frazier and Roark held prayer meetings at each stop. The pair reported back to the home church that "in every place people bade them farewell with tears, imploring God's blessings on their labors in that distant field." In January 1840 Amos Roark took the first census in Austin, Texas. He counted 856 residents and 75 families. The 145 black slaves made up 17 percent of the population. A measly 5.6 percent of the total, or 48 people, attributed to themselves a religious denomination, which may explain the motivation behind Roark's effort. Perhaps the preacher planned especially to target the twenty men in his survey calling themselves professional gamblers.[12]

Blue skies and balmy weather greeted early Sabbath riser A. B. Lawrence in Austin January 12, 1840. The Philadelphia resident washed, ate breakfast, then strolled pleasantly past closed shops on empty streets until he reached the capitol building. Entering the Senate chamber, Lawrence felt mild surprise that so few seats remained. After settling in he surveyed the room and recognized many familiar faces, including most of the members of Congress, department heads, and their families. The crowd quieted as William Burnet, six-year-old son of Vice President David Burnet, received baptism. Worshipers then listened attentively to a sermon from Reverend Lawrence of New Orleans. Reverend J. F. Crowe of Indiana presided over a communion service for nineteen people, one of whom, a black slave, "these Christians publicly acknowledged in the brotherhood of Christ." That afternoon Lawrence returned to hear an address by a Methodist minister to a group of citizens organizing a Sunday School society. Attendees donated a total of $129 toward this purpose. Evening services were "solemnly and faithfully" conducted by Reverend Crowe. The day's events greatly impressed A. B. Lawrence, who wrote, "Such facts related of a town situated upon the outmost borders of civilized population, and not yet six months old, must, to every reflecting mind, be as gratifying as they are uncommon and surprising."[13]

Pious Austin residents fretted over the city's lack of a proper house of worship. The two congregations in town, one Methodist and the other Presbyterian,[14] met in the Senate chamber of the capitol.[15] The Presbyterians gained an early lead by beginning construction of a dedicated building in the spring of 1840.[16] The builder was Abner Cook, who, along with James Burke, Richard Bullock and his wife, and two others had founded the congregation at Bullock's hotel October 13, 1839.[17] Cook had a short commute to the job site, which lay adjacent to his own house on West Bois d'Arc Street.[18]

Although the Presbyterian congregation had raised two thousand dollars in subscriptions to build their church, the actual cash trickled in slowly.[19] Cook's progress was therefore sporadic and stopped altogether in October 1840. A year later the editor of the *Texas Centinel* attempted to shame the congregation into finishing the job:

> It is well known that a church was commenced in this city some eigh-teen months since; and it is also well known, that for the last twelve months, it has been used, in an unfinished condition, as a carpenter's shop. . . . We see that the old building still remains in its dilapidated con-dition, not the abode of owls, for they would hardly live in it—but a monument of the folly of our citizens, in allowing a piece of property, which is of no use or value in its present state, to run to waste, when a few hundred dollars would finish it.

Shortly thereafter Cook had the building ready for use but it collapsed during a severe storm in 1844.[20]

Success came quicker to the Methodists, despite a later start. Once completed in 1841, their pine building won distinction as the first church in the city. The structure measured thirty by forty feet and stood on the northeast corner of Congress and Cedar. The absence of a ceiling prob-ably gave worshipers the impression of a roomier facility than its modest size would have otherwise indicated. Churchgoers listened for the clang-ing sound of a large steel triangle to call them to services. Made by a lo-cal blacksmith and attached to a wooden post in front of the church, the imposing piece of metal soon had residents calling the corner "Triangle Hill."[21]

Austin's earliest critics loved to point out the difficulty involved in trans-porting goods to the frontier. As John Eldredge of the *Morning Star* noted, "Every comfort and almost the necessaries of life must be sent from Houston in wagons, and the cost of transportation . . . when added to the high prices which groceries &c. bring here, must render them difficult to be obtained, except by a few."[22] No one starved that first summer; after all, game abounded and area farmers successfully raised great quantities of corn.[23] But lack of dietary variety was a fact of life. The *Morning Star* editor poked fun at this in a facetious lament that he hadn't been invited to the dinner welcoming President Lamar to Austin by allowing that the

(Left) Twenty-three-year-old Julia Lee arrived in Austin from Cincinnati with her sister and two brothers in May 1840. Shortly thereafter she wed postal clerk George Sinks. Years later, Julia Sinks wrote a series of detailed newspaper articles describing life in early Austin. Courtesy of De Zavala (Adina Emilia) Papers, CN12187, the Dolph Briscoe Center for American History, University of Texas at Austin.

(Right) George Sinks was President Lamar's chief post office clerk and one of Austin's first residents. He married Julia Lee shortly after her arrival from Cincinnati in 1840. Courtesy of Mr. Sinks De Zavala (Adina Emilia) Papers, CN 12184, the Dolph Briscoe Center for American History, University of Texas at Austin.

oversight "must have occurred in the extent of the preparation of cornbread and beef." Frank Brown, who moved to Austin at age thirteen in 1846 and later compiled a detailed history of the city, claimed that boarding houses like Bullock's served mostly cornbread, beef, wild honey, and game. When the City Restaurant opened for business in October 1840, its owner promised only "a choice supply of provisions, of the best that can be procured, which will at all times be served up in a style to suit customers."[24]

Those unwilling to rely upon market availability sought any opportunity to supplement their corn-and-beef diet. Settler John Holland Jenkins recalled going on a fall pecan hunt led by a man named Foxhorn. Participants aimed "to gather pecans and 'lay in' as much buffalo, bear, and deer meat as would last their families during the winter." Jenkins fondly remembered that "no meat is more palatable and better than good fat buffalo meat." Fruits and vegetables remained particularly elusive. According to William Walsh, "There was not one can to be had of any kind of fruit, vegetable, or fish." As late as 1845 Thomas William Ward had to order lemons, potatoes, onions, and beans from Houston.[25]

Meat was plentiful. Every restaurant and boarding house, such as that run by John Woodruff, seemed to offer buffalo, venison, and turkey. Almost everything else came on wagons from Houston. William Walsh recalled watching brown sugar being unloaded and spread out on a long platform with a receptacle underneath to catch the dripping molasses. Coarse salt required crushing prior to use. And, "strange as it may seem in a country filled with cattle, milk and butter were almost unknown." Even so, Brewster Jayne found a steady enough supply to write, "You know I am a dear lover of milk, and I live mostly on it."[26]

Flour arrived in large barrels, when it arrived at all. Once, again according to William Walsh, rain and muddy roads kept the delivery wagons in Houston as the day of an Austin wedding approached. The families involved despaired because "a pound cake with a wedding ring inside seemed to be an absolute necessity." Finally, an older woman insisted on attempting the cake using coarse cornmeal. Be painstakingly sifting the meal with a flannel cloth, she was able within two days to procure fine enough flour to successfully bake the desired cake.[27]

As beautiful as its situation was, early Austin offered little entertainment. Creative residents therefore made their own. One morning a group of young boys stationed themselves at regular intervals along Congress Avenue where it runs past the government offices. As they knew he would, President Lamar soon ambled absentmindedly down the street, hands clasped behind his back. The first boy he passed shouted a cheery "Good morning, Mr. President!", a greeting which Lamar returned. Within moments though he passed the second boy, then a third and fourth, all of whom offered up the same salutation. Catching on to the joke at last, the president wheeled about, bowed extravagantly while removing his hat, and exclaimed, "Good morning, gentlemen. In the name of God, good morning to you all!"

Another group of young men sought amusement by organizing the "Congress Extraordinary of the Rounders," which met at George Dolson's for the first and only time on Christmas Day 1841. A notice in the

Daily Bulletin invited all to attend, but added that two rules must be strictly followed:

> If any member is too drunk to rise from his seat to speak, the Chair shall appoint a committee of three to hold him up.
>
> No member shall absent himself from the House, unless he have leave to be sick.

After abolishing the Republic of Texas and its Congress and placing the country under "new and more efficient government," the Rounders began their deliberations. They quickly adopted another rule that stated, "No member should be required to speak with any relevancy to the subject under consideration." The body then passed several bills "to benefit the people a great deal and the Congress much more, a course for which there is plenty of precedent." The Rounders spoof sparked enough interest that thirty years later Frank Brown encountered Austin residents still able to discuss it.[28]

At Austin's founding Shoal and Waller Creeks flowed year-round. Before farming filled them with sediment, each stream ran through deeper and narrower channels. Deep pools at intervals along their lengths provided excellent fishing and bathing opportunities.[29] William Walsh recalled swimming as a boy in Shoal Creek near its junction with the Colorado.[30] The river itself also teemed with fish and turtles but was harder to reach because of its steep, jungle-like banks. This proved no impediment to settler George Grover, who wrote to his brother in Kentucky, "I have made some of the *prettiest hauls*, that have been made about here." Grover eagerly joined the fish from time to time, telling his brother, "It is truly a luxury to enjoy a good swim."[31]

Men staged shooting contests in which they competed for prizes of beef or turkey. Or they organized groups on horseback to chase jackrabbits. Hunting was popular, especially south of the river west of Barton Springs. Horse races occurred about a mile east of town.[32] Cockfighting provided bloody entertainment as well as gambling opportunities. Saloons and faro banks never lacked for business. The gambling houses were already earning reputations for trouble, as one unfortunate congressman discovered in February 1840: "An affray took place at Austin, in which the Hon. Stephen H. Everitt was severely wounded in the forehead, with a Porter bottle. The difficulty occurred in a dispute at a Faro table!!!"[33]

Those seeking diversion often made trips into the countryside. Barton Springs and present-day Mount Bonnell were popular destinations. Before composing a letter back home to Kentucky, George Grover made such a journey, "endeavoring to find something to write about." Grover and his riding companion encountered a group fishing at Barton's, which he described as "the greatest springs that I ever saw." Anyone who has visited the modern Barton Springs pool will understand what happened next: "One of the boys could not resist the temptation, so *in he dove*; I followed his example and it was . . . 'much good.'"[34]

Austin women also sought relief from the tedium imposed by frontier life. Dance parties to fiddle music proved popular. Ladies were frequent observers at congressional debates. They also attended lectures and debates at the newly formed Austin Lyceum, which met in the Senate chamber. The speakers seemed to always be men, which might explain the debate topic for the September 29, 1840, meeting: "Are the minds of females susceptible of as high cultivation as those of men?"[35] The Senate chamber witnessed numerous complimentary balls given in honor of various male heroes. Groups of women organized details and decorations. Mary Bullock often catered the food. For one such occasion honoring William Cooke, organizers first removed all of the Senate furniture, then:

> the room was arranged and beautified with a degree of taste and elegance we have seldom seen equaled. The railings, tables, desks, and lobby seats were removed, the walls were beautifully decorated with festoons, pyramids, wreaths, and stars of evergreen, and with drapery of blue, white and red colors; while, in addition to these, the western wall was adorned with the flags of Texas, of the U. States and of France, tasteful disposed in juxtaposition one to the other. An immense Texian flag formed a panoply on the ceiling over head. Through the centre of the hall, a stand of muskets, polished to dazzling brightness, with bayonets fixed, ranged from one end to the other, leaving only space sufficient at each end for a promenade around the stand. The festoons, pyramids and stars were most of them interwoven with swords and cutlasses, the sheen had glare of which made a rich and imposing contrast to the deep green in which they were imbedded. The room was illuminated by two large chandeliers, formed by inverted bayonets, rising in a conical form.

Mrs. Bullock received high praise for her "three tall pyramids [of pastry] which were respectively crowned with the national banners of the United States, France, and Texas."[36]

Austin enthusiastically celebrated the Fourth of July, Texas Independence Day, and San Jacinto Day. Alcohol played a prominent role in these affairs, as noted in the *Morning Star.* "By a correspondent in Austin, we learn that they did up the 4th there in fine style—a procession, oration and dinner, of course, were among the proceedings. At the dinner, many speeches were made, and much wine drank, and it is said a *pretty considerable* portion of the company were fuddled; the latter *may be* a slander."[37] The Travis Guards, a volunteer militia constituted in March 1840, led an annual San Jacinto Day parade on April 21 in the early years. As is the case in modern Austin, such processions marched to the head of Congress Avenue for speeches, music, and other celebration. Texas Independence Day on March 2 elicited similar festivities. A terrible accident marred the first Independence Day celebration in Austin. Thomas William Ward, who lost a leg at the Siege of Bexar in December 1835, suffered a shattering wound to his right arm when a cannon he was loading discharged prematurely. The unfortunate Ward, already nicknamed "Peg Leg," lost another extremity when doctors found it necessary to take the damaged arm off at the shoulder.[38]

Austin lost one of its most notable settlers in the spring of 1840 with the death of William Barton, named in his obituary as "the Daniel Boone of Texas." Barton had moved to the property enclosing his famous springs to get away from encroaching settlement. He first watched the construction of Waterloo, then Austin on the opposite bank of the Colorado River. His acquaintances knew him as "frank and confiding . . . he was emphatically an honest and upright man."[39] Considered elderly by area residents, Barton died on April 11, 1840, at age fifty-eight.[40]

| Chapter 13 |

MOCCASIN TRACKS

There's but two tribes any how in this country. One is the moccasin and the
other the boots. In those days the moccasins had the county and I was on the trail;
now the boots have it, and the moccasins have disappeared, but blamed if
I know whether the country is any better off.

Early Austin resident Ben Gooch, Brown, *Annals of Travis Country*, ch. 11

Sometime during the 1810s a Georgia schoolboy named Mirabeau Lamar took up his pen while pondering the question, "Were the Europeans Justified in Conquering and Taking Possession of America in the Manner They Did?" The idealistic youth began by noting, "It must be acknowledged . . . in the conquest of America many daring and outrageous acts of barbarity were committed by the Europeans." Europeans had been guilty of "neglecting the laws of humanity and their god. . . . The fact is, that, the Europeans finding America a fruitful and advantageous Country, and allured by their thirst for conquest, and wealth, sought the destruction of the natives that they might open a road to their own aggrandizement and profits." Denying the validity of the rights of discovery and conquest, Lamar argued, "As well might the natives of any land in the ocean who have not yet discovered Europe fit out a ship, land on the coast of England or France and finding no inhabitants but poor peasants or fishermen, drive them from their lands, and claim the whole country by right of discovery." In summarizing, the young man left no doubt about his answer to the question under debate, "It is self-evident and clear and that it was absolutely unjust."[1]

Decades later this same schoolboy addressed his countrymen in quite a different tone:

> If the wild cannibals of the woods will not desist from their massacres:
> if they will continue to war upon us with the ferocity of Tigers and
> Hyenas, it is time we should retaliate their warfare, not in the murder of
> their women and children, but in the prosecution of an exterminating

war upon their warriors, which will admit of no compromise and have no termination except in their total extinction or total expulsion.[2]

From the start President Lamar pursued a stern policy against "the wandering tribes that infest our borders." He denounced a soft approach toward "the debased and ignorant savages" and their "atrocious cruelties": "As long as we continue to exhibit our mercy without shewing [*sic*] our strength, so long will the Indian continue to bloody the edge of the tomahawk." Contrary to Sam Houston, whose friendliness toward the Indians in general, and the Cherokee in particular, aroused accusations of treason from Lamar partisans, the new president did not concede "that the Indians, either Native, or Emigrant, have any just cause of complaint. That the Emigrant Tribes have no legal or equitable claim to any portion of our territory is obvious." Even the Native tribes "shall deport themselves in a friendly manner; being subordinate to our laws."[3] Lamar believed this despite the fact that *he* had immigrated to Texas fifteen years *after* the Cherokee, and only three years before this speech.

When Lamar assumed office, relations between the Texas government and the Cherokee were peaceful. This quickly changed. Lamar, like many Texans, suspected the Cherokee of conspiring with Mexico against the new republic.[4] Chief Bowles, the elderly leader of the Cherokee and a close friend of Sam Houston, professed good will toward Texas, but Lamar thought him a liar. His suspicions seemed confirmed after Manuel Flores's courageous death on the North San Gabriel River in May 1839.[5] In Flores's saddlebags were letters from Mexican officials containing an invitation to the Cherokee to join Mexico in ousting the Anglo-Texans.[6] Lamar demanded that the Cherokee leave the republic. When Bowles refused, Lamar sent an army to evict him. The inevitable battle destroyed Cherokee military power. A wounded, unarmed Bowles had his brains blown out by one of the Texans.[7] Another then cut strips of flesh from the chief's body to make a belt. The old man's trademark hat was shipped to Sam Houston in mocking tribute.[8]

Lamar's treatment of the Cherokee triggered ethnic warfare. While many Texas tribes reacted violently to their eviction, the Comanche in particular saw in Lamar's actions proof that the whites intended to destroy them. Anglo settlers, including those in and around Austin, suffered under the ensuing barrage of brutal attacks, which seemed to them pointless and cruel. They fought back without pity, attacking and burning villages, killing indiscriminately while taking no prisoners. Scores died on both sides. Under the circumstances most Texans were unapologetic in

their ferocity. "Life sits lightly on the borderer," wrote settler Jane Cazneau. "Neither his own nor his friend's is spared any risk, and as for the
Indians, in his eyes they were only made to be killed."[9]

Readers of the *Morning Star* chuckled over a humorous frontier anecdote
in the newspaper's February 28, 1840, edition. When a Tonkawa scout
employed by Edward Burleson in the vicinity of Austin strayed from
camp he was spotted by a local man hunting turkey. The hunter immediately leveled his rifle "when the Indian accidentally turned. . . . Had he
turned to run or even to fall to the ground, his fate would have been decided; without hesitating, he lifted both hands and ran towards his opponent, exclaiming me Tonk! me Tonk! Bobasheelee heap. The hunter
dropped his rifle and met his red friend with a roar of laughter."[10]

As the Tonkawa scout's narrow escape demonstrates, belonging to a
"friendly" tribe provided only flimsy protection to Indians in the Austin
area. Three Indian nations, the Tonkawa, the Lipan Apache, and the Comanche, figured most prominently in Austin's earliest history. Militarily
insignificant by the time of Austin's founding, the Tonkawa quickly threw
in with the Anglos in an effort to gain protection from the Comanche. The
Tonkawa had lived in the region since at least the seventeenth century.
Decades of warfare, first with the Lipan Apache and later with the Comanche, had vastly decreased their population. As their strength declined, so did their access to the buffalo herds, weakening them further.
As a result, Anglo settlers collectively had no reason to fear the Tonkawa.

Before the Comanche swept onto the southern plains in the seventeenth and eighteenth centuries, the Lipan Apache had dominated the
region. But, fueled by their desire to harness the riches of the plains for
themselves, as well as to control the lucrative trade markets of San Antonio and eastern New Mexico, the Comanche preyed ceaselessly on
Apache towns and villages, eventually driving their enemy into south
Texas and Mexico. The Lipan initially responded by seeking shelter in
Spanish missions. Later they looked to Mexican and Anglo-Texan authorities for protection. As Austin sprang into existence Texas military leaders like John Moore and Edward Burleson had little difficulty recruiting
Lipan Apache scouts for punitive expeditions against the Comanche.

Comanche acquisition of the horse in the late seventeenth century
sparked a radical cultural transformation that enticed individual Comanche bands to leave the Rockies for life on the Great Plains. The initial
migratory trickle became a great flood, the result of which was the development of a nomadic lifestyle perfectly suited to its environment. Co-

manche women learned to utilize horses for the efficient long-distance cargo transport necessary for following buffalo herds. Comanche men mastered mounted warfare. The more settled Lipan Apache had no effective defense against the swift surprise attacks of their enemy. Even the Spaniards had been unable to overcome Comanche military might, eventually opting for accommodation over continued futile efforts at conquest. By 1839 Comanchería, as Comanche territory was known, included vast stretches of what is now Texas, Oklahoma, New Mexico, and Colorado. Generations of Comanche had fought, bled, and sacrificed to build this empire. They would fight to preserve it. In 1839 Comanchería reached as far south as the Balcones Escarpment, or within a few miles of the city of Austin. But President Mirabeau Lamar and his fellow Texans viewed this new city as lying at the center of a Texas empire rather than on the edge of a Comanche one.[11]

In early 1839 a group of Lipan Apache hunters stumbled upon a large Comanche camp on the San Saba River about fifty miles above the seat-of-government site. They informed white settlers, who selected Colonel John H. Moore to lead an expedition against the village. The combined Texan and Apache force caught the Comanche completely off guard. Attacking at dawn on February 14, the Texans fired mercilessly into the buffalo-skin tents of their enemy, "killing indiscriminately a number of all ages and sexes."

Four days later Elizabeth Coleman and her five-year-old son Tommy were working in the garden of their home on Webber's Prairie when a large band of revenge-minded Comanche charged out of the brush. Mrs. Coleman's concern for her boy proved fatal. As she stopped to assist him in running to the house an arrow pierced her throat. She nevertheless made it inside. Tommy did not. An attacker scooped the child up and carried him off. The dying Elizabeth gasped, "Oh, children, I am killed," then told her oldest son, "Albert, my son, I am dying, get the guns and defend your sisters." Fifteen-year-old Albert fought bravely and managed to kill or wound several attackers before receiving a fatal wound himself. His two younger sisters escaped when the attacking band rode off at the calls of their comrades engaged in plundering the nearby residence of Joel Robertson.[12]

Edwin Waller and his workmen thus built the Texas capital in a war zone. Most settlers hated Indians, or at least the perceived insecurity they brought. Few took great pains before firing to ascertain the hostile status of a target. To some it made no difference. While on the road to Austin in 1840, A. B. Lawrence encountered two young men practicing their rifle skills:

> Their language and conversation smacked strongly of the spirit of border fighting and hatred to the Indians. They had learned but a few hours before, from a traveller [sic], that Indians had been seen further up the country, (whether friendly or not they seemed not disposed to inquire,) and hence they were thus preparing for such emergencies as they supposed might likely transpire.

A bit farther up the road Lawrence met a similar attitude in a family with whom he stayed the night:

> In answer to a suggestion that the Indians mentioned by the travelers might be a company of friendly Indians, and not disposed to do mischief, the young husband, with a mingled frown, sneer and angry laugh, answered, "friendly! Yes, they will all be friendly enough if once they come in the range of my rifle." This remark was received by the junior members of the family with a laugh of pleasure. It required but little penetration to discover that our hosts were accustomed to the vicissitudes attendant upon settlers in the borders of the haunts of savages, and that to them sporting and the killing of Indians were merely synonymous terms.

Nor was such talk merely idle boasting, as another of A. B. Lawrence's hosts illustrated:

> In many instances, he said, the greatest troubles with which the Texian army had to contend, were the depredations and robberies practiced by the Indians who were professedly friendly. These were constantly lurking about the camps and stealing everything of value within their reach. . . . He mentioned that once being left in charge of the camp equipage, while his messmates were abroad on duty, he left his place for a few moments to procure water from the river Guadalupe, which was just at hand. While here, he caught a glimpse of an Indian gliding swiftly through the thickets towards the river above him, with a blanket he had just stolen from the camp. He immediately fired upon the savage with a rifle, but without effect, as the Indian pressed on into the stream. By the time he could seize another gun, and be ready to fire, the red man had nearly attained the middle of the river with his booty. He again fired,

and it would seem with better aim, for the thief sunk and was seen no more, while the stolen blanket was observed floating down the current. How the narrator's mind was affected by such events did not appear other than by an apparent perfect indifference.[13]

Despite the armed forces screening his work crews, Waller lost at least two men to Indian attack during construction. The two were camped along Waller Creek at the time of their deaths. They were buried on the far side of the creek near Sabine Street and between Hickory and Mulberry Streets.[14] Many whites acknowledged that Indians, and the Comanche in particular, possessed justifiable motive for such aggression, but most agreed that Comanche patriotism must yield to manifest destiny:

> It is doubtless better for the world of industry that this vast region of the Comanches should be converted from the theatre of hunting and of war, into smiling fields and verdant meadows. But we should not forget at the same time that this is doing, that this country is the olden home of the Indians, that his father and his father's father are buried here. Let us not be surprised then if the savage adheres to his old hunting ground, with great tenacity. . . . It is submitted whether it is not the only proper policy for Texas to pursue toward the Comanches, to carry a war of extermination into the heart of their country.[15]

Senator Anson Jones slept only fitfully the night of March 12, 1840. He had fallen asleep without difficulty in his bed at Edwin Waller's house at Mulberry and Congress, but at ten o'clock awoke to the loud cry of "The Indians are upon us; turn out!" echoing through the streets. Then he listened agonizingly to the tormented screams of a man named James Headley dying at the hands of Comanche raiders. He learned the next day that the butcher William Ward had also perished and that the raiders had made off with all of the town's horses from the corral near Waller Creek.[16] Vowing revenge, Edward Burleson immediately organized a pursuit party. Recruiting posed no challenge because the townspeople "seem resolved to exterminate the bloody and thieving rascals: they will shoot them down whenever and wherever they are met."[17]

Already skittish Austin residents clamored for action. Samuel Whiting claimed in the *Austin City Gazette* that if the attackers had only known of the town's weak defenses they could have burned it down. He also decried the lack of town organization in the face of such threats. Whiting called for permanently stationing mounted troops east and west of Austin and placing a third group, assisted by Tonkawa scouts, in the foothills to the northwest. He also urged further arming of the citizenry and the creation of an armory and fire company. Prussian army veteran H. Moll-hausen wrote immediately after the raid to President Lamar to offer him-self as commander of the town's cannon. He wanted to move the weap-on from the capitol to President's Hill so it could be fired as a warning signal without endangering lives and property. There is no record of the piece being moved but in June Mollhausen was placed at the head of a sixty-man volunteer artillery company.[18] By then the cannon had attract-ed practical jokers, which aroused the chivalrous sentiments of the *Austin City Gazette*:

> One night last week the citizens of this place were roused from their slumbers by the discharge of a piece of artillery—on hastening to the spot it was discovered to be only a false alarm.

> Although it might seem to the perpetrators to be a very fine joke, they ought to show at least some respect for those few numbers of the fair sex who have located their head rights within the bounds of this city.[19]

Constant fear of Indian attack terrified many residents, especially non-combatants. Julia Lee Sinks recalled a party at the president's house on a beautiful August evening in 1841: "The young people flitted in and out and stood in merry groups around the hilltop, lapped in the soft, sat-iny folds of a Texas moonlight whose whiteness seemed almost palpable to the touch." Suddenly from the distance burst the loud clatter of hoof beats and the shout, "It is Indians!" Sinks wrote: "Then was executed by the ladies what was known in Texas as a stampede. All at once there was a sudden breaking away from the beauties of the night. They flew to the house for shelter like a flock of pigeons, while the gentlemen lingered behind, listening for other advancing sounds." Although the alarm proved false, Sinks explained, "We relate these trivial alarms to show how, min-gled with all our mirth, were lurking the ever present undertones of prob-abilities, or at least possibilities."[20]

Julia Sinks cited Mrs. Bullock's piano parlor as a common gathering place of women during Indian alarms. Some sought to ease the tension with jokes and music; others reproached them for such mirth in the face of danger. Two-time War Department Secretary George Hockley, "with pistol in hand . . . would come among us, saying: 'Don't get frightened, ladies, don't get frightened; there are enough men here to whip all the

Indians between here and Santa Fe.'" But even with an "all clear" signal "the uncertainty of the need made all go in crowds, those who feared, and those who feared not."[21]

Attacks came suddenly and unexpectedly, but usually on a small scale. In early July 1840 a Mr. Clapton of Gilleland Creek sent for town physician Richard Brenham to tend to a wounded slave. A group of three or four Indians had attacked the unfortunate woman, first disabling and then scalping her and leaving her for dead. Once she was alone she was able to stumble back to her master's, where Brenham patched her up before announcing a good prognosis.[22]

Austin's detractors seized upon every Indian attack as proof that the location was a poor one for the government seat. Their eagerness to find fault sometimes resulted in fanciful exaggeration, such as the story about the aftermath of an attack by Colonel Moore upon a Comanche village appearing in Sam Houston's hometown newspaper, the *San Augustine Journal and Advertiser:*

> A party of Comanches followed them, and after parading at midday through the streets of the great metropolis of Texas, raising their war-hoop [sic] on the square of Austin, holding the good people of our seat of government in great bodily fear and cutting various other extraordinary capers in that *warlike* city, which contains the public documents of the Republic, very much to the relief of its inhabitants, quietly marching on after their former conquerors, retook 25 of the captured horses, and returned again to their prairie homes.[23]

In denouncing the story, the *Austin City Gazette* scolded those responsible: "Editors in Texas ought to remember, ere they lend themselves to the propagation of such false and malicious rumors, with intent to injure the present location of the seat of Government, that, as far as Austin is concerned, their slanders avail them naught, but such misstatements are but too well calculated to injure the interests of their country abroad, and to deter men with families from emigrating to Texas."[24]

John J. Linn had never seen so many Indians. Accustomed to visits from small parties of Lipan Apache, he and his Victoria neighbors at first assumed only that a particularly large band of Apache had gathered about the town to trade. But when word arrived of two area murders by this army of Comanche raiders, Linn knew that Victoria faced "overwhelming numbers of these implacable enemies of the human race."

Victoria was lucky. After gathering up all of the horses around Victoria, the Comanche force bypassed the town and headed toward Lavaca Bay, where it encircled the coastal village of Linnville. Startled residents fled in boats to the safety of the bay and could only watch as the raiders ransacked and burned their homes. Laden with plunder and captives, the Indians reversed course to return to the plains.[25]

Four days later, on August 10, 1840, the Reverend Z. N. Morrel was driving an ox wagon over the divide between the Guadalupe and Lavaca Rivers when he recognized the trail made earlier by the Comanche on their way to the coast. He raced to La Grange to inform Edward Burleson of his discovery. At about the same time word arrived in La Grange of the Linnville attack. Organizing quickly, the Texans soon had a force of about two hundred men under Felix Huston waiting to intercept the Comanche about thirty miles southeast of Austin at Plum Creek.[26]

On August 12 the Comanche rode into view. Texan Robert Hall recalled:

> As the long column marched across the prairies it presented a ludicrous sight. The naked warriors had tried to dress themselves in the clothing they had stolen. Many of them put on cloth coats and buttoned them behind. Most of them had on stolen shoes and hats. They spread the calico over their horses, and tied hundreds of yards of ribbon in their horses' manes and to their tails. . . . They all had new white shields, and many of the warriors had long tails to their headgear.

Hall estimated that the column of Comanche horses and pack mules stretched over seven miles. Comanche fighters outnumbered the Texans by at least two to one. Despite this numerical advantage and remarkable individual bravery, the Comanche suffered what the whites viewed as a crushing defeat. The ease of the victory surprised Robert Hall:

> It has always been a mystery to me why the Indians became so terribly demoralized in this battle. It was fought on the open prairie, and they could easily see that they greatly outnumbered us. It is rather strange that they did not make a stand. . . . Our boys charged with a yell and did not fire until they got close to the enemy. The Indians were panic stricken, and fled at once. The Texans followed them over the prairies for fifteen or twenty miles. . . . The Comanches were greatly superior to us in number, but the battle was a crushing defeat, and was the end of the long reign of terror of these terrible red devils in Texas.

Hall's use of the word "devil" in describing his Comanche enemies meshed with the world view of his comrades-in-arms. One Texan soldier recalled a conversation between French Smith and his father Ezekial after the older man shot and killed an unarmed, wounded Comanche woman:

"Well, Father, I would not have done that for a hundred dollars."

"Done what," says the old man.

"Why, kilt a woman, a human being."

"That aint a human. Thats an injun and I come to kill Injuns, and all the rest has out ran me and got away."

General Huston reported: "We have given the Comanches a lesson which they will long remember; near four hundred of their brave warriors have been defeated by half their number, and I hope and trust that this will be the last of their depredations on our frontier." Felix Huston was overly optimistic. Comanche military power in Texas survived the Battle of Plum Creek by three decades. Nevertheless, the Anglo-Texans had won a decisive victory, one which conferred much greater security on the city of Austin. The Comanche, realizing that Anglo-Texans offered much stouter resistance than the inhabitants of northern Mexico, thereafter aimed their largest raiding expeditions south of the Rio Grande. Although no one yet knew it, the Battle of Plum Creek rendered residents of the seat of government safe from major attack by the Comanche they had displaced. [27]

Chapter 14

THE PIG WAR

These people, M. le Comte, are unbelievably inexperienced and ignorant in all that concerns external politics. They have no idea of the respective situation of different nations, of the rules and the usages that govern the relations amongst these nations; besides, begin Americans, they have boundless vanity and presumption.

Alphonse Dubois de Saligny, letter to M. le Comte, April 20, 1839

Pity poor Eugene Pluyette. The unlucky French servant could not have been thrilled to follow his employer, Alphonse Dubois de Saligny, chargé d'affaires of the Kingdom of France to the Republic of Texas, to the backwater town of Houston in 1839. Now, two years later, he found himself in even more disagreeable surroundings on the very edge of civilization. He and his master had reached Austin only by attaching themselves to an armed escort, so dangerous was the countryside around his new home. Once in the capital the official representative of one of the most powerful nations on earth could find no better quarters than the rough log shack masquerading as a hotel suite owned by a ruffian named Richard Bullock. After leaving Bullock's hotel the French entourage had at least secured its own private building, if only an unimposing frame structure made of sawed pine. But the location on Pecan Street three blocks west of Congress Avenue[1] placed Pluyette and his countrymen along the main western approach to the city beyond the immediate protection of Austin's other residents. And, while Pluyette worried primarily about Indian attack, it was from his former landlord Richard Bullock that he received the beating that ignited an international controversy.

Jean Pierre Isidore Alphonse Dubois, the self-styled comte de Saligny, first arrived on Texas soil early in 1839. While Lamar's commissioners busied themselves along the Brazos and Colorado Rivers, de Saligny, at the behest of the French government, toured Galveston, Houston, and the Texas coast to Matagorda. Along the way he encountered Sam Houston, in whom he saw "a certain dignity, in spite of the strange garb in

Austin residents welcomed French Chargé d'Affaires Alphonse Dubois de Saligny's 1840 arrival as a sign of legitimacy for their new city. De Saligny strove unsuccessfully for passage of the Franco-Texian bill, which would have established a line of French-financed forts along the Texas frontier in exchange for land grants for French immigrants. Subsequently, he left town in disgrace after a personal dispute with Richard Bullock. Courtesy of Prints & Photographs Collection, Saligny, C. de, CN01265, the Dolph Briscoe Center for American History, University of Texas at Austin.

which he is always muffled," but also negligence, laziness, and adminis-
trative incompetence. In Mirabeau Lamar he perceived a "little, ugly,
awkward, and ordinary" man. Lamar's famous reticence struck the
Frenchman, who wrote, "Unbelievable effort must be made to pull from
him the few words that he lets fall heavily and with difficulty." But if Texan leaders failed to impress the count, average Texans did not. In marveling about the rapidity with which these "men of rough and almost fierce
manners" had built the city of Houston, de Saligny gushed, "I shall show
Your Excellency what kinds of men inhabit this country. . . . What a race!
What can the Mexicans do against men of this character!" In summarizing his Texas experience for his superiors, de Saligny made clear his recommended course of action:

> If there had remained in my mind any doubts on the situation of the
> New Republic, on its resources and the means by which it could main-
> tain its independence, this trip that I have just made would have dissi-
> pated them. Everywhere I saw people a little uncivilized, perhaps, and
> sometimes crude, but intelligent, industrious, and determined, who at
> the first signal, would all run to arms and against whom all the forces of
> Mexico would not be able, I believe, to hold out for so long.[2]

On the strength of Alphonse de Saligny's glowing report, the French
government recognized Texan independence in a treaty signed September 25, 1839. As he had hoped, de Saligny received his king's appointment as chargé d'affaires to the young republic. On January 19, 1840, he
wrote in an official dispatch from Houston that "the recognition of the
new Republic by the government of the King has caused universal joy in
this country." Two days later he left for Austin.

De Saligny and his companions spent five days slogging along muddy roads to reach the capital. One of his horses died of fatigue en route,
while another drowned crossing the Brazos River. Excited Austin residents, led by James Pinckney Henderson and Mayor Edwin Waller, met
the French procession five miles east of town. Waller delivered a welcoming speech, then escorted de Saligny and his train into the city. A
pleased de Saligny noted, "The welcome that I received in this country . . . leaves nothing to be desired. Everybody demonstrates a sympa-
thy and preference for France."[3]

De Saligny's first stay in Austin was a short one. The Fourth Congress
adjourned February 5, 1840, and the capital soon emptied itself of most
of its important men. On March 12 the French chargé d'affaires left the

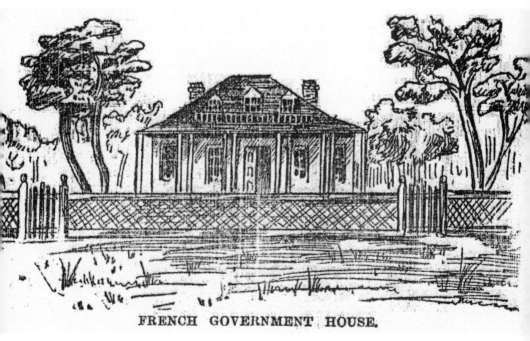

FRENCH GOVERNMENT HOUSE.

Alphonse de Saligny had left Austin by the time his intended French Legation
was completed in 1842. Julia Robertson, the artist responsible for this sketch,
lived in the house for many years. Courtesy of the *Galveston News*, February
1896, Center for American History, University of Texas at Austin.

city for Houston, where he stayed only briefly before continuing on to
New Orleans. The steady stream of immigrants into Texas greatly impressed de Saligny. He passed one three-mile convoy of five hundred
wagons carrying 1,800 people, including three hundred slaves. During
the journey he cultivated his relationship with Sam Houston, who was en
route to New Orleans with his new bride Margaret. In June he stopped in
Galveston to visit President Lamar, who intended to spend the summer
there recuperating from an unnamed illness. He felt duty-bound to accept
an invitation from Galveston citizens to a public dinner in his honor. Finally, in mid-July de Saligny headed back toward Austin, but not before
complaining of the city's lack of proper facilities: "I have not been able
yet to find other lodging than a sort of miserable wood cabin composed
of three rooms for which I pay the *small sum* of 500 francs a month! I
would like to try to set myself up in a manner a little more comfortable
and above all more suitable, and I fear I will not succeed except by having
a house built."[4]

Back in Austin de Saligny immediately fell ill due to "the terrible effects of the burning sun of this country." One of his black slaves died from the same illness, and two others in his employ almost followed suit. Whatever the cause of his affliction, de Saligny lay bedridden until October, but by early November felt well enough to formally address the House of Representatives at the Fifth Congress. By then he had also purchased twenty-one acres atop a hill east of Waller Creek, where workmen had already commenced construction of a residence worthy of the representative of France.[5]

While waiting for more elegant surroundings, Alphonse de Saligny transformed his simple frame house on West Pecan into an Austin social hub. Beginning in November 1840 he entertained at least twice a week, plying his guests with cigars, French wine, fine food, and an air of cultured refinement temporarily distracting the company from its primitive frontier reality. Cabinet officers, congressmen, senators, and "the most important people of the Country" frequented these gatherings, which allowed de Saligny the opportunity of cultivating relationships with those in a position to push policies favorable to France. So extravagant was de Saligny's hospitality that the editor of the *Texas Centinel* complained, "Truths were wasted on the desert air—for the thing was arranged over the fuming bottles and smoking dinners of M. Saligny." Nevertheless, Sam Houston accepted many of the Frenchman's invitations, and wrote home proudly to his wife Margaret of his newfound ability to abstain from alcohol. Mirabeau Lamar became a close friend as well. When the president left Austin to seek medical treatment in the United States in December 1840, he made a point of stopping at de Saligny's house on his way out of town.[6]

Of course de Saligny sought to accomplish more than making friends and enhancing France's reputation. His true motive appeared in the form of the Franco-Texienne bill, which would grant large swaths of frontier Texas land to a French corporation set up by de Saligny and others to bring French immigrants to the republic. In exchange for tax breaks, trade rights with Mexico, mineral rights, and duty-free importation of certain goods, the French would build and maintain a line of twenty protective forts between the Rio Grande and Red Rivers. De Saligny therefore aimed to exploit Texan dreams of frontier expansion to France's, and his own, advantage. The magnitude of this advantage seemed clear to one French newspaper editor, who wrote, "Texas will become, so to speak, an independent French colony, appertaining to herself alone and costing us nothing."[7]

De Saligny privately enlisted several key supporters before making

Sofa brought from France by M. Alphonse Dubois de Saligny

At a time when many Austin residents made do with furniture fashioned from rough lumber and rawhide, French Chargé d'Affaires Alphonse de Saligny arrived with elegant pieces such as the sofa pictured here. The letter press at left also belonged to de Saligny during his time in Austin. Reprinted by permission of the Austin History Center, Austin Public Library, PICA 04888.

his intentions public. One of them, Congressman James Mayfield of Nacogdoches, might have been a less willing convert had he known de Saligny's private opinion of him. The French chargé d'affaires enlisted Mayfield's assistance despite his unflattering description of the congressman as "of a less than mediocre capacity and of an extreme ignorance . . . [because of] his gross and brutal manners . . . his surly and trouble making disposition . . . his lack of honor and loyalty . . . and his indecency in violating the most sacred engagements."[8] Nevertheless, Mayfield agreed to introduce the Franco-Texienne bill in the House and did so January 12, 1841.

De Saligny did not rely solely on the allegedly incompetent Mayfield to sway House members. Appearing in the chamber himself, he produced "a most splendid map, about six feet square, representing in rainbow colors, those various tracts of country proposed to be granted . . . with twenty fortifications thereon, plotted with all the ingenuity [sic] of a politecnic graduate."[9] Subsequent debate provided more fodder for Mirabeau Lamar and Sam Houston's personal enmity. Lamar's dream of western empire did not include handing over valuable trade routes to a foreign power. Houston's practical nature saw perfect sense in allowing French immigrants to shoulder the cost of protecting the frontier.

While House members argued, de Saligny dipped repeatedly into his entertainment budget, staging elaborate dinner parties with free-flowing wine and other European luxuries. The *Texas Centinel* complained:

> To . . . Saligny's mind, he had not been wasting his French wines, Principe Cegars, West India Sweetmeats, and lusty promises, upon our unsophisticated Congressmen to no purpose . . . and how far these things may have influenced any freeborn Texian's vote, we leave for others to judge; one thing is a matter of history, and that we can speak; that the bill was rushed through congress in a gag-law manner . . . much to the discredit of those who sustained it.

De Saligny's efforts paid off on January 23 when the House voted 19–12 in favor of passing the Franco-Texienne bill. Senate passage seemed assured when President *pro tem* Anson Jones announced his support, giving proponents a 7-to-6 advantage. Acting President David Burnet, however, let his intention to veto the bill be known through like-minded Senator Francis Moore, who stood on the Senate floor to praise the "virtue, integrity, and firmness" of the stand-in chief executive. The dismayed advocates of the bill gave up the fight, failing even to call for a final Senate vote.[10]

David Burnet's threatened veto of his beloved Franco-Texienne bill only confirmed Alphonse de Saligny's impression of the man. Of Burnet, de Saligny had the previous December bemoaned "the inflexible and brittle character of the Vice-President, his pedantry and vanity, his smallness and pettiness of mind, his utter lack of candor—not to mention his secret antipathy for France concealed by pleasant and intimate relations that have so far existed between the Legation of the King and the government."[11] Burnet's victory, and de Saligny's humiliating defeat, must have strained to the breaking point the patience and tact of the French agent. How else to explain De Saligny's subsequent overreaction to a minor, unrelated annoyance that ultimately extinguished his dream and ended his Texas career?

Richard Bullock raised hogs. He evidently made little effort to confine them to his property as "no garden in town escaped their incursions."[12] Alphonse de Saligny, or at least his servants, grew vegetables. These vegetables proved a magnet for Bullock's hogs, as "every morning one of my [de Saligny's] servants spends two hours repairing and re-nailing the boards of my fence that these animals break in order to come eat." The hungry animals were not picky diners. Three of them one day broke into de Saligny's bedroom, where they ate his bed sheets and some of his official papers. On another occasion, several burst into the French stable to get at the horses' corn and in the process injured one of de Saligny's servants.[13]

Angered and humiliated by his failure in the Texas Congress, Alphonse de Saligny vented his frustrations on Richard Bullock's pigs. Claiming that he was only following the example of his Pecan Street neighbors, the chargé d'affaires ordered his servants to kill any animal straying onto his property. Several unlucky pigs soon succumbed. De Saligny later argued that he had not singled out Bullock's livestock for such treatment with the plausible explanation that the pigs "did not carry on their backs the name of their master."

Even before learning of the fate of his pigs, Richard Bullock despised Alphonse de Saligny. He accused his former tenant of an unpaid bill totaling $270.75. De Saligny acknowledged a debt but claimed that Bullock's amount represented price gouging. He had offered a smaller sum on several occasions, only to be repeatedly spurned. Thus, while de Saligny may not have intentionally targeted Richard Bullock's pigs for destruction, he most likely would have seen a certain sense of just retribution for perceived misdeeds. Against this swirling backdrop of ill will de Saligny hosted another of his famous dinners, at which the main dish was a whole roasted pig. Knowing of Richard Bullock's stable of hogs, one mischievous guest later complimented the innkeeper on the delicious treat he had enjoyed at the Frenchman's table.[14] The thought that he had supplied a free meal to the deadbeat who had wronged him enraged Richard Bullock. To de Saligny servant Eugene Pluyette's misfortune, it was he who crossed the innkeeper's path to catch the brunt of his fury.[15]

Early on the morning of February 19, 1841, Richard Bullock spied Eugene Pluyette walking along the street past his hotel. Bullock charged

BULLOCK'S HOTEL.

Richard and Mary Bullock's hotel on the northwest corner of Congress and Pecan was the social center of early Austin. The fort-like complex also served as a place of refuge during threatened Indian attack. Note the "Loafer's Logs" in front of the complex. Courtesy of the *Galveston News*, February 1896, Center for American History, University of Texas at Austin.

into the street to verbally confront the man, then "[threw] himself upon him with a stick." Pluyette dodged the initial attack and attempted to continue on his way. Bullock would have none of it. According to de Saligny "this miserable man, without the *sangfroid* and presence of mind of my domestic, undertook to follow him, and the affray was commenced again in a more serious manner." In a bit of hyperbole, de Saligny elevated the incident from a minor scuffle to "one of the most scandalous and outrageous violations of the Laws of Nations."

De Saligny now faced a dilemma. The logical person for him to direct his complaint to was new Secretary of State James Mayfield, recently appointed by David Burnet. But only three days earlier de Saligny had written, "Mr. Burnet could not possibly have made a worse choice from every point of view. Despite his pretentious bearing and affected manners, Mr. Mayfield is a very incapable and extremely ignorant man." De Saligny therefore had to entrust his case to the very man he deemed incapable of passing competent judgment. He nevertheless delivered an official letter presenting his side of the story to the secretary only hours after hearing it himself from Pluyette.

James Mayfield's February 20 reply to the French complaint assured de Saligny that his government would address the matter and punish any person who had broken the law. Mayfield may also have tipped off Bullock, who submitted a petition to David Burnet that same day. Bullock first complained of the debt owed him by de Saligny. He then hinted that the French agent had taken his revenge on Bullock by having fifteen to twenty-five of his hogs killed "most maliciously and wantonly . . . with pitchforks and pistols." Bullock swore to the animals' innocence. Claiming that de Saligny had illegally failed to properly maintain the fence around his property, he added that the hogs "only went under Saligny's horse trough, fed for the most part in an almost open lot, there being no garden or kitchen that they either molested or disturbed."

An impatient de Saligny answered Mayfield on February 21 with the demand that Bullock be immediately punished. He added that, fearing for his servants' lives, he had ordered them not to leave the house unless armed and to use those weapons if challenged by Bullock. Mayfield replied coolly that he had referred the matter to the appropriate law officer, who had arranged for a judge to hear testimony at the Senate chamber on February 23. An annoyed de Saligny countered that, although he *could* deign to allow his employee to supply a simple declaration, his duty and the dignity of France would *not* permit him to agree to the man appearing as a witness in a court of law. Mayfield promptly washed his hands of the matter by claiming, "the Government has no further control."

De Saligny would have been wise to drop the matter at this point or, at the very least, to write to his superiors for instructions. Personal pride intervened, however, after he came across a copy of Richard Bullock's petition to David Burnet. A self-righteous de Saligny could not resist writing to the secretary of state to counter Bullock, who, according to the Frenchman, "has not ceased to vomit forth against me the grossest insults, to spread about from door to door the most outrageous calumnies." Then, on March 25, as de Saligny attempted to visit the American chargé d'affaires Colonel George Flood in his quarters at Bullock's hotel, Richard Bullock stopped him at the door. According to de Saligny, "he [Bullock] shook his fist at me threateningly and acted as though he wished to hit me. . . . Then he took me first by the collar, then seized me by the arm violently." Bullock let his adversary go with the warning, "The first time that you come back here, I shall beat you up."

Austin residents watched with dismay the simmering feud between their respected innkeeper and the representative of the King of France. The *Austin City Gazette* claimed impartiality in an early report on the "spicy" dispute, then added, "The French Minister is altogether mistaken in our laws, and in the character of Texians if he supposes that either one or the other will permit a man to be punished without being first tried and found guilty of the alleged offence." De Saligny again appealed to James Mayfield for action, only to be rebuffed. Highly offended, the French minister suspended relations with the Texas government "until I have received further orders from the Government of the King." An equally miffed Mayfield replied that he would furnish traveling papers to the French delegation upon request and—since de Saligny had chosen to suspend his activities as France's representative—his immunities and privileges as that representative had been revoked. President Lamar, having recuperated from his illness and back at his post, instructed the Texan chargé d'affaires in Paris to request de Saligny's recall.[16] With as much dignity as he could muster under the circumstances, de Saligny packed his things and left Austin, never to return.

Alphonse de Saligny couldn't have invented a more satisfying postscript to his entanglement with Richard Bullock and James Mayfield than the one that played out in the city of Galveston in June 1842. Mayfield, no longer secretary of state but still a congressman, was staying at a Galveston hotel when Richard Bullock turned up to demand payment of a six hundred dollar bill for room and board in 1841. Mayfield expressed astonishment and indignation at the request in light of his previous support of Bullock in his dispute with de Saligny. During the ensuing argument the two men exchanged blows. Bullock attempted to impound Mayfield's horse and carriage as payment, but was stymied by the fact that Mayfield's current landlord had already done so. An irate Bullock could only storm off amid mumblings of lawsuits to come. Finality arrived a few days later when Bullock died of "brain fever" on the road back home.[17]

A shortage of cash forced the French chargé d'affaires to sell his unfinished Austin mansion in December 1840. The purchaser, Father Jean Marie Odin, agreed to allow de Saligny right of occupancy through April 1842 in exchange for his promise to complete construction. On August 19, 1841, the *Texas Centinel* announced that "his [de Saligny's] house in this city has been newly fitted up of late, and furnished with costly furniture, wines, provisions." Indeed, Anson Jones visited the showpiece and marveled at the beautiful gold, orange, and damask Parisian furniture. Alphonse de Saligny never saw the completed house. Instead, it brought him one final indignity from the Texas capital. Having invited fellow countryman Henry Castro to temporarily use the residence while formulating French immigration plans of his own, de Saligny could only complain from afar when:

He [Castro] began to act as if he actually were in his own house. He gave *in my home* and at my expense, dinners, and small suppers to which he invited not only the President, his cabinet, and the members of Congress favorable to France, but also two or three individuals who for nearly a year have been continuously conspicuous for the impudence of their invectives against France and her representative.[18]

Who were these offensive individuals enjoying Henry Castro's hospitality? De Saligny doesn't say, but imagine his tortured fury while pondering from afar toasts made with *his* wine around *his* table in *his* house by James Mayfield, David Burnet, or, *la horreur!*, Richard Bullock![19]

One of Alphonse de Saligny's first projects after his 1840 arrival in Austin as the French chargé d'affaires involved the construction of this house just east of town. John and Lydia Robertson acquired the property shortly after de Saligny fled Austin in 1841. Their twelve-year-old daughter Julia painted this portrait of her family's home in 1858. Courtesy of the French Legation Museum Committee, Daughters of the Republic of Texas, Inc.

| Chapter 15 |

FIASCO

After months of wallowing in a Mexican prison, Hugh McLeod craved something stronger than water to quench his thirst. He stepped off the *Rosa Alvina*'s gangplank onto a Galveston pier and scanned the waterfront for possibilities. A group of similarly parched Texans, all veterans of the failed Santa Fe Expedition led by McLeod, accompanied the happy man. Following their former commander into the closest bar, the party smiled gratefully as McLeod, on the strength of a doubloon he claimed in his pocket, ordered a round of drinks for his companions. Joyful toasts and satisfied smacks of pleasure embellished the men's drinking. But suddenly McLeod's smile gave way to a look of consternation. Nervously and repeatedly sticking his hands into various pockets, he cried, "What have I done with it—with the doubloon!" As the men fidgeted in embarrassing silence, the captain of the ship arrived and, overhearing McLeod's exclamation, reminded him that he had given the coin to his friend William Cooke before departing Mexico. The generous bartender forgave the debt and bade the celebrants a cheery farewell.[1]

Walking among the weed-choked streets of his frontier capital, President Mirabeau Lamar envisioned the imperial grandeur that was Austin's destiny. One day not far in the future the city would welcome endless trains of wagons bearing Mexican goods from Santa Fe. These wagons would rumble through paved streets to a bustling waterfront, where dockhands would transfer the precious cargo to waiting steamships. An easy trip down the Colorado River into the Gulf of Mexico would deliver these goods to Galveston warehouses, which in turn would supply the ever-increasing number of American merchant ships calling at the Texas seaport. The trade would transform an anemic Texas economy into a financial powerhouse and Lamar's humble village of Austin into the grandest metropolis in the west. Not only that, as Edward Hall wrote to Lamar, "If the Santa Fe Expedition succeeds it will immortalize you."[2]

Few Texans doubted this scenario. As the commissioners selecting Waterloo as the seat of government had remarked, "The commissioners confidently anticipate the time when a great thoroughfare [through Austin] shall be established from Santa Fe to our Sea ports." The *Austin City Gazette* echoed the sentiments of many with its prediction that "the time is not very far distant when the waters of the Colorado will be rendered navigable to this place, above here the rapids will ever present an insurmountable barrier to further progress. Austin, therefore, at some future day is destined to be a place of some importance as being located at the head of navigation." Early signs encouraged optimism. Shortly after Mirabeau Lamar's triumphant 1839 entry into Austin, a merchant named Thomas Grayson advertised a claim that appeared to vindicate the town's Colorado River location: "The subscriber being perfectly convinced of the safe navigation of the Colorado, has now on the river two keelboats, to wit: the David Crockett and Tanterbogus. Mr. Editor—I came up in the last boat, and found no obstacle greater than I found from Richmond to Groce's, on the Brazos river."[3] And, whereas Grayson's trip upriver originated at "the head of the raft," another citizen publicized his intention to bring goods all the way from the coast:

NAVIGATION OF THE COLORADO.—A respectable gentleman living in the vicinity of this city, has requested us to state, that if he can get the sum of five thousand dollars subscribed, to warrant him in the expense he may be put to in cleaning out the river, &c., he will agree to navigate the Colorado with a keel boat, from the city to Matagorda.[4]

Mirabeau Lamar therefore entertained no doubts about a vast trade one day bestowing riches upon his newly created capital. Furthermore, he saw no reason to leave the source of this wealth in the hands of a government still technically at war with his own. Indeed, while speaking against annexation in his inaugural address to Congress in 1838, Lamar laid bare his imperial ambition: "When I view her [Texas's] vast extent of territory, stretching from the Sabine to the Pacific and away to the South West as far as the obstinacy of the enemy may render it necessary for the sword to make the boundary." Lamar supporters encouraged the president's dream. Former campaign manager William Jefferson Jones urged Lamar to action by pointing out the huge tax revenue sure to flow from a trade estimated to be worth at least twenty million dollars. The necessity of an arduous and lengthy overland trek from Santa Fe to St. Louis severely limited profits; traders would leap at the chance of taking an easier route along the Colorado. Jones advised as a first step toward capturing this trade the sending of a "politico-military mission" to Santa Fe. He addressed, and quickly dismissed, every possible opposing argument.

Guessing correctly the future site of the seat of government on the Colorado, he claimed that an already existing wagon road from there to Santa Fe was only five hundred miles long. Trappers in the Santa Fe vicinity would quickly recognize the advantage of shipping their furs under Texan protection. Hostile Indians along the trail could easily be bribed into submission. And the people of Santa Fe "are prepared to unite with us, and this is the favorable moment to cement the friendship they have offered to reciprocate."[5]

High-minded talk of friendship undoubtedly helped Texans like Jones convince themselves of the purity of their motives. Such words also provided political cover to President Lamar. But the ugly nature of the greed and racial bigotry actually driving these men rose to the surface in this January 1842 newspaper account confirming the expedition's failure: "Why should a land abounding in many of nature's favors be occupied by men who appear incapable of either moral or political advancement? We will not be disappointed if this proves, too, but the prelude to the occupation of that country by the Anglo-Saxon race."[6]

American merchant William G. Dryden arrived in Austin in the spring of 1840 to add fuel to Mirabeau Lamar's inner Santa Fe fire. When Dryden confidently informed the president of the desire of Santa Fe citizens to join Texas, Lamar quickly drafted a letter of invitation for the merchant to carry back to that city. In his missive Lamar elaborated grandly on the republic's bright future, with its "commerce extending with a power and celerity seldom equaled in the history of nations." He promised to send commissioners to explain the advantages of a Texas union in more detail. An armed body would accompany the commissioners, but only "for the purpose of repelling any hostile Indians that may infest the passage." Lamar concluded with this promise: "Under these auspicious circumstances we tender to you a full participation in all our blessings. . . . We shall take great pleasure in hailing you as fellow citizens."[7]

Lamar next turned to the Fifth Congress to implement his plan. In November 1840 the House approved funding for a trade expedition with military escort to Santa Fe. However, when Lamar left Texas the following month to seek medical treatment in the United States, the effort foundered under acting president David Burnet. By the time of its adjournment February 5, 1841, Congress had still not given approval to actually sending the expedition it had already funded. A frustrated Lamar pressed on. As friend and apologist Edward Fontaine later wrote, "the President was compelled . . . to assume the responsibility of independent action, leaving the people to decide upon his conduct."[8] In other words, convinced of his rectitude, Lamar decided to send the expedition with or without congressional blessing.

Lamar faced little opposition from ordinary Texans. The *Austin City Gazette* spoke for many in offering its support: "Shall our government and citizens look tamely on and see other countries deprive us of a trade which by rights belongs to Texas? All who study the true interests of Texas cannot but answer, NO." And Lamar's friend James Webb reported from Houston, "The Santa Fe expedition seems to meet with general favor all through the country." Bolstered by public opinion, President Lamar directed Treasury secretary John Chalmers and quartermaster William Cazneau to organize the expedition. He sent George Howard to New Orleans to buy supplies and recruit volunteers. He selected long-time friend and supporter Hugh McLeod to lead the hundreds of merchants and soldiers across the prairie to Santa Fe. Lamar even hired a man named Mengle to engrave mottoes on the expedition's artillery pieces.[9]

Although recruits rallied to the cause, the excitement was not quite universal. James Durst wrote to Lamar from Angelina[10] that "it is impossible to raise a single man now in this country." While conceding local objection to McLeod as commander, Durst thought he perceived cowardice in those declining to enlist. He also blamed Lamar nemesis Sam Houston, whose friends "have tried to impress it on the minds of the people that it is a very dangerous expedition."[11]

Durst's experience proved exceptional. So many men soon gathered at Austin that expedition organizers set up three separate camps to hold them all. Two of the camps lay east of town near the junction of Walnut Creek and the Colorado River. The third was north of the city about five miles up Walnut Creek. One company of volunteers from Houston greatly impressed Austin residents upon arrival by marching directly from town to one of the eastern camps "without stopping at any of the groceries to refresh themselves."[12]

In early June illness severely curtailed Hugh McLeod's activity and caused the expedition's delay. Illness forced another prominent military leader, Edward Burleson, to drop out altogether. Writing from his sick bed in Mount Pleasant, Burleson informed Lamar of his incapacity by noting, "I am Scarcely able to Set up to wright [*sic*] a Line."[13] But, given the popular view that the journey to Santa Fe would be "nothing more than a pleasant hunting excursion,"[14] other men flocked to the camps around Austin to enlist in the "Santa Fe Pioneers." By mid-June McLeod had assembled a force of about 270 armed men to escort approximately fifty traders, teamsters, journalists, and servants.[15]

Before gathering at the final rendezvous point on Brushy Creek,

McLeod and his men thrilled Austin residents with a parade down Congress Avenue.[16] They marched under a banner made by the ladies of Austin and presented on their behalf by Mrs. Cazneau. Simple in design, the small flag consisted of a blue background with a central white star underneath the words "Santa Fe Pioneers." Near the river the men halted under a stand of oak trees to be reviewed by President Lamar and Secretary of War Branch T. Archer. Archer's ensuing speech "was loudly cheered by the assembled soldiery."[17]

McLeod's men may have anticipated a "pleasant hunting excursion," but their commander did not. Shortly after leading the triumphant parade down Congress Avenue, Hugh McLeod wrote to Mirabeau Lamar requesting payment of his salary to date in order to settle his debts before departing. McLeod justified his request by pointing out that "there is at least a possibility of my being killed in this Campaign."[18] A terrible accident in camp then gave credibility to Hugh McLeod's concern. On June 12, a Houston volunteer named Andrew Jackson Davis reached for his gun to demonstrate military maneuvers to his comrades. As he drew the piece toward his body the hammerlock caught in a hole in an adjacent salt bag and fired the gun, killing Davis instantly.

Accompanied by Mirabeau Lamar, the last detachment of soldiers left on Austin June 18 for the camp on Brushy Creek. When the company stopped for lunch, the president impressed the men by staking his horse and preparing his own meal. After supper Lamar imitated the volunteers by spreading his blanket on the ground to sleep in the open. The following morning Lamar addressed the cheering men, bade farewell, and rode back to Austin, perhaps contemplating the long weeks of waiting he must endure before learning the fate of his dream.[19]

With nothing to do but wait, Mirabeau Lamar left the capital for Galveston. On July 14 he received his first scrap of news about the expedition, and this was only a report from Samuel Roberts stating that there was no significant message yet from McLeod. Shortly thereafter, however, Thomas Blackwell sent encouraging news. Blackwell had heard from William Dryden, the American trader who had stoked the president's passion for expansion in 1840. In his March 10 letter Dryden claimed to have spoken with Santa Fe's governor, who had offered the extraordinary view that "he as well as the people were willing that Texas might establish her law and hold her Government over that country." Furthermore, the expedition should have no trouble from the Comanche, who had conveniently traveled north to negotiate a treaty with other tribes.[20] A month later the

Austin City Gazette quoted this passage from Dryden's wildly optimistic letter:

> We have been looking for some news from Texas, because every American and more than two-thirds of the Mexicans and all the Pueblo Indians are with us, heart and soul, and whenever they have heard of your sending troops, there has been a rejoicing; and, indeed, I have talked many times with the Governor, and he says he would be glad to see the day of your arrival in this country, as he feels well assured that no aid will be sent from below, as *they have no means,* and *he* himself *will offer no resistance.*[21]

Of the many valleys in Mirabeau Lamar's life the month of December 1841 must rank among the deepest. As his presidential term drew to a close, Lamar knew that the fate of his beloved city of Austin would largely define his legacy. Austin's early reputation leaned heavily on its two major public buildings. Now after only two years one of those edifices, Lamar's own presidential mansion, teetered on the brink of decrepitude. In his hurry to complete the government buildings in 1839, Edwin Waller had of necessity used unseasoned Bastrop pine in constructing them. As the green timbers dried the inevitable warping produced ugly cracks in wall plaster and large defects in the roof. A December 1, 1841, editorial in the *Austin City Gazette* pointed out the obvious fact that the house required major repairs to "render it tenantable, which it, in its present condition, is not."

To worsen Lamar's gloom, Sam Houston rode into Austin December 8. This would have meant little to Lamar except for the reason for Houston's arrival, the upcoming inauguration ceremony that would reinstall the despised man in the presidency. After a bitter campaign marked by personal invectives flying in both directions, Houston had trounced Lamar's man, Vice President David Burnet. That Lamar supporter Edward Burleson had gained the vice presidency offered small consolation. Sam Houston's antipathy to Austin was well known. Many westerners and Austin supporters feared he would attempt to relocate the seat of government once again, an act which would destroy one of Lamar's crowning achievements.

But of all the heavy burdens endured by Mirabeau Lamar that gloomy month, a newspaper article containing this particular passage must have triggered terrible chills down his spine: "There is a rumor in town that the

Santa Fe Expedition has been captured. It is said to have been derived from a Mexican journal which purports to give the particulars of the capture, and says that they were taken without the firing of a gun."[22] The writer of this report added, with typical Anglo hubris, that the rumor could not be true because no number of Mexicans could capture armed Texans and that at least three thousand would be required to finish off a force the size of McLeod's. Certainly, the writer concluded, the rumor had to have been concocted by the enemy "for some sinister effect in Mexico."

But it was true. The entire Texan force had indeed surrendered without firing a shot. Over three hundred men now languished in Mexican jails as a prelude to being force-marched to Mexico City. Several others were dead, having perished on the journey or been shot by the Mexicans after capture. Confirmation came in the form of a December 16 letter from U.S. envoy Powhatan Ellis to American Secretary of State Daniel Webster. A more fanciful and, to Texans, more believable report came from Galveston port collector Alden Jackson, who claimed to have received his information from a schooner arriving from Yucatan. According to Jackson, Hugh McLeod and his men fought a fierce battle against 1,600 Mexicans about sixty miles from Santa Fe. The Texans surrendered only after running out of ammunition, but not before killing 320 of the enemy while losing just two of their own.[23] But even if Mirabeau Lamar found comfort in such fantasy he had to admit that his grand imperial scheme had collapsed.

Why? What had happened? It had seemed so easy to reach out and pluck Santa Fe from Mexico's grasp. Wasn't the road to the prize relatively short and easy? Weren't the traders and trappers of the southern Rockies happily awaiting just such a move from the Texans? Didn't the people of Santa Fe dream of joining the Republic of Texas? And hadn't the governor himself assured the American Dryden that his forces would offer no resistance?

Unfortunately for Hugh McLeod and his comrades, every assumption about the journey to Santa Fe had been completely wrong. There was no well-marked trail from Austin to Santa Fe; the expedition's route was significantly prolonged when the Texans repeatedly got lost. The distance between the two cities is actually about seven hundred miles, rather than five hundred as claimed by Dryden. Little water and game existed along significant stretches in what is now the Texas panhandle. A number of men vanished after wandering away from the main body in search of food. The Texans may have encountered relatively few Comanche, but there were plenty of Kiowa who, on one day alone skewered

George Hull with lances, killed and scalped James Dunn, Sam Flenner, and Francis Woodson, and crushed William Mabee's skull before carving his heart from his chest.[24] Once the Texans reached Santa Fe they found no throngs of happy citizens anxious to throw off Mexican rule. Instead, there was only Governor Manuel Armijo, loyal to his government and in no mood to listen to protestations of peaceful intent from armed soldiers.

Austin residents anticipating a joyful Texas Independence Day March 2, 1842 tasted a bit of vinegar in their celebratory punch. The day's *Austin City Gazette* carried an extract from a letter dated February 16 in which the writer blamed Hugh McLeod's surrender on the treachery of Texan artillery commander William P. Lewis. The Spanish-speaking Lewis had evidently made a deal with the Mexicans to help arrange a Texan surrender in exchange for his own freedom. Now, according to the letter, William Cooke, the man who had fallen for Lewis's guile, and his comrades "are working on the streets of Mexico, chained together like felons."[25]

Newly installed president Sam Houston inherited Mirabeau Lamar's Santa Fe mess. With assistance from the United States he obtained the release of all but one prisoner by June 13, 1842. The solitary exception was José Antonio Navarro. Born in San Antonio and a signer of the Texas Declaration of Independence, Navarro served as one of Lamar's commissioners to Santa Fe. But whereas Santa Anna viewed the Anglo-Texan members of the expedition as hostile invaders, he thought Navarro a traitor to Mexico. Hugh McLeod and the other surviving Texans had been free for over a year by the time Navarro escaped from a Vera Cruz prison in December 1843.[26] Two years earlier these men had set off on their doomed adventure from a thriving capital city. Now those that returned to Austin found a town hovering near extinction.

| Chapter 16 |

RETURN OF THE RAVEN

I consider Sam Houston's Elevation would be a National Calamity.
Edward Hall, letter to Mirabeau Lamar, August 8, 1841

Is Burnet a western man when he is opposed to western measures? . . .
Fellow citizens, believe him not, trust him not.
Austin City Gazette, August 25, 1841

Mirabeau Lamar had reason to feel satisfied with his presidency as it wound to a close in the fall of 1841. His eviction of the Cherokee from Texas represented a major step toward his goal of cleansing the nation of its indigenous people. Only two years from its founding an already thriving Austin seemed about to become a major commercial and political center. And the recently departed Santa Fe Expedition would soon deliver vast new territory to the Republic of Texas and untold wealth to its treasury. Now that he had planted the seeds of national greatness all that Lamar needed was a successor to nurture his handiwork.

Only one obstacle loomed on the immediate horizon, but it was a big one. Sam Houston was running for president. Houston, who in Lamar's view had proved traitor to his race by attempting to grant the Cherokee permanent title to land which rightfully belonged to Anglo-Texans. Houston, who had bitterly opposed moving the seat of government to the west and had branded the Santa Fe mission folly.[1] Houston, the immoral, drunken lout and the one man Lamar could count on to destroy everything he had achieved so far as president.

Lamar's hopes of averting this catastrophe rode with Vice President David Burnet. Like Lamar, Burnet hated Sam Houston and, like Lamar, his hatred transcended politics. The stern and devoutly religious vice president had little tolerance for Houston's gregarious socializing, drinking history, and aborted marriages. Their like-mindedness regarding Houston led Lamar and Burnet years later to coauthor a scathing indictment of their enemy's career. This was their later portrait of the man now threatening Mirabeau Lamar's accomplishments:

> General Houston is a demagogue. His mind, heart, manners; all conspire to fit him for distinction in that odious character. Superficial in knowledge; flippant and witty in small talk; studied and sometimes agreeable, though too theatrical in manners, with a physique somewhat imposing; polite in his social intercourse and seemingly warm in his professions of regard to all; he is an isolated, heartless egotist; incapable of one abiding feeling of attachment to any; artful and intriguing; sometimes apparently candid, but never sincere; a *Proteus* in form and a *chameleon* in color.[2]

Houston possessed an equally low opinion of Burnet. In a letter to wife Margaret written in January 1841 he referred to Burnet's "imbecility" and "selfishness" before adding, "The poor creature will be execrated in the mouth of Babes."[3]

Sam Houston's weakness lay in the west. His pro-Cherokee views found no favor among voters who made no distinction between friendly and hostile Indians. His retreat to San Jacinto in 1836, though ultimately successful, still rankled less cautionary Texans, who by nature now congregated on the frontier. And his earlier opposition to placing the seat of government at Austin spawned rumors that, as president, Houston would move it back east. Anyone privy to his private thoughts would have had good reason to believe this rumor. Writing home to his wife Houston ridiculed the fact that his friend Colonel Flood and family had no better quarters in Austin than a room fourteen feet square: "Tis a great city! Just such as savages wou'd not live in! As a city its days are number'd and its glory will pass away!"[4]

Just as he had done in 1836, Sam Houston in 1841 pretended disinterest in becoming president. He reassured Margaret that he would not accept a nomination without her consent. Writing eloquently of their recent joyful weeks together, the lifelong politician insisted that he desired only her company, which held for more allure than any position of power on earth. But when he had confided the possibility of not running to his friend Mrs. Flood, she had reacted with astonishment, exclaiming that the people would elect him anyway. Thus, "If I were to declare that I wou'd not serve, if elected, I assure you that it wou'd be deemed a national calamity."[5]

Margaret must have eventually assented, for when a group of citizens gathered in San Augustine in April 1841 and nominated him for president, Sam Houston accepted. Almost immediately, the candidate struggled to minimize political damage from his earlier stance against moving the government to Austin. In May he wrote a letter to William Wallach, editor of the *Colorado Gazette and Advertiser*, outlining his position with respect to the capital. Admitting his opposition to the removal from Houston, he stressed that this stemmed from concerns about the cost of *any* removal as well as the previous law placing the government in Houston until 1841. He also claimed to have acted in obedience to the wishes of his constituents which, after all, was his duty as their congressman. Finally, with an eye toward the related issue of frontier protection, he stated that "the seat of government being *now* at Austin, would present many considerations connected with any change in its removal in future. I have no prejudice against Austin; I have no interest in its removal to any other place. . . . I deem the efficient protection of the frontier against the Indians, as a desideratum in the policy of Texas. And should I be elected, it shall be protected!!"[6]

Houston's denials of intent to move the seat of government failed to assuage his enemies, who continued leveling the charge right up to the election in September. The *Texas Sentinel* published what it considered damning evidence of Houston's duplicity in the form of a letter from "a gentleman of Houston." The anonymous writer claimed to have overheard a promise by Houston to remove the archives from Austin whether or not the seat of government remained there. Furthermore, the candidate had supposedly exclaimed that he "would not risk his scalp, up in that d——d hole called Austin!" Another rumor had Houston stating that if he were elected president, "Austin should be desolate, and the grass should grow in the streets." This one stung enough that Houston submitted a letter of denial to the *Austin City Gazette*. But the very next day the *Texas Centinel* ran a variation of the same quote: "Gen. Houston said last summer, 'In less than three years, if *I* am elected, the streets of Austin shall again become the feeding place for the buffalo, and the hunting ground of the red man.'" Meanwhile, hoping to take advantage of the controversy, David Burnet publicly announced his support for keeping the government at Austin.[7]

Both candidates were guilty, but David Burnet in particular attempted to gain votes through personal assault. Using the pseudonym "Publius," he authored a number of vicious letters attacking Houston's character.[8] Houston responded with five separate letters signed "Truth." In one of them, he hurled Burnet's charge of drunkenness back at the accuser by citing several examples of Burnet's own drunken behavior. Scornfully referring to his opponent as "Davy" throughout, Houston concluded his last letter with this blast: "You prate about the faults of other men, *while the blot of foul unmitigated treason rests upon you.* You political brawler and canting hypocrite, whom the waters of Jordan could never cleanse from your political and moral leprosy."[9]

Others fretted about the outcome of the upcoming election, but Sam Houston did not. Confident of victory, he even ordered a special inauguration outfit through the French Chargé d'Affaires Alphonse Dubois de Saligny. To be made of green velvet embroidered in gold, the suit would be complemented by an embroidered velvet cape and plumed hat. Saligny knew of Houston's penchant for flamboyant dress but was startled nonetheless. He wrote, "It is in this strange outfit that the future Head of the Republic of Texas intends to take his seat in the Presidential armchair."[10]

Judging from the results of the September 6 election, David Burnet never had a chance of winning. With 7,508 votes, Sam Houston trounced his opponent by a 3-to-1 margin. Interestingly, despite the campaign rhetoric about Austin, Houston carried the district with 286 votes to Burnet's 164. More reflective of western sentiment were the counts in Bastrop and Gonzales, each of which went heavily for Burnet.[11] The popular Edward Burleson easily outdistanced Memucan Hunt for the vice presidency.

Sam Houston rode out of his namesake city in late November 1841 ready to step back into the spotlight. By December 2 he had reached Washington, where he paused to write a letter to Margaret. He once again bemoaned their separation, because "the sacrifice [is] greater than the honor is agreeable." Nevertheless, he wrote that he "must not disappoint the 'big doins' which are to take place on the occasion." Houston promised to behave. He assured his wife that "I will do *no act whatever* if *truly* reported to you, that cou'd cause . . . one painful emotion in your heart." And, to ease Margaret's greatest specific worry, he added, "I need not tell you that my arch enemy never dares to approach me! I mean 'Grog' in any shape or character."[12]

Six days later Sam Houston arrived at Austin. The usual gathering of dignitaries, onlookers, and friends assembled to meet his party two miles east of the city. After several welcoming speeches the Travis Guards escorted the President-elect back into town, where he was greeted by an artillery salute before stopping at his quarters at the Eberly House. Houston reported excitedly back to his wife, "On yesterday I rec'd the most elegant and hearty greeting that I have ever done. Speeches and a party at night!"[13]

Houston did not wear his fancy velvet suit at the inauguration. He had already given up drinking and dancing for his wife and perhaps ad-

David Burnet was the first acting president of the Republic of Texas and vice president under Mirabeau Lamar. In 1841 Burnet failed badly against bitter rival Sam Houston in a presidential contest marked by political and personal invective from both sides. Courtesy of Prints & Photographs Collection, Burnet, David Gouverneur, CN00450, the Dolph Briscoe Center for American History, University of Texas at Austin.

opted more restrained dress in deference to her wishes as well.[14] The president received his oath of office December 13 in a late morning ceremony at the rear of the capitol. A telegraph signal notified soldiers at the arsenal of the precise moment of Houston's swearing the oath.[15] The instantaneous artillery salute booming in the distance thrilled and baffled the crowd. Houston then delivered a lengthy speech. Outgoing president Mirabeau Lamar, who by now knew better than to compete with the oratorical master, had previously notified organizers that he would not speak. Edward Burleson also declined to say anything and in a manner which amused Houston greatly. After his oath the vice president placed his hand over his heart, informed the crowd that he would defer making a speech until taking his place in the Senate, bowed stiffly, and sat down. In relating this to Margaret, Houston told her to "take one laugh at it, but only one, and then—'Mum is the word.'"[16]

Sam Houston believed he was inheriting a disastrous state of affairs from his predecessor. A few days before the inauguration he confided to Margaret, "Our country is on the brink of disolution [sic], and if I can save it, it will be a greater work than I have before achieved." He knew whom to blame. "Poor Lamar is in a pack of troubles and pity can only save him from impeachment, but is unable to redeem him from contempt & derision!" But, if he had to wade into the political mess left by Lamar, he refused to live in the physical one bequeathed to him. "I will not go to the White House to live. . . . I hate the pollution!"[17] After taking an invoice of the mansion's contents, Houston notified Congress:

> I respectfully submit to the attention and consideration of the honorable Congress, the enclosed statements in relation to the furniture purchased by the government for the use of the Executive. . . . The present Executive has no disposition to appropriate the same to his use, on account of its ruinous Condition. . . . There are no locks on the Presidents House, and what remains there is exposed to pillage, which has already commenced as he has been informed: The building itself is in a ruinous and dilapidated condition, and not in a situation to be tenanted with any degree of comfort to the occupant.[18]

Houston's concerns about pillaging were well founded, judging from this newspaper notice:

GOVERNMENT PROPERTY TAKEN

The person who has taken away without leave, from the late President's dwelling, one mattress, one pillow, one bolster, and two linen sheets marked "Lamar," will return the same without delay, otherwise a prosecution will be instituted—the *present* Executive not being disposed to encourage such practices.[19]

One can also imagine, given the personal nature of the missing items, that Sam Houston was merely having a bit of fun at his predecessor's expense.

Chapter 17

CHAOS

There was no such thing as settling permanently in those days. In the judgment of the people everything was on the wing or ready to be, at the shortest notice. It was expected almost continuously to fort or flee the country.

Reverend Josiah Whipple, in diary entry for July 10, 1842

Austin residents in the early 1840s did not relish the prospect of braving city streets at night. Methodist preacher Josiah Whipple, while claiming divine protection, nevertheless wrote, "And although man may be immortal until his work is done, I have concluded not to travel after night in the Indian range after this." Swiss-born John Wahrenberger, however, was out of meal. The trip to the mill proved safe and, after achieving his objective, Wahrenberger slung his meal sack over his back, thanked the miller, and began the walk home. Suddenly, out of the darkness, the unmistakable whirr of an arrow zipped past the startled man. Wahrenberger sprinted for his life. He reached the home of Louis Cooke just ahead of the pursuing Indians, where the occupant stepped out of the house, fired his pistol, and frightened the attackers away. As an exhausted Wahrenberger slumped to the ground he noticed an arrow stuck in one arm. Relief replaced distress, however, when he looked at his meal sack, which had numerous arrows stuck therein. "Oh! Mine Got!" exclaimed Wahrenberger, "What a Texas dis is! I tink I go back to Sweetzerland!" The noise attracted all within earshot, many of whom came running with loaded weapons. Searching frantically for Indians to shoot, "the men ran through town like a gang of wild mustangs. . . . Reason had completely forsaken them." One resident, Colonel Clendennin, suffered from the chaos. When he failed to respond quickly enough to a hail from Captain Nicholson, the captain shot him. Fortunately for the victim, the wound was slight.[1]

Margaret Houston worried constantly about her husband living in a city that hosted Indian battles in its streets. In his many letters to her, Sam promised his wife that he was watching out for himself. Nevertheless, just days after his inauguration he wrote her of sending out a search party for a mail carrier gone missing on the road from Bexar. The body was found scalped and partially eaten by wolves just twelve miles from town.[2] But, Sam assured his wife, such dangers were temporary, because "you may confide in the trust that the seat of Government cannot and will not remain at this point."

John Welsh of Webber's Prairie could not have liked the results of the 1841 presidential election. On January 7, 1842, he sat down to write a letter to his new president, whom he initially addressed as "Old Sam," but later on in the letter as "you Dam old drunk Cherokee" and "you dam blackgard Indian drunk." Welsh thought Sam Houston a cowardly liar because "we did heare that you was goin to move the seat of government. . . . You swore you would do it, and then when you come to Austin and found out the boys would not let you do it you sed you never was goin to move it . . . the truth is that you are afeard." Welsh confidently predicted that local residents would forcibly prevent a removal and dared Houston to attempt one: "Now old fellow if you want to try Ned Burlesons spunk jist try to move these papers, and old Ned will serve you just as he did your Cherokee brother when he took the Hat what you give to your Daddy Bowles." Finally, to let Houston know that he was a force to be reckoned with, Welsh informed the president, "You shall hear more from me when I am ready."[3]

If John Welsh read the January 18, 1842, copy of the *Daily Bulletin*, he most likely conceived of a few more colorful epithets for Sam Houston. The paper informed its readers that two bills regarding the seat of government had just been introduced in Congress. One allowed the president to move the national archives and related public property to any place he deemed proper. The other authorized the House and Senate by joint decision to relocate the government seat.[4] Houston, of course, still remained above the fray since he could claim that he had nothing to do with the proposals. But once he realized the bills would not pass before the legislature adjourned on February 5, he confirmed John Welsh's suspicions with a presidential message to Congress:

> Previous to your adjournment, I deem it my imperious duty to present to your consideration, the exposed condition of the national archives. . . . I have every reason to believe that the available remaining force at Austin will not be such as to guaranty the undoubted safety of the archives and other public property. . . . Therefore, to the representa-

tives of the people, I submit the question as to the measures proper to be adopted for the protection and security of an object so important to the whole nation.[5]

After sending this letter, Sam Houston saddled up his mule Bruin and rode to Houston, never again as president of the republic to see the city of Austin.

Houston's message to Congress and subsequent hasty departure from Austin triggered a new round of rumors regarding his intentions. On February 23 the *Austin City Gazette* scolded its readers by suggesting that, given Houston's emphatic denials about removal, interested persons "should keep quiet until some demonstration has been made." Furthermore, because Houston was not a man easily alarmed, he would surely make such a move only if the archives were truly threatened.[6]

Reverend Josiah Whipple despaired for the people of Austin. Attendance at his sermons was sparse and those that did come often mocked him. One local judge complained of Whipple's "unhappy effort at preaching." An elderly lady started a lively step during another sermon, declaring that if the preacher hadn't come at least there could be a dance. Whipple prayed for God to "send salvation to this wicked town" because "I feel too weak to preach to such sinners." A beautiful March day then arrived to brighten Whipple's spirits and inspire him to conduct one of his best services so far in Texas. But while taking a little refreshment awaiting the afternoon service, Whipple heard a cannon booming in the distance. An express rider had arrived; the Mexicans had captured San Antonio! Citizens dashed aside any thought of further worship that day. Reverend John Haynie made a quick "war speech," after which women gathered their children and men raced for their arms. A disappointed Whipple recalled, "two hours before there was a fair prospect of conversions, and quite a number thought of joining the church."[7] But that would have to wait.

Mexican General Ráfael Vásquez and several hundred armed men had disrupted Reverend Whipple's Sunday service by parading into San Antonio March 5, 1842, raising the Mexican flag, and declaring the supremacy of Mexican law. The next day Secretary of War George Hockley wrote from Austin to Sam Houston in Galveston to inform the president that "if not checked, the next move of the enemy . . . will be against this place, to destroy the archives." But he assured Houston that "I will defend the archives to the *Knife*." Hockley sent another letter to Houston March

7 to report that he had buried the archives under various government offices to keep them safe. And he issued this proclamation:

> Martial law becomes necessary for the preservation of the Archives of the Government and for the safety of the Citizens of Austin and their property.
> It is hereby declared and will be rigidly enforced. All good citizens will obey it. Retailers of Spirituous liquors will forthwith close their doors and cease vending them. [. . .]
> No person will leave without receiving permission [. . .]
>
> By Order of the President
> Geo. W. Hockley
> Secy of War and Navy[8]

Austin residents banded together to fight the Mexicans. They elected William Cazneau civil commander and placed Thomas William Ward in charge of ordnance. Ward promptly ordered George Dolson, engaged in organizing a company of volunteers, to assign a detail to guard the magazine at the capitol. Dolson was to allow no one within twenty steps of the gunpowder, and to take care that "no fire from sigars [*sic*] or of any other character shall be permitted within the Stockade." Residents sent to Bastrop for Colonel Henry Jones, commander of the Fourth Regiment of Travis and Bastrop Counties. Several men placed the twelve-pound brass cannon "El Dragon" at the capitol to guard the city's western approach. Others rolled the Twin Sisters to the top of President's Hill and aimed them south at the river. The Travis Guards under Joseph Daniels mustered for service. After the arrival of Jones, he and Edward Burleson inspected all available troops, finding four hundred ready for service. They took two hundred with them toward San Antonio, leaving Daniels and Dolson in Austin with the remainder.[9]

Civilians reacted with alacrity. Families loaded all they could on wagons and sped out of town. Desperate shopkeepers pressed every available conveyance into service and followed the train of evacuees heading east. Men of fighting age remained. Some enjoyed the camp-like atmosphere resulting from the evacuation of their wives and children. One recalled, "Although it was painful to see the women obliged to part & leave us in tears & in haste . . . yet *some of us* did glory in it." At the same time, this writer bemoaned Hockley's ban on liquor, especially since "the Travis Guards were on their *taps* as usual."[10]

Suddenly, as quickly as it had appeared, the threat vanished. Before any Austin troops reached San Antonio, General Vásquez evacuated the city and retreated back across the Rio Grande. Josiah Whipple noted that, while noncombatants evacuating Austin were relieved, the troops under Burleson and Henry Jones expressed disappointment because "they desired to show them once more with what dexterity back-woodsmen can handle their rifles and Bowie knives." The Mexican occupation appears to have been nothing more than a nuisance raid in retaliation for the Santa Fe Expedition and a statement by Santa Anna that he had not yet given up his claim to Texas. Sam Houston recognized this, but seized the opportunity he had been waiting for to remove the government from Austin. On March 10 he ordered George Hockley to transport the archives to Washington. Hockley put Thomas Ward in charge of the deed and notified Henry Jones to assist. Jones evidently voiced reluctance because Hockley told Houston, "He [Jones] was informed of the order and required to obey it. This caused a discussion between himself, Col. Ward, and me. We parted for the night, and I was under the impression that he was favorably disposed to the measure."[11]

Houston's order stirred up a hornet's nest. Samuel Whiting chaired a committee of angry Austin residents asking Hockley to rescind the order and, when Hockley refused, organized under Henry Jones and the Fourth Regiment to resist.[12] Jones ordered his officers to occupy the quartermaster's department and arsenal, where they seized control of government ammunition and artillery. Supporters pulled one of the artillery pieces to a shed in the second lot on the east side of Congress Avenue above Pecan Street with the understanding that it should be fired in the event of an attempt on the archives.[13] Jones also ordered inspection of all wagons leaving Austin to guard against anyone bringing the archives out surreptitiously. Upon receiving word of these activities, President Houston sent a note to the rebellious Jones threatening him with charges of treason and insurrection. Jones responded by notifying Thomas Ward of his readiness to remove the archives "whenever the republic of Texas is invaded by a foreign foe."[14] Meanwhile, seeing that further effort at removal would lead to determined resistance, George Hockley quietly suspended plans to carry out the presidential order.[15] In obedience to the president, cabinet officers and most clerks left town. The exception was Thomas Ward, in charge of the Land Office, which contained the most important documents. But although the archives stayed put, State Department chief clerk Joseph Waples did manage to sneak the official seal past inspectors on April 5.[16]

Bastrop citizens were no less aroused than their Austin counterparts. They also formed a committee of protest, which met under the leadership of L. C. Cunningham, G. D. Hancock, and G. W. Glascock, and composed this dramatic message for Sam Houston:

> Your committee are fully advised that the present is not a time of war, as contemplated by the constitution, and, therefore, your committee are compelled to come to the conclusion that if the order should be considered an official act of the President, it is a direct violation of the constitution, and subversion of, the liberties of the people; and in that view, your committee can look on it in no other light than as a deliberate act of usurpation, misrule, and abuse of power.

Furthermore, as had Austin residents, Bastrop denizens pledged to protect the archives against Indian or Mexican attack. They promised to assist in removal if the archives were truly threatened or if the people of Texas declared this as their wish. Otherwise, they would fight to preserve the status quo.[17]

With the archives in Austin paralysis gripped the Texas government. Most Texans favored pursuing the retreating Vásquez across the Rio Grande. Vice President Edward Burleson, defending his support of invading Mexico, publicly proclaimed, "For one, I am free to admit that seven years' patient endurance of insult and injury—of outrage and oppression, from our Mexican enemy, makes me exceedingly anxious to end this war." But President Houston did not share Burleson's war fever, concerning himself instead with safety of the archives in Austin. On March 18 Attorney General George Terrell informed President Houston that "all the Archives [are] packed up—and business of every kind in all the offices [is] suspended." A week later Terrell wrote from Austin that "civil war [is] just ready to break out at the seat of Gov't. The state of things here are lamentable indeed. . . . In one week more there will not be twenty men left in this place." Houston attempted to reestablish control. He called on all government officers to gather in Houston, adding, "Should any refuse to come, their offices will be considered vacant and accordingly filled." He gave Hockley permission to lie low on the archives removal by maintaining, "I will not remit my purpose, but I wish no violence or bloodshed." Houston had no intention of allowing anyone but himself to assess the situation. He emphatically claimed, "I am the sole judge of the emergency." Furthermore, "It is beyond endurance to suppose that the very liberties of Texas are to be sacrificed to the interests or wishes of less than one tenth of the nation." And he once again disparaged Austin as a government seat: "Austin is no defence to the frontier, as the three last years have demonstrated, in the number of persons killed there and horses stolen."[18]

Houston's anger failed to frighten the people of Austin. When Hockley refused to rescind his order to remove the archives they went over his head with a direct appeal to the president. Houston rejected their request in a March 24 letter explaining his position and offering the hope that "the reasons now assigned . . . will sustain him in the course which circumstances have compelled him to adopt." In response, Samuel Whiting, editor of the *Austin City Gazette* and an earlier Houston supporter, wrote defiantly, "Old Sam Houston and David G. Burnet have played the very devil here. . . . We are holding on to the Archives like death to dead negro and are determined they shall not be taken from here 'till ordered by a higher power than Sam Houston." On April 11 Whiting chaired a meeting at which citizens aired their grievances against the president:

> Whereas, in the history of warfare, it is a novelty that the first military order given, should be the abandonment of the Capitol of the nation, and to retreat from an embecile [*sic*] and flying foe, and the consequent breaking up of the settlements of the frontier; therefore
> Be it resolved, That the order of the Executive for the removal of the archives of the Government was wholly uncalled for.[19]

But although Houston may have been unable so far to pry the *records* of government away from Austin, he did manage to transfer government *function* elsewhere. Washington Miller noted as early as April 13, "The President and Col. Hockley and Judge Terrell are now here. . . . The offices of course have not been opened *in executive*, but upon a *small* scale—for instance a pigeon hole to each department!" Then, under presidential directive, the Sixth Congress convened a special session in Houston on June 27 to formulate a response to the Vásquez invasion. The resulting bill authorized the president to draft up to one-third of the eligible population to carry an offensive war into Mexico. Sam Houston's veto enraged westerners and easterners alike.[20]

On August 17, 1842, those few citizens remaining in Austin found nothing but bad news in the *Austin City Gazette*, including the obituaries of two of its most popular residents. Friends had warned John Black and George Dolson against a trip to Barton Springs, but, feeling safe in the possession of fast horses, the pair went anyway. Two hours later both horses ran back into town, saddles empty save for an arrow stuck in one. Searchers found the stripped and scalped bodies along a narrow path on the opposite riverbank.[21] The newspaper that day also carried a transcript of Sam Houston's letter to Congress justifying his veto of the Mexican war bill. And finally, editor Samuel Whiting notified his readers that the August 17 issue would be the City Gazette's last. Noting that he still possessed a large stock of paper and printing material, Whiting explained that "it is rather dead weight for us to carry at this time, but as we have expended some thousands in puffing Sam Houston into office under false promises, and the only reward we have as yet received from him has been his curses, we will expend what spare means we have to give the public his character in its true light." Whiting then recapped events following the recent Mexican occupation of San Antonio. He charged that Sam Houston had acted unconstitutionally in ordering the government and archives out of Austin. Because Vásquez had quickly retreated, his invasion had constituted no emergency, but had merely served as an excuse for Houston to carry out something he had intended all along. Whiting cried betrayal:

> Gen. Houston has disappointed the hopes of all those who have placed their trust in him; he has deceived and betrayed the interests of his best friends—capricious, insincere, and unjust, as he is, we can place no further confidence in him. We know, too, that he entertains against the people of this part of the country the most malignant, the most envenomed animosity, whatever power he may have he will wield it to do us injury. We appeal to the sense of right and justice on the part of the people of the Republic against this rancorous hostility of the President; and we depend upon the people at large to sustain us, and to have justice done.[22]

Another Mexican incursion gave President Houston even greater excuse to move forward with his push to remove the seat of government from Austin. At dawn on September 11, 1842, startled San Antonio residents wakened to the thundering roar of a single cannon shot. Texans hiding near the town square peered through a dense fog to see a party of armed soldiers dash up the street. These skirmishers turned right at the square, but behind them rode General Adrian Woll leading a much larger column. Woll continued through the square toward the concealed Texans, who fired their weapons, killing a drummer and wounding several horses. When Woll halted to deploy his forces the Texans cheered loudly. But as the fog lifted they saw that they were trapped. One raised a white flag. The Mexicans had returned![23]

This time the Mexicans seemed more determined to stay. They still occupied San Antonio a week later when two hundred volunteers led by Captain Matthew Caldwell united with Jack Hays and his fourteen-man ranger company to oppose Woll's 1,500 men. The Texans took cover along Salado Creek outside of town, lured the Mexican force into the open, and inflicted a decisive defeat. Woll took the hint and struck out for the Rio Grande. Swollen rivers and atypical indecisiveness among their leaders slowed the Texan pursuers enough that the Mexicans successfully reached Coahuila.[24]

As fall approached Texans wondered where the Seventh Congress would convene. Practically no one wanted to return the seat of government to Houston. Many legislators remembered with disdain their earlier discomfort in that city. And Congressman Richardson Scurry pointed out to the president how poorly war-hungry Houston citizens had been treating him: "For my own part I am extremely averse to seeing the business of the Nation transacted at a place [Houston] where citizens attempt to control the officers of the government by clamour [sic] and mobs." Spurned in 1839, Washington town leaders recognized their opportunity. They offered not only to pay the expenses of relocating the government, but to provide meeting halls for Congress free of charge. Sam Houston took the bait. He called on Congress to convene at Washington November 14, 1842, but by the appointed date reluctant legislators had not formed a quorum. Houston didn't press the issue, but met with more success after releasing another call to Congress to begin its regular session on December 5.[25]

Whereas Sam Houston interpreted Adrian Woll's attack on San Antonio as vindication of his attempt to move government out of Austin, that city's residents saw the Texan victory at Salado Creek as proof that the archives were safe with them. Thus, while Houston was telling Thomas Ward, "You will fully understand having the archives removed to some place of greater safety than Austin," people in Austin remained intransigent. With Woll in San Antonio, Henry Jones and his men notified Thomas Ward of their willingness to assist the removal, but only "to a place which *they* deem safe." After Woll's defeat, however, Austin citizens once again resumed their opposition to Houston's order. A frustrated Houston told Congress that

> acts of the most seditious and unauthorized character have been perpetrated by persons styling themselves the "*Archive Committee,*" positively refusing obedience to the orders of the Executive. . . . This flagrant vi-

olation of all civil rule inculcates the indispensable necessity of some congressional enactment for the purpose of suppressing insurrectionary acts toward the authorities of the country.

A divided Congress failed to act.[26]

By 1842 Ashbel Smith had been a teacher, practicing physician, and Texas surgeon general. He had roomed with Sam Houston, negotiated a treaty with the Comanche, published numerous medical papers, founded a hospital, and chaired the republic's first medical board. He was in Paris in 1832 studying medicine when a cholera epidemic flared up. Smith temporarily set aside his studies to treat victims, then wrote and published a treatise on the disease. Now Smith found himself back in Paris, this time as a diplomat charged with repairing the havoc wreaked by the recent Pig War. In December 1842 he opened a letter from a friend in Texas which told of an even greater looming crisis.

In his letter to Ashbel Smith, Washington Miller summarized the president's frustrations with respect to the seat of government and the people of Austin. Miller at the time was postmaster general and a confidante of Sam Houston. He told of "dissension and distrust among the people," lawlessness, talk of secession, and a congress paralyzed by a stubborn, irrational western minority. He feared imminent invasion from Mexico. Money was worthless, the Navy lay rotting in New Orleans, and the treasury was empty. And the government attempting to address these formidable challenges had to operate without its records, because "as error is frequently stubborn, so the citizens of Austin tenaciously hold on to [the archives]." Miller agreed with Sam Houston that Austin was no place for the archives. Frequent Indian attacks and the Mexican threat had combined to almost depopulate the town. Yet those "desperate" few remaining, "who have invested all they have in the world in city property," obstinately blocked every attempt by the president to bring the archives away. Miller feared civil war if Houston persisted. Or, perhaps worse, "they would apply the torch and make one great bonfire of the whole catalogue." Not wishing to provoke a violent encounter, Sam Houston had attempted to persuade the Seventh Congress to act, but this effort failed due to western members absenting themselves from the session to prevent a quorum. Miller noted, "He [Houston] has a decided and clear majority in either House, but the vituperation, denunciation, and abuse lavished upon him is apparently increased by the hopelessness of the minority. . . . The Western members, seeing [their situation] have left and gone home." The result, according to Miller, was that "nothing has been done; and I think it quite possible that nothing will be done, and that the session will break up in a row, without making any appropriations or provision for the carrying on the operations of government for the ensuing year. . . . We are in collapse, perfectly prostrate and powerless."[27]

Sam Houston didn't give up. He remained convinced that Austin provided too little safety given events of the preceding months. In October 1842 he sent John W. Hall and William "Uncle Buck" Pettus to bring out the state department records. The pair openly loaded two wagons before repairing to a local saloon for cards and refreshment. The next morning Hall exited his boarding house to find an angry crowd pointing a loaded artillery piece at the wagons. He fetched Pettus to back him up, but Uncle Buck, pointing to one of the townspeople, could only say, "See here, Hall, I know that lady, and she will shoot." Admitting failure, Hall and Pettus prepared to leave without their cargo. Pettus's bald horse—for during the night someone had shaved Old Ball's mane, tail, and ears—soon had local residents referring to Austin as "Shave-tail country." On December 10 a determined Sam Houston ordered Major Thomas Smith and Captain Eli Chandler to go to Austin, load up the archives, and fetch them to Washington. Houston estimated that the task would require ten to fifteen wagons and teams. This time he wanted secrecy, suggesting, "You might raise your men as if for an Indian excursion." He cautioned the men to guard not only the archives but themselves "so as to suffer no detriment," but added, "Do not be thwarted in the undertaking." At the same time Houston notified Thomas Ward to expect Smith and Chandler's arrival.[28]

A nearly deserted Austin awaited Sam Houston's next move.[29] Christmas came and went. Around midday on December 30 someone beat the Indian alarm drum, summoning all able-bodied men to give chase to the suspected intruders. As was usual women and children gathered for protection at Bullock's. Physician John Robertson, an elderly Benjamin Craig, and Dennis Walsh, on crutches with a broken leg at the time, remained with the women. Half an hour later a group of about twenty armed men rode into town from the east. Several teams and wagons followed the men, who entered Congress Avenue via Hickory Street before stopping in the alley behind the General Land Office on the intersection's northeast corner. Curious, Dr. Robertson ambled up the street to ask the men their business, only to be told brusquely to stay out of the way. Returning to Bullock's, he and the others watched the men begin loading large crates from the Land Office onto the wagons. Angelina Eberly, proprietor of a boarding house one block west of Bullock's on West Pecan, recognized immediately that the men had been sent by President Hous-

Thomas William Ward served as American consul to Panama from 1853 to 1857. He constructed the capitol building in Houston in 1837 and was land commissioner during the Archives War in Austin in 1842. Courtesy of *Prints & Photographs Collection*, Ward, Thomas William, CN01248, the Dolph Briscoe Center for American History, University of Texas at Austin.

ton to remove the archives. She urged Robertson to action. When the doctor professed helplessness, Eberly pointed across the street and cried, "What is that cannon for?" Robertson and several bystanders ran across the street to the shed in which the piece was stored, removed the chucks holding it in place, and rolled it out onto Congress Avenue. Mrs. Eberly dashed into Bullock's and returned with a lit fuse. Seeing that Robertson's aim was too far to the left, she gave the piece a shove eastward, then applied the fuse and sent a round of grapeshot flying.

Fortunately for Eli Chandler and Thomas Smith, for it was indeed these two carrying out their orders from President Houston, the shot went wide and slammed into the Land Office building. Land commissioner Thomas Ward, who lived in his workplace, heard someone shout,

MORELAND HOUSE.   QUARTERMASTER'S DEPARTMENT.

The quartermaster's department sat on the northeast corner of Hickory and
Ash Streets. Immediately behind it is the multi-storied land office central to the
1842 Archives War. Courtesy of the *Galveston News*, February 1896, Center for
American History, University of Texas at Austin.

"Blow the old house to pieces!" Ward later counted eight holes in the side
of the building. Startled teamsters urged on their animals and, with Smith,
Chandler, and their men following, the wagons and the archives raced out
of town. The train headed north toward Brushy Creek so as to avoid the
potentially hostile residents of Bastrop, finally stopping after sixteen
miles to rest at Kenney's Fort.

Meanwhile, the men of Austin, having heard the cannon blast, sped
back to town. Infuriated at the disappearance of the archives, they scram-
bled to organize pursuit. When Dr. Marsden refused to yield his horse,
John Noland threatened to shoot him. A woman screamed as Noland
lowered his weapon, which was quickly knocked away by Captain Mark
B. Lewis. Marsden fled the scene, but, minutes later, when he raced back
past the gathering, two of the men did indeed fire at him.[30] The pursuit
party then hitched the cannon to four fresh mules and followed Captain
Lewis out of town to chase after Smith and Chandler. Some rode eastward toward Webber's Prairie and Bastrop to spread the alarm. Individually and in small groups, men hurried northwest throughout the night to
join Lewis, who by morning commanded a force of forty-nine armed and
angry frontiersmen. Rain fell as the temperature plunged on the prairie.
Buckskin moccasins became "flabby and distorted," thus offering little

protection to the feet. Many of the men, not having expected an overnight trip when riding out of Austin, now suffered from the cold due to lack of adequate clothing. Nevertheless they pressed on until, shortly before dawn, advance scouts found Smith and Chandler's unguarded camp along Brushy Creek behind a shelter of cedar posts.

Imagine Thomas Smith's sinking feeling as he raised his chilled body from the damp earth at dawn, rubbed the sleep from his eyes, and found himself staring at the mouth of a loaded cannon pointed directly at his encampment. Then follow his surprised gaze along the near horizon as he spotted Lewis and his men aiming their weapons at him. Someone shouted for Smith to surrender. Smith refused, instead demanding a parley with his enemy. After a brief conference among the Austinites, two of them trotted over to Smith. When they insisted that Smith return the archives to Austin he again refused and invoked the authority of his order from the president. But now many of Smith's men had gathered around their commander. One of them stepped forward and announced that he had signed up with Smith to defend the archives against Mexicans and Indians, not fellow Texans. He would not fight. When others quickly agreed Smith had no choice but to yield.

Mark Lewis sent a rider back to Austin with word of his success before turning the wagons around and beginning the slow trip back to town. Hours later, tired but victorious volunteers paraded onto Congress Avenue, where jubilant townspeople had prepared a feast of "all the substantials and luxuries that could be found." Fiddlers played, couples danced, and children "flew here and there eating everything in reach and dodging under the feet of the grownups." Embarrassed government clerks who had accompanied Smith as he fled Austin maintained low profiles, which was difficult as their faces were well known to city residents. "They were treated with politeness and no word or sign showed that they were unwelcome, but no woman in the house was aware of their presence. They were 'wall flowers' and, without doubt, welcomed the end of the event."[31]

A disgusted Thomas Ward reported Smith and Chandler's failure to Sam Houston. He had only been able to watch as Lewis's men brought the archives back into town and unloaded them at Angelina Eberly's house. Ward then had observed the crates being carried off to another house on Pecan Street but "whether with the papers, or empty, I cannot say." Residents refused Ward's request to put the papers back in the Land Office. Anger at the land commissioner devolved into ugly threats, but support from two brave friends, Mr. Sutton and Mr. Hunt, shielded him. Ward faulted Major Smith for much of this antagonism. According to him

Smith "excited [people] against me by some tale that [he] was so unkind as to tell in seeking his own safety, supported as he was by twenty-six riflemen."[32] But, whatever happened to Land Commissioner Thomas William Ward, one thing was clear. The archives would stay in Austin.

Not long before Angelina Eberly's famous cannon shot, Austin's first newspaperman sent a letter to Secretary of State Anson Jones. Samuel Whiting, editor and owner of the now defunct *Austin City Gazette* and *Daily Bulletin*, needed money. Whiting had used his printing press to fill several orders from Congress and hadn't yet been paid, a deficiency he blamed on President Houston. Because of this, Whiting told Jones, "I am now in as tight a place as I wish ever to be." Then Whiting shared a sentiment that could have been written by many a western man and, although he didn't say so, was also attributable to Sam Houston: "Another trouble now stares me in the face—have lost all hopes of the seat of government remaining here, and I must away, but where to go God only knows."[33]

Chapter 18

DESOLATION

It was in the spring of 1845. . . . The capital of the republic was desolate, vacant
houses on all sides. People moved into whatever tenement they thought most
conducive to safety or convenience. . . . We had walked to President hill . . . once occupied by the President's mansion, to gather some of those chalky daisies that grew
there. Climbing the hillside among the tussocks of lemon balm, leaving the radiant
scarlet phlox on the sandy slopes below, we stood on the gallery of the deserted
and vacant house. . . . The spring winds sighed mournfully through the broken case-
ments. No footprints, no signs of human life were to be seen.

Julia Lee Sinks, Vertical File

dwin Waller built the city of Austin on the site of Mirabeau Lamar's successful 1838 buffalo hunt. After shooting the large
beast, Vice President Lamar had allowed himself an admiring
view of nature's handiwork before turning his eye toward a prosperous
future of *man's* creation. The buffalo herds, which for millennia had crisscrossed the Texas prairie, occupied no place in Lamar's vision. Of necessity would they yield to the march of progress, their former grazing
grounds converted to a bustling metropolis surrounded by rich and boun-
tiful farms. Lamar dreamed of civilizing what to him was untamed wilderness, symbolized by its largest denizen, the buffalo.

Mirabeau Lamar would therefore have anguished at the sight greeting the few remaining Austin residents in April 1844. Attentive onlookers
first noticed a large cloud of dust on the southern horizon. The green
spring grass beyond the river became spotted with individual black dots,
which gradually coalesced to form a massive dark cloud approaching the
water. Some of the dots stopped at the river's edge; the majority pushed
across the current and entered the town. People scurried out of the way
of hundreds of buffalo ambling through the streets of Austin. The beasts
meandered up Congress Avenue, stopping now and then to pluck clumps
of grass from the weed-choked thoroughfare. Pawing at the ground, they
scraped their massive bodies against buildings, urinated in the streets,
and left droppings behind for curious dogs to sniff. The quickest-thinking

townsmen brought out loaded weapons to fire at the slow-moving targets. A number of animals thus perished within yards of Mirabeau Lamar's 1838 kill. The entire city population dined that night on fresh buffalo meat.[1]

Austin may have won the battle for the archives but, for a while anyway, it appeared to be losing its war for survival. With hardly a western man in his camp, President Sam Houston nevertheless seemed always to have just enough votes to have his way. When late in 1842 some members of the Seventh Congress attempted to force the government back to Austin from Washington, they met a narrow defeat. In response, a group of eastern senators introduced legislation to permanently establish the seat of government at Washington. Only Vice President Burleson's negative tie-breaking vote stopped the measure. The paralyzed session stumbled to a close in January 1843 with debate over a resolution tendering thanks to the citizens of Bastrop and Austin for opposing Houston's ill-fated attempt to sneak the archives out of Austin. The resolution failed by a single vote.[2]

Englishman William Bollaert came to Texas at the behest of his friend William Kennedy, later British consul to the republic, in 1842. He was pleased to find excellent roads upon which to travel, noting that an acquaintance had been able to ride from Houston to Austin in a buggy with only the occasional tree stump to avoid. A year later on this same road Bollaert encountered quite different conditions. Even before reaching La Grange he noticed that many previously prosperous plantations consisted primarily of untilled fields. Furthermore, "the roads are choked up with the wild sun-flower and weeds, so much so that other roads are made by the side of the old ones, for the little transit there is in this direction. . . . The sun-flower roads are called 'Sam Houstons.'"[3]

Although he liked the appearance and comfort of La Grange, Bollaert also commented on the apparent lack of industry about the place, which he attributed to the government's abandonment of Austin. And upon reaching the one-time capital, he wrote

> Lo! Dreariness and desolation presented themselves; few houses appeared inhabited and many falling to decay. The "Legation of France" empty, its doorsband windows open, palings broken down and appearing as if it would soon be in ruins. The President's House looked gloomy, the streets filled with grass and weeds and the western people say all this "through the vindictiveness of Old Sam."

Visited the "President's House." It is falling to pieces, and now the residence of bats. The Capitol is the abode of bats, lizards, and stray cattle. These buildings having been built of green wood and run up with great expedition, the timbers have dried and become loose, the plaster peeling off, and the "Austin soft stone" cracking.[4]

Austin residents knew who to blame for this sorry state of affairs. One wrote to his relatives in New York: "Texas is in a bad fix and no mistake old Sam Houston has eternally damned himself, and I don't believe he has a *true* friend in the county—his action in relation to the removal of the Seat of Government and to offensive operations towards Mexico are enough to kill and forever damn him."[5] With the object of their anger out of reach in Washington, the people of Austin turned their fury on each other. A *Cincinnati Gazette* correspondent wrote in 1844 of a town devolving into social anarchy. Numerous cliques sprang up, only to subdivide further into even smaller hostile groups until "each man is the enemy of all others. . . . It constitutes hell." In July 1843 this rancorous atmosphere exploded in deadly fashion. The instigators were Mark B. Lewis, leader of the Austin contingent in the Archives War, and John Noland, described by Noah Smithwick as "a big Irish bully." Smithwick claimed that Noland had been spurred to action by "a certain lawyer whose inordinate vanity and ambition could ill brook the favors lavished upon" the popular Lewis.[6] Or perhaps Noland carried a grudge against Lewis for knocking his gun away when he tried to commandeer Dr. Marsden's horse to chase after the archives the previous December. The confrontation occurred on East Pecan during an election for militia officers. While violently arguing with each other, both Lewis and Noland drew pistols, fired, and missed. Noland reached for his Bowie knife, which broke in his hand as a shot from Lewis's second pistol slammed into his body, killing him instantly. Lewis immediately surrendered to the sheriff, who promptly locked the prisoner away for the night.

On the following morning the sheriff brought Mark Lewis into the street to escort him to a preliminary hearing. At a crossing Louis P. Cooke, who may have been the lawyer referred to by Noah Smithwick, and John Noland's nephew George Barrett stepped from behind a building and ordered the sheriff to stand out of the way. When Lewis asked for a chance to defend himself, his adversaries again warned the sheriff to move. Lewis appealed to his protector, who responded by shoving him farther into the open. Realizing his hopeless position Lewis broke and ran for a nearby house, but Cooke and Barrett shot him down. They also shot and killed Angelina Eberly's son Aleck Peyton as he attempted to intervene on Lewis's behalf. Both attackers were arrested; both later escaped and fled to safety.[7]

After his disastrous attempt to sneak the national archives out of Austin, Sam Houston threw up his hands in disgust. Convinced of the grave danger he saw in maintaining the country's records on the frontier, the president pointed a finger at the city's citizens and proclaimed, "Whatever of evil may befall the nation from the loss or destruction of its archives, must *fall upon the people,* but not by the agency of their President. . . . The Executive, having thus far discharged his duty, will use *no further exertions on the subject,* but leave the matter to the people *and their Representatives.*"[8]

Stubborn Austinites, already feeling the economic effect of the government's exodus, remained defiant. Early in 1843, when Commissioner Thomas William Ward proposed reopening the General Land Office in Austin, the "Archive Committee of Travis County" refused to turn over the papers without a written pledge that Ward would provide notification of any government order to remove them from the city. Citing lack of authority to give such assurance, Ward declined. Austin advocates thereby perturbed even those Texans inclined to sympathize with westerners. The *Morning Star* editor complained, "It is important that the office should be opened, as a great many persons have not yet obtained their titles, and are subjected to great inconvenience for want of them. Although we fully admit the right of the citizens of Austin to prevent the illegal removal of the archives from that city; they certainly have no right to prevent any officer of government from opening his office."[9]

A year later, Ward had still not opened his department. Concerned, the House of Representatives sent two of its members to Austin to inspect the records. A testy Thomas Ward, perhaps succumbing to the stress accompanying his status as the government's sole agent in Austin's hostile environment, responded by picking a fight with one of the congressmen. Ward had prepared a list of Land Office holdings, which Congressman John Grammont was using to go through some of the boxes. Something caused Ward to brusquely demand that Grammont hand over the list; the Congressman refused, instead handing it to his House colleague Frederick Ogden. Incredibly, Ward then obtained a warrant for Ogden's arrest. Evidently he found no one willing to execute the warrant, as Ogden and Grammont finished their inspection and left the city. This pair then returned Ward's pettiness with their own by unsuccessfully attempting to bring charges against him in Travis County District Court. Nevertheless, the Land Office finally resumed business shortly thereafter.[10]

Complaints about the Land Office, and thus about Austin, now shifted from its failure to operate to the inconvenience of its location away from the rest of the government. In April 1845 the *Morning Star* related the story of a veteran who had traveled from Houston to Austin to obtain a land patent, only to be informed that he first needed approval from the Secretary of War in Washington: "Thus the poor soldier is compelled to make a regular campaign-marching and countermarching about three hundred miles before he can get the patent. . . . This is one of the many disadvantages arising from the separation of the heads of departments and the archives."[11]

Samuel Whiting, owner and publisher of the *Austin City Gazette*, had enjoyed immediate and growing success after setting up shop in Austin in 1839. Early immigration to the city steadily expanded his readership; a later successful campaign to become public printer seemingly guaranteed ongoing success.[12] Then came the Mexican invasion of 1842. Whiting temporarily abandoned Austin during the panic, ending his three-year run of weekly editions. He soon returned but was never able to resume regular publication of his newspaper. The August 17, 1842, appearance of the *Austin City Gazette* proved to be its last. Months later a despondent and frustrated Whiting wrote to Secretary of State Anson Jones: "Poor me, I have gone through troubles enough since you left here to have put an end to almost any other mortal man living. . . . I have nearly had my life teased and fretted out by duns of printers for work done for last year's Congress, and for which our worthy President will not suffer me paid." Like many others in his position, Whiting blamed Sam Houston. While mentioning hope that Comptroller James Shaw would soon approve payment of some of his government accounts, he asked Jones, "Will you be so kind as to assist him, should he find any difficulty in doing so from orders of His Majesty." And to make sure that Jones took him seriously, Whiting concluded, "I am now in as tight a place as I wish ever to be, and require your friendly aid to extricate me. Pray put your shoulder to the wheel and help me out of this suck." That Whiting's experience was no exception among Austin residents is clear from Anson Jones's comment in the margins of this letter: "This is a fair specimen . . . of the thousand and one letters of a similar kind I have received within the year, and a fair sample of the times in 1842."[13]

Samuel Whiting's editor, George Teulon, also suffered because of the city's dwindling population, but struggled to hold on nevertheless. In February 1843 he teamed with James Webb to introduce Austin readers to the biweekly *Western Advocate*. The newspaper sputtered on through the rest of 1843, enduring Teulon's serious illness that summer, to finally expire a year after its founding. Like Whiting before him, Teulon poured out his woes to Anson Jones: "I am attached to Austin,—I love its mountain seat, its beautiful scenery, and even its very atmosphere; it was my first abiding-place in Texas—it shall be my last. If the Congress and the Government do not come here, I must leave and seek another clime. When I quit here I quit Texas." Privately in opposition to his president's policies regarding Austin, Jones commented in response to Teulon's note, "I *have had* nothing to do, I *will have* nothing to do with the policy which has contributed to desolate the fairest portion of Texas—the West." Those remaining in Austin would have agreed with Jones's description of a desolate west, as proven by Edwin Morehouse's 1844 observation from the city, "We are beyond the pale of news, save rumor."[14]

Shortly after the Mexican scare of 1842, Thomas Shuff, who lived on Barton Creek just west of Austin, determined to visit a neighbor about a cow. When he told his wife that he would take their young son with him she replied, "No, don't wake him, he is asleep." Later that day Mrs. Shuff heard her husband shouting loudly in the distance but ignored this, thinking he was merely calling the cow he was bringing home. She realized her mistake when Shuff's riderless horse sprinted up to the house. A search party found Shuff's corpse but not the Indians who had killed him. A mourning Mrs. Shuff took solace in the nap that had undoubtedly saved her son from capture or death.[15]

Incidents such as this fueled the hatred most Austin residents felt toward Sam Houston. Even before the government's exodus to Washington, westerners had complained that Houston neglected their safety. Now they saw the president's removal of the government as proof of his disregard. Of course, Houston had always stated that the government had no business on the frontier precisely because of the inherent danger. So when western advocates clamored for Sam Houston to return the government to Austin to alleviate the danger faced by its citizens, the president argued that this very danger prevented him from doing so. And, although the large-scale Indian attack feared most by Austin residents never materialized, there was yet enough violence to stoke everyone's anxiety.

One fall day in 1842 a Mr. Davis, while riding his horse northeast of Austin, spied a group of Indians riding rapidly toward him.[16] Fleeing across Waller Creek, he caught the attention of Judge Joseph Lee, who was approaching from the north.[17] Lee raced into town to spread the alarm.

Giving up on Davis, the Indians veered to the northwest, pausing briefly to pursue a man named Larabee, who eluded them by hiding in the thick brush. They next encountered the house of Judge Brewster Jayne. Jayne saluted the seemingly friendly party and approached with one son in his arms and another by his side. During the ensuing conversation one of the Indians attempted to grab the youngest boy from his father's arms. Jayne turned with his son to go back to the house when one of the Indians shot him and then a nearby field hand. The raiders forced the older boy onto a horse and sped off. Jayne died in his wife's arms in the doorway of his house; his youngest son survived with an arrow wound.[18]

That same year two men named Baker and Souls met their deaths near Manchaca Springs south of Austin. While searching for some lost cattle the two were ambushed by several Indians. Baker died with the first volley; Souls killed or wounded several of his attackers before succumbing in turn. The search party found both corpses scalped, but only Souls's heart had been cut from his body, most likely consumed by his killers in an effort to incorporate his bravery into their own bodies.

Alabaman Gideon White proved a tough opponent as well. Although he knew better, White set out on foot one day to hunt some wandering livestock near his cabin on Shoal Creek.[19] His lack of a horse proved fatal when a group of mounted Indians attacked. White put up strong resistance before his death. Searchers later found multiple bullet holes and arrows in the tree he hid behind during the fight. Several yards away they noticed a circle of trampled grass darkened with clotted blood.[20]

Although these incidents occurred outside the city limits, they terrified Austin residents nonetheless. Julia Lee Sinks recalled many an evening during which "the frightened women gathered when the cry of 'Indians,' whether true or false, made the night hideous." Huddled together for protection in Bullock's hotel scared women and children passed countless tedious hours in each other's company, anxiously awaiting the "all clear" signal. Some cried and some sat in fearful silence, while others strove to lighten the mood with awkward jokes. A few brave souls even attempted to dance, only to elicit angry cries of protest and prayerful admonitions. On one such occasion George Hockley strode through the crowd, pistol in hand, calmly intoning, "Don't get frightened, ladies, don't get frightened; there are enough men here to whip all the Indians between here and Santa Fe."[21]

Then came an 1842 attack that struck terror into even the stoutest hearts among Austin's citizenry. One afternoon a widow named Simpson sent her twelve-year-old son Tommie and fourteen-year-old daughter to fetch the family milk cows to their house in the 300 block of West Pecan.

About 150 yards west of the house Indians surprised and carried off the children. Citizens responded almost immediately to Mrs. Simpson's cries; some pursued on foot while others raced for their mounts. The kidnappers sped past the site of modern-day Woodlawn on their way toward Mount Bonnell.[22] The chase party lost the trail in the rocky foothills, allowing the Indians to escape to Spicewood Springs to the northwest.[23] Once safe from their pursuers the Indians paused to deal with the now frantic teenage girl. Tommie recalled later that he tried unsuccessfully to calm his sister. Then one of the Indians led the girl away from the group, only to return a bit later with her bloody scalp hanging from his saddle.[24]

The Simpson girl's killer played a key role in an 1845 attack that highlights the chasm of cultural ignorance which separated Indian and Anglo communities. Reuben Hornsby's son Daniel and his friend William Adkisson, an Austin resident, struck out from the Hornsby home one day to fish on the Colorado River. While they stood on the bank, Indians speared them from behind. Both fell into the river; the attackers riddled Hornsby with arrows, killing him instantly. Adkisson made it to the opposite bank, but died within a few feet of the water.

Austin residents received the news of these murders as further proof of the senseless savagery of the Indians. And if, as with most Indian attacks, no further explanation had arisen, this conclusion might have been understandable. But in this case another explanation *did* arise which, while not easing anyone's pain, at least explained a motive for the attack.

The man who killed Daniel Hornsby and the Simpson girl had been shot by a Captain Coleman during a skirmish on the Pedernales River. Thereafter he mistook Daniel Hornsby for Coleman at Torry's trading house, despite assurances from a Delaware Indian at the store that the man was not Coleman, but Hornsby. The alarmed Delaware warned the local Indian agent, Mr. Sloat, of Hornsby's danger. Sloat in turn went to the man threatening Hornsby and warned that his own family would suffer if he attempted to harm Hornsby. At this the Indian scoffed that no white man could kill him and boasted that he had been the one to kill the Simpson girl. He persuaded several comrades to join him in the revenge attack that resulted in the deaths of Hornsby and Adkisson. Sloat caught up with and confronted the killer in a Comanche camp of about six hundred people on the San Gabriel River north of Austin. Achieving no satisfaction he rode to Washington to confer with the president. Meanwhile Hornsby's friends and relatives formed an armed gang to attack and destroy the Comanche camp if the murderer was not given up. According to the Houston-based *Morning Star*, the episode "shows how difficult it is to preserve peace between the Indian tribes and our frontier settlers."[25]

Most westerners, assuming that peace between themselves and Indians was impossible, instead saw proof of the perils imposed by Sam Houston's policies.

One commodity that destitute Austin residents of the early 1840s had in abundance was food. Those refusing to leave in the wake of the government lacked for many things, but they had plenty to eat and no one starved. The Houston *Morning Star* attested to this in 1843 and 1844 with notices of large wheat crops being raised around Austin. Traveler Francis S. Latham, passing through Austin in May 1842, noticed that "there seems to be a good supply of corn and provisions. . . . The people everywhere I have been are remarkably healthy and fat looking." Frank Brown highlights a likely explanation for this in his *Annals*: "Every acre of enclosed land in or near town was utilized [for crops]. There was not an idle man to be found. Every one turned planter and went to cultivating the soil. There was nothing else to do."[26]

Despite the well-fed condition of its populace, Austin impressed Texans and foreigners alike as a doomed city. In a letter to Mirabeau Lamar at Galveston, James Webb bemoaned Austin's reduced population, lack of commerce, and poor living conditions, adding, "Poor Austin has sadly changed since you saw it." Tennessee newspaperman Francis Latham noticed deterioration as early as May 1842, when he included Austin in his tour of Texas. He claimed that many families had been financially ruined by the Mexican invasions of 1842, first through the burden of quartering Texan soldiers, then by losses incurred while fleeing the perceived threat. Prices had skyrocketed due to the lack of currency, always a problem on the frontier but particularly severe after the spring of 1842. Like others before him, Latham paid tribute to Austin's great beauty and the fertility of its countryside. But in the city he encountered only a plain capitol building and encircling palisade amid 150 lonely houses, two-thirds of which were built of rough logs. Commenting on Sam Houston's having "deserted" Austin, he observed that "more than five-sixths of the people have also left, and there are now scarce two hundred people in the city." Latham nevertheless enjoyed his stay, which included a ball attended by "some 25 or 30 ladies . . . many of them elegant and accomplished."[27]

Englishman William Bollaert arrived in Austin during its nadir in 1843 marveling at the stunning scenery and vast potential wealth of the region. Ignoring the recent Santa Fe Expedition fiasco, he parroted earlier predictions of Austin as the linchpin of a great future trade route. Texans, in particular western Texans, impressed him. According to Bollaert, "They have never failed in any one of the duties of patriotic citizens. Industrious and thrifty . . . they are generous and brave . . . [and] moral in their habits. . . . Texas may well be proud." But in Bollaert's view prosperity lay in the future, for the present looked bleak. "Alas! Poor Austin, thy seven hills are nearly deserted," the Englishman wrote. He mourned the decrepit, crumbling appearance of Austin's government buildings, the tiny population, frequent Indian attacks, and even the people's health, for "this year [Austin was] visited by considerable sickness, until then it was proverbially healthy." And Bollaert pointed out the obvious, that the only residents left in the city were those who had staked everything they had on its success. "Those cling to the spot who assisted to rear it," he wrote, "for they have their property there. They hope for better times."[28]

One who didn't stay was New Yorker William Abell. During the panic of the Mexican incursions of 1842, he packed up his store merchandise and joined the stampede out of town. Abell came back, but: "When I returned to Austin it was painful to see the desolation but a few families remained—Maj. Brighams—Mrs Wooldridges & Mr. Eberlys and a few others—I stayed but a day or so and then went out on a *mustang hunt* for 3 or 4 days and two days after—I left old Austin." Once back in his hometown he wrote lyrically of his time in Texas:

> Oh dear I almost get the Blues in thinking over the old fellows & times we used to have after all dident we live as happily in Austin as we can expect in this world—I have wished a great many times since my return home that I was back in Austin and everything going as smoothly *as it used to did*—what do you say for a stroll around Coombs hill & gather some flowers or down into the cooling waters of the old never-to-be-forgotten Colorado.

And in lamenting those lost, idyllic times Abell expressed the bitterness shared by many along the Colorado: "He [Sam Houston] came to Austin, we used him well & he used us *mean*. d——d mean in the end."[29]

Chapter 19
SALVATION

The first session of the Legislature, after the adoption of this Constitution by the Congress of the United States, shall be held at the city of Austin, the present seat of Government, and thereafter, until the year one thousand eight hundred and fifty; after which period the Seat of Government shall be permanently located by the people.

Article 3, Section 33, Constitution of the state of Texas, 1845

If westerners could have read Anson Jones's private diary in 1844, they might not have feared the prospects of a Jones presidency quite so much. As President Sam Houston's secretary of state, Jones was widely held to be a member of the Houston party. Voters therefore assumed that, if elected, Jones would continue the policies of his predecessor. But months before the election of September 1844, Jones had confided in his journal, "I have had nothing to do with the 'seat of Government policy,' and have been opposed to Gen. H.'s course upon it; knowing this, he has ceased to counsel with me upon it."[1]

Houston's policy, of course, was to keep the government in Washington or, at least, away from Austin and the frontier. Westerners hated him for this. William Cazneau articulated the prevailing sentiment of his fellow Travis County residents when he wrote that "the apparent determination of [Houston] to desolate and destroy the west, arrayed that portion of his constituents against him." President Houston's removal of the government from Austin in 1842 nearly ruined Cazneau. Like others, the merchant had reluctantly abandoned Austin as a means of financial survival. His tale of woe mirrored dozens of others in the early 1840s. Government removal, wrote Cazneau, "so completely paralyzed the business operations and pursuits of those who remained, that many . . . were left destitute of the means of providing for themselves and families. Of this number I was one."[2]

Anson Jones certainly did not see himself as a Houston man. Over the years his feelings toward his political benefactor fluctuated, but ultimately he judged Houston's impact to be negative. Like Mirabeau Lamar,

ANSON JONES.

See p. 259.

When he ran for president in 1844, Doctor Anson Jones was widely perceived to be in the Houston camp. Jones's true feelings were decidedly mixed. His diary contains frequent criticisms of Sam Houston, and he eventually concluded that his presidential predecessor's overall influence had been negative. Reprinted by permission of the Austin History Center, Austin Public Library, PICB 10944.

Jones personally disliked Sam Houston, and, like Lamar, Jones allowed this to influence his views of the great man's political acts. Of their first meeting in 1835 Jones wrote, "I formed a very unfavorable opinion of him . . . regarding him as a miserable sot, without dignity of character, and without principle of any kind."[3] While serving in the Senate during Lamar's presidency, the future president observed: "I had hoped something from General Houston, but he appears only intent upon making Lamar's administration as odious as possible, in order that the contrast with his own may be favorable to him. He is willing the Government should be a failure, in order that he may have it to say there is no one but 'old Sam' that the people can depend upon." And, a year into his own presidency, Jones privately accused Sam Houston of jealousy: "I very much fear I have given mortal offence to Gen. Houston, in having succeeded in my administration thus far. He will only omit to persecute and hate me, as he has so many others, on condition that I will let him appropriate all the credit of my acts as President to himself."[4]

Anson Jones therefore bristled at being called a Houston man. But the campaign of 1844 put him in a bind. Since many of his own supporters loved Sam Houston, to publicize his true feelings about the man would have been political suicide. And yet to remain silent seemed to confirm the suspicions of the anti-Houston faction so dominant in the west. As one supporter informed Jones: "In *these* [*western*] *settlements,* as a matter of course, the talented General Burleson stands fair, as they say he is to bring back, without difficulty or hesitation, and irrevocably *fix* the seat of Government at Austin, and Dr. Jones' policy is of Sam Houston."[5]

Anson Jones indeed faced a formidable challenger in Edward Burleson. Western voters revered "Old Ned," in whom they saw a man capable of standing up to the might of the hated Houston. Of above-average height and solidly built, the blond, blue-eyed Burleson looked the part of a leader.[6] His soft-spoken, decisive manner endeared him to other frontiersmen. They had repeatedly followed him into battle against Indian and Mexican forces and now looked to him as their savior in the struggle to return prosperity to Austin and the west.

In September 1843 a group of citizens in Columbus formally nominated Edward Burleson for the presidency. Although he accepted the challenge, Burleson tried to make it clear that he ran as his own man: "I do not consider myself a candidate of a party nor can I in any event be made subservient to the purpose of any party."[7]

A committee of Independence residents nominated Anson Jones in October. Like many politicians then and now, Jones publicly affected an attitude of indifference to high office, claiming to seek it only at the behest of his friends. Unlike many, however, his public protestations matched his private feelings: "I have no expectation that the presidential chair will be any thing else than one of thorns; nor do I desire the office; and my only object in consenting to take it is, to consummate a policy which has already cost me great labor and great sacrifices, and thus give peace, security, and happiness to Texas."[8]

Despite the efforts of Burleson and Jones to prevent it, the presidential campaign of 1844 turned into a fight between the Houston and the anti-Houston parties. As the editor of the *Morning Star* put it, "On the one hand, Dr. Jones is to be forced upon the people by the merits of Gen. Houston; and on the other hand, Gen. Burleson is to be sacrificed by the demerits of Gen. Lamar." One never-ending point of contention that dogged both candidates, but especially Jones, was where to locate the government seat. No one doubted that Burleson would return it to Austin. This was an easy position to defend, as the law placing government in that city still stood. Jones's position was more precarious. If he announced opposition to an Austin return he would vadidate charges of being Houston's lackey. If he publicly favored Austin he would risk support from his base. He therefore remained as quiet as possible about the issue. When on the eve of the election he finally did indicate support for Austin, Burleson partisans cried foul:

> Well, our correspondent is right; Dr. Jones has at last . . . declared himself an advocate for the removal of the Seat of Government back to Austin. . . . This is certainly a bold stroke for Western votes. Heretofore Jones' supporters have poured upon us all the vials of their wrath and most unmitigated abuse for the very opinions now expressed by Jones himself. Strange things happen in these latter days. He is evidently in alarm lest his weight may be too great even for Old Sam to carry him successfully through, and he therefore shifts one leg upon Old Ned's shoulders, by adopting part of *his* circular.[9]

Jones defended himself by claiming respect for the will of the people: "I have said that wherever Congress and the people determined the Seat of Government should be established, I should acquiesce in their decision—that this was a position of local domestic policy entirely about which the people of the country and their Representatives could be judge."[10]

As the election approached, the race between Anson Jones and Edward Burleson appeared close. Jones revealed private resentment of what he perceived as tepid support from many in his camp when he wrote, "I expect the *support* of my friends, not apathy and discouragement. After James Wilson Henderson aligned himself with Jones in June 1844, the candidate sarcastically commented, "After trying to bring out, one after another, every *available* man in the country, the Houston clique finally, on the 20th of June, finding I would be elected with or without their support, concluded to *take their stand* for me in preference to Gen. Burleson and the Opposition. How patriotic and magnanimous!!!"[11]

Within weeks of the election Anson Jones may have thought his victory certain, but few others shared that view. One big reason was that the man most closely identified by the public with Jones's cause had so far remained quiet. An insecure Jones felt certain that Houston's silence betrayed opposition. When in May rumors that Houston had been pushing the candidacy of Supreme Court Justice John Hemphill reached him, Jones observed, "*Crawfishing* about, trying to defeat my election."[12] And even though Houston did finally endorse Jones in August, Jones complained in his diary, "That Gen. H. preferred Gen. Burleson to me as his successor is well known to me." There may have been some truth to Jones's musings, given Houston's less than passionate endorsement: "I am not opposed to his [Jones's] election. If I have not been a noisy advocate for his success, it has not been because I did not confide in him. . . . I have confidence that if the choice of the people should devolve the duties of President upon him, he would consult the true interests of the country."[13]

Results of the September 2 election reflected the sectional nature of the contest. Burleson dominated in the west, but the more populous east coast swung the outcome in Jones's favor. Although Burleson carried twenty of the thirty-six counties, he earned only 44 percent of the total vote. Jones's popularity was particularly apparent in densely settled regions, including Montgomery, Red River, and Nacogdoches Counties, where his aggregate majority of 1,364 votes almost equaled his overall victory margin of 1,370. Writing from San Augustine, easterner William Ochiltree crowed, "The East, Middle and North, did their duty gloriously. I rather think that Gen. [Burleson] returns to the West in no very good humor."[14] But James Morgan, who apparently voted for Jones, evinced less enthusiasm: "Dr. Anson Jones is certainly elected to the Presidency. . . . He had no popularity of his own, rode in on Old Sam's shadow! His opponent Burleson is a very illiterate man & would have disgraced the Republic in that office. . . . Old Sam can beat the D——l himself when he trys [*sic*] and make anyone President."[15]

Washington, Texas, in the 1840s offered no more comfort to the nation's lawmakers than had Austin or, for that matter, any of the other previous seats of government. In an 1842 letter to his wife, Congressman Asa Lewis of Colorado County joked, "About noon I received a note of invitation to dine with the President and will now give you an account of all, and when you have read it I presume you will make no more complaint about our furniture." Lewis reported seeing uncovered sofas, rawhide chairs, a patched, unpainted armchair, and mismatched glassware. The

Undated photograph of Frank Brown and his wife Georgiana. In 1846 twelve-year-old Frank Brown moved with his family from Washington to Austin. Later in life he drew upon his own experiences, as well as those of some of the city's original residents, to compile an invaluable history of the Texas capital. Courtesy of Prints and Photographs Collection, Brown, Mr. and Mrs. Frank, CN03318, the Dolph Briscoe Center for American History, University of Texas at Austin.

food was "good but not fine." Lewis and the other guests enjoyed pork, roast turkey, fried chicken, turnips, and corn bread. But the presidential table lacked wine; diners washed their meal down with water.[16]

Six-year-old Frank Brown moved with his family to Washington in 1839. Years later he recalled a lively town of about three hundred inhabitants. The local ferryman stayed busy carrying goods and passengers over the Brazos River into town. Steamboat traffic began even before the arrival of the government in 1842. The *Mustang* and the *Lady Byron* were soon joined by others making their way upriver. They could go no farther than Washington because of an obstruction just above town known as Hidalgo Falls.

After losing out to Austin in 1839, Washington residents did not expect to host another government. Accommodations in 1842 were therefore scarce. Townsfolk spruced up an abandoned two-story hotel and packed it with as many out-of-towners as possible. President Houston found a small room on Main Street to serve as the executive office. He also managed to secure a cottage three hundred yards down the street as his residence. As there was no building large enough to hold both houses

German immigrant Francis Dieterich was among the first residents of Austin. He supplied beef to Edwin Waller's work crews in 1839 and to the Santa Fe Expedition in 1841. Like many others facing financial ruin after the government left Austin in 1842, Dieterich moved to Washington. He returned with the government three years later and opened a dry goods store on Congress Avenue. Courtesy of Bonham (Dora Dieterich) Papers, CN122188, the Dolph Briscoe Center for American History, University of Texas at Austin.

of Congress, the Senate and House met in separate structures about one hundred yards apart.

Frank Brown remembered many Washington neighbors in the early 1840s originally from Austin. Prominent among them was Asa Brigham, Austin's mayor in 1842. Senator James Shaw was one of scores who followed the government out of Austin in response to Sam Houston's directive. Future Austin mayor John "Rip" Ford spent time in Washington, as did House clerk James Raymond and Sam Houston protégé Washington Miller. Mrs. James Smith, whose husband had been killed by Indians just outside of Austin in 1841, left the depopulated city in 1842 for the relative safety of Washington. Meat dealer Francis Dieterich, supplier of the Santa Fe Expedition, trailed after his customers to the Brazos River town.[17]

When Frank Brown put his Washington recollections to paper in later life, two exciting events stood out in his mind. In the summer of 1844 a group of about a hundred Indians came to Washington at Sam Houston's invitation to confer with the president. They erected their buffalo-skin tents about three-fourths of a mile outside of town. Houston provided the visitors beef and corn to supplement what they had brought themselves. Washington residents wore out a path walking to the camp to trade trinkets for honey, bear oil, and wild game. Curious Indians wandered freely through Washington's streets, poking around shops, visiting acquaintances, and occasionally dining as guests in the homes of residents. Brown found amusement at the awkwardness of the Indians as they attempted to use unfamiliar utensils. One man held a piece of corn bread and a fork in the same hand; each time he tried to take a bite of the bread he poked himself in the eye with the fork. The Indians showed more ability on their own turf when townspeople gathered to watch exhibitions of skill with lance, tomahawk, and bow and arrow. Evening brought games and dancing. Conversation was either in the Indians' native tongue or Spanish, as few of the Indians spoke English.[18]

The other Washington event impressing Frank Brown took place December 9, 1844, when Anson Jones received his presidential oath of office. By then the eleven-year-old was working as a delivery boy for the *Texas National Register*.[19] He and most of the town population gathered in front of the House of Representatives at 11:00 a.m. to watch Anson Jones, Vice-President-elect Kenneth Anderson, Sam Houston, Houston's cabinet, and a joint congressional committee march ceremoniously to the front of the crowd. Tod Robinson, Brazoria County representative in the Seventh Congress, presented Jones and Anderson to House speaker John Lewis and the man defeated by Jones, Senate president Edward Burleson. Jones and Anderson were led to seats on an elevated platform, to be joined moments later by the American chargé d'affaires and consul.[20]

At noon, after a prayer by the House chaplain, outgoing president Sam Houston rose to speak. Affecting an air of humility, he thanked the people of Texas for entrusting their affairs to him three years beforehand. He recognized the differences between his opinions and those of many in Congress, but added that the resulting conflicts had regrettably arisen from his patriotic sense of duty. Nevertheless: "In my retirement . . . I take with me no animosities. If ever they existed, they are buried in the past; and I would hope that those with whom it was my lot to come in conflict, in the discharge of my official functions, will exercise towards my acts and motives, the same degree of candor." And then, somewhat laughably given his lifelong predilection for assuming the spotlight, Houston closed by remarking, "I shall bear with me, into the retirement in which I intend to pass the remainder of my life, the grateful and abiding recollection of your many favors."

It was now Anson Jones's turn to tackle the unenviable task of following brilliant speaker Sam Houston. After receiving the oath of office,

Jones talked only briefly. He provided no specifics; to the contrary, he maintained: "It belongs not to the present occasion to discuss the various subjects connected with the present or future policy of the country. Other occasions will occur for the appropriate performance of that duty." Guests at the inaugural ball that evening could therefore only speculate about whether this would be the last such gala in Washington, or the first of many to come.

German immigrant Francis Dieterich had been a Texan for five years when he showed up in Austin in 1839. Working from a butcher pen on Waller Creek near the crossing of College Avenue (now Twelfth Street), Dieterich and business partner Jacob Harrell sold beef at fourteen to sixteen cents per pound to feed Edwin Waller's work crews. Two years later Hugh McLeod and his men carried thousands of pounds of meat from Dieterich on their ill-fated trip to Santa Fe. Business was good enough that Dieterich purchased three Austin city lots in May 1841. But when his customers fled east with Sam Houston and the Texas government in 1842, Dieterich had little choice but to follow. Setting up shop in the building that had witnessed the signing of the Texas Declaration of Independence in 1836, he opened a dry goods business, recording his first sale of twelve dollars' worth of sperm candles to the House of Representatives in December. For the next three years, Dieterich supplied many of the needs of government officials and other Washington residents. When Sam Houston gathered area Indians for the council witnessed by Frank Brown, he likely purchased their provisions and gifts at Independence Hall.[21] Such was the extent of his business with the government that Dieterich's descendant, Dora Dieterich Bonham, titled her biography of him *Merchant to the Republic*.

By late 1844 Texans had been arguing so long about where to put the seat of government that many gave up hope of ever putting the issue to rest. Referring to "this vexed question," the editor of the *Telegraph* despaired, "Is it now of any earthly consequence to the people where the next Congress meet, since the only law upon the subject has been abrogated? . . . Will the people tolerate any more stock jobbing and speculation, and corruption, and intrigue under Executive influence?"[22]

The Ninth Congress opened in Washington December 2, 1844, but some of its members were determined to close it in Austin. On December 19, the *Morning Star* noted that "appearances at present prognosticate that the Congress is again to be agitated with stormy contentions upon the seat of government question."[23] This comment elaborated on a report of the most important matter then being debated, namely a House bill introduced by Travis County representative William Cazneau requiring that the president and all department heads return to the seat of government, which for Cazneau naturally meant Austin. Robert Williamson of Washington County countered this with a proposed bill requiring that all government property be brought from Austin to Washington. It stretches credulity to think that after years of debate anyone hadn't yet chosen sides, but that didn't forestall the many long-winded, self-righteous speeches that followed. No new reasoning appeared. Richardson Scurry of Red River accused his colleagues of wasting taxpayer money with further arguing because "the mind of every member upon this floor, [is] perfectly settled with regard to this question."[24] Finally, on December 20, Cazneau's bill came to a vote; it passed, barely, 20 to 18.

That Congressman John "Rip" Ford rose immediately to protest the bill's passage is ironic given later events in his life. A future Austin mayor, Ford subsequently gained fame fighting with the Texas Rangers; his name is now synonymous with the rugged Texas frontier. But at the time, he represented Sam Houston's home county of San Augustine and could hardly have been expected to act otherwise. Eight other congressmen, all easterners, joined Ford's official complaint.[25]

No one at the time was certain how President Jones would react to the proposed law. He had opposed situating the capital at Austin in the first place, then, as a member of Houston's cabinet, offered no public support when his boss moved it to Washington.[26] Now, forced to take a stand by the new legislation, Jones quashed the return to Austin. In explanation the president cited a clause in the bill's preamble that stated, "Whereas, the emergency having ceased for the removal of the Heads of Departments from the city of Austin."[27] Like Sam Houston, Jones claimed sole authority of declaring a state of emergency and could not agree with Congress that Austin was out of all danger. Furthermore, if Congress disagreed with him, it had the power of removing him from office. As a sop to the western contingent, Jones closed by suggesting an appropriation of five thousand dollars, rather than the two thousand dollars allotted in the vetoed bill, for a removal to Austin in case he changed his mind later about returning to that city.

There was subsequently no serious attempt to override the presidential veto. Both the House and the Senate focused instead on mandating a popular vote to determine a permanent government seat. But the debated legislation *did* appropriate money for a return to Austin and directed a return to Austin by the president when he determined it to be safe enough. Dissenters feared that, once the government was back in Austin, Congress would repeal that part of the act calling for the national election.[28] Ultimately nothing happened; the Ninth Congress closed February 3, 1845, without changing the status quo.

Practically as the last rifle shot echoed into stillness at San Jacinto had Texans argued about attaching themselves politically to the United States. At the same election that installed Sam Houston as the republic's first president, citizens also voted overwhelmingly to seek a union with their northern neighbor. But when US President Martin Van Buren opposed the idea, Texas withdrew its offer.

Annexation found no friend in Mirabeau Lamar after his 1838 election to the presidency. The issue therefore lay dormant until Sam Houston, always a proponent, took back the reins of state from Lamar. This time, however, Houston played it coyly, at times even speaking out against annexation. He aimed to play Great Britain, the United States, and Mexico against each other in an effort to achieve not only the best annexation deal possible, but also peace with Santa Anna's government. This drew anger from those supporters less politically shrewd than the president.

Feigning reluctance, Houston signed a treaty of annexation with the United States in 1844. Antislavery advocates in the US Senate gathered enough support to kill the deal. In response, President John Tyler, worried that an independent Texas would eventually function as a British satellite, successfully guided a conditional annexation offer through Congress. This joint resolution passed February 28, 1845. At about the same time, Great Britain convinced Mexico to offer peace to Texas if it would agree to remain independent.[29]

Anson Jones had no intention of shouldering the entire responsibility for accepting or rejecting the American offer. On April 15, 1845, he issued a proclamation calling the Ninth Congress back into special session June 16 at Washington.[30] Jones and everyone else knew, however, what the outcome of this session would be. He therefore issued a proclamation on May 5 for another convention beginning July 4, this time for the purpose of "adopt[ing] a Constitution with a view to the admission of Texas as one of the States of the American Union."[31] And, although this may or may not have been his intention, by calling for this assembly at Austin, he paved the way for returning the seat of government to the west.

Public opinion in 1845 still heavily favored joining the Union. One dissenting voice expressed itself in verse not long after the United States' offer became known. The poem highlighted the resentment felt by many

Texans over having been spurned twice before as well as the *conditional* nature of the latest offer. Describing Cupid's attempts to convince the reluctant American damsel to accept the pleas of her ardent Texan suitor, the poet lamented,

Cupid turn'd in disgust from the sport he had started;
Broke his bow and his arrows—thus Hymen departed.[32]

American Chargé d'Affaires Andrew Donelson understood that his country's offer might offend more sensitive Texans. He therefore adopted a conciliatory tone but, nevertheless, stressed that *neither* side found *all* aspects of the proposed merger to its liking:

> But reference is made to such objections, not to ascertain their justness or unjustness on this occasion; but to remark, on the part of the United States, that much was conceded to obtain the passage of the resolution. And it was also believed that a like spirit would induce Texas to overlook minor considerations, relying on that high sense of honor and magnanimity which governs both the people and the representatives of the United States, to secure to her hereafter, all that she can reasonably desire, to place her on the most favorable footing with the other members of the Union.[33]

Congress opened the special session June 16, 1845. Both houses heard Donelson's letter and the American resolution before beginning deliberations. Santa Fe Expedition leader Hugh McLeod, now the Bexar County representative, charged Anson Jones with "attempting to thwart the people in their well known wish to reunite themselves to the great political family of the United States, and throw them afloat again upon the troubled sea of a separate existence." To prevent this he wanted to void the republic's government and replacing it with an *ad interim* administration that would rule until statehood took effect. The House declined his revolution. On June 19 members of both houses voted on a proposal to accept statehood. Not a single one said no.[34]

As his friends said good-bye to Vice President Kenneth Anderson at the closing of the special Senate session June 28, 1845, many figured that they would next greet him as "Governor." With Sam Houston's assistance, Anderson's star had risen continuously in the republic since his arrival from Tennessee in 1837. During a stint as San Augustine County sheriff he studied law, then served as a customs collector in the Lamar administration before being elected to Congress in 1841. After gaining the House speakership, he endeared himself further to Sam Houston by leading an unsuccessful attempt to impeach President Lamar and Vice President Burnet. Anderson faced no serious opposition in his vice presidential campaign after the death of his chief rival, Patrick Jack. Now he struck out for home after closing the Senate session as a leading candidate for the governorship of the nascent state of Texas.

Anderson made only eighteen miles before stopping at Fanthorp Inn to rest from the fever that had gripped him since the Senate adjournment. There he died on July 3, the day before the constitutional convention was to open in Austin. The remains of the last vice president of the Republic of Texas now rest in the Fanthorp Cemetery not far from the inn.[35]

After a rushed journey from New Orleans, Sam Houston learned on the road outside of Nashville, Tennessee that his lifelong benefactor was dead. That Andrew Jackson was in frail health was common knowledge. Nevertheless, Houston had planned his trip from Texas anticipating a chance to say good-bye. Once at Jackson's bedside the Hero of San Jacinto therefore broke down and cried. He picked up two-year-old Sam, Jr., held the boy above the bed, and urged him to remember the face of the one man the ever-confident Houston likely saw as his better.[36]

Less than a month after Andrew Jackson's death, elected delegates on July 4, 1845, gathered in Austin in obedience of Anson Jones's call for a constitutional convention. While they cheered the anniversary of the US Declaration of Independence, the few remaining residents of their nation's nominal capital must also have experienced joy at the opening of the first government session held in their dying city in three years. And they would have celebrated wildly a week later to read Section 32 in the newly proposed Texas state constitution then under debate: "The first session of the General Assembly; after the adoption of this Constitution by the Congress of the United States, shall be held at the city of Austin, the present Seat of Government, and thereafter, until the year one thousand eight hundred and fifty, and until the Legislature shall otherwise provide by law for a temporary or permanent Seat of Government."[37] Not long thereafter, one newspaper report suggested that Austin's salvation was not yet a sure thing: "The members of the Convention are becoming a little more excitable as time progresses. . . . The seat of government question, I think, is destined to raise a row, the 'West' having divided upon it, between La Grange and Austin."[38]

Within days of the convention's opening in Austin, delegate William Ochiltree already disliked what he saw of the proceedings. On July 8, 1845, he wrote to Anson Jones urging the president to come to the city as soon as possible because "your enemies are actively, busily at work to undermine you." Ochiltree felt that, given the absence of the administration, convention delegates were making decisions that properly belonged to the chief executive and his cabinet. Jones did not yet feel the time was right for his presence, but promised in a note to himself, "I will go to Austin in good time and crush this revolutionary plan—but not just now."[39]

William Ochiltree was not the only delegate sensing danger at the convention. On July 25, James Farquhar wrote to a still absent Jones to report, "I find considerable excitement among the members of the Convention. I am certain of one thing, that is, if you do not come up we will get into confusion."[40] Van Irion's warning was more explicit: "From what I have seen, I believe it is the intention of some of the members of the Convention to make an attempt to destroy and abolish the present existing Government, and to establish in its stead *one* of a provisional character."

Ochiltree again expressed alarm on August 6:

We have been very anxiously expecting you up for several days past, and your friends are much disappointed that you have not come. The Convention is rapidly drawing to a close, and I find the opinion gaining ground, that on the passage of the Constitution by the Convention it will operate as a *supersedeas* of the present Government. . . . Your presence would do much to allay the feeling which a few persons are most industriously endeavoring to get up.

Jones privately affected contempt for the threat to his government: "This letter is important as showing how far the arts of emissaries had extended. I stayed, however, long enough from Austin to show I was not to be frightened, and went up there soon enough to save the country from anarchy."[41] Finally, on August 14, the Washington-based *Texas National Register* reported, "The President, accompanied by the Secretary of State and Treasurer, set out on Monday, on a visit of a few days to the city of Austin." With his arrival in what he saw as the lawful capital, President Anson Jones brought national government back to Austin and ended what he had derisively called "the Hegira from the city."[42]

Whatever interest some western delegates had in La Grange as a state capital fizzled. A newspaper report toward the end of the convention noted, "Various places were nominated, in committee of the whole, but utterly failed."[43] When the assembly adjourned on August 28, Section 35 of the new state constitution elated those who had stuck it out in Austin. Their city would host state government until 1850, at which point a statewide election would determine a site until 1870. What would happen after that remained unclear. But no matter, the delegates' choice of Austin for now breathed new life into a city on the brink of extinction. Austin mattered once more.

By the fall of 1845 the United States had formally invited Texas to join its union, and the Republic of Texas had accepted the invitation and written a state constitution, but until that constitution gained acceptance in the US Congress, Texas continued as an independent country. President Jones returned to Washington, but only to prepare for the government move back to Austin. In early September Travis County voters reelected William Cazneau as their representative to the Tenth Congress, which never met. The following month Washington residents read a newspaper notice of their town's imminent demotion: "We are authorized to state that the government offices at Washington on the Brazos, will be closed on the 4th inst., preparatory to their removal to Austin." An indication of Austin's regained status appeared in the same edition: "A company of U. S. troops will shortly be stationed at Austin. The proper officers have already arrived there. The troops will occupy the arsenal buildings as barracks."[44] And with the October 9 issue of the *Texas National Register*, a news blackout engulfed Washington: "The Register will hereafter be published at the City of Austin. . . . We respectfully request that our exchanges be addressed to us at that place, instead of Washington."

Early Austin settlers looking for adventure in the 1840s often traveled into the hills west of town. After taking in the spectacular view from the crest of the tallest peak, the more intrepid ones could ride a bit farther north to a 150-foot tall cliff towering above Bull Creek. A thrilling scramble about ten feet down the cliff face brought the traveler to a small ledge fronting a small cave entrance. By then a steady drone emanating from the cave competed with the rumbling of the creek below. A continuous stream of black dots whizzed into and out of the cave mouth. Once inside the cavern, visitors marveled at the sight of countless masses of bees and honeycombs, stretching back as far as vision in the dim light allowed. Area residents saw a potential fortune in that cave, for "if its treasures could be extracted readily, they would doubtless be found far more valuable, than the contents of any silver or gold mine, that adventurers have been seeking for years, in that section."[45]

Likewise, Texans once again saw fortunes to be extracted from doing business in the once moribund city of Austin. Samuel Stone set up a twenty-four-hour ferry across the Colorado near the home of a man named Luckett. John "Rip" Ford acquired the *Texas National Register* at

On February 19, 1846, Anson Jones lowered the Texas flag in a ceremony at the capitol in Austin to mark the end of the Republic of Texas. Regarding the subsequent raising of the American flag, Noah Smithwick observed, "Methinks the star in the lower left hand corner should have been especially dedicated to Texas." Courtesy of Prints & Photographs Collection, Annexation, CN03085, the Dolph Briscoe Center for American History, University of Texas at Austin.

Washington, moved it to Austin, and resumed publication under the banner *Texas Democrat*. Augustus Fischer advertised legal services, mentioning in particular a willingness to transact business at the Land Office or the Supreme Court, "where members of the bar have too far a distance to travel to attend to the same."[46] And Francis Dieterich returned to the city he had helped feed in its infancy.

This time Dieterich merely shifted his location and not his product line. By November 15, 1845, he was operating a dry goods and grocery in the old store building of Alexander Russell.[47] A few weeks later Dieterich notified newspaper readers of his purchase of W. W. Thompson's one-time tavern. Promising good service and reasonable prices, the new innkeeper foresaw that "if steady attention, and a determination to do every thing in his power to please, will avail any thing, the undersigned conceives his portion of patronage will be flattering and *profitable.*"[48]

When the United States Congress approved the state constitution sent to it by the Republic of Texas on December 29, 1845, that independent country technically ceased to exist. But it was not until the following February 19 that Anson Jones, the last president of the republic, performed his last official act. Three days into the first legislative session of the newest American state, President Jones ascended the steps of the capitol and, while watched in breathless silence by a large crowd of spectators, lowered the Lone Star flag. As the president reverently folded the beloved banner, he evoked the tears of onlookers by pronouncing, "The republic of Texas is no more." But a roar of approval at the hoisting of the Stars and Stripes quickly transformed the somber mood into one of wild celebration. Nevertheless, proud Texans at the time would certainly have agreed with Noah Smithwick's later comment, "Methinks the star in the lower left hand corner should have been especially dedicated to Texas."[49]

March 8, 1846, found every resident of Austin straining their eyes eastward from the bank of the Colorado River at the foot of town. As the steamboat *Kate Ward*—the first to visit Austin—came into view, a United States Army officer named Beal gave an order and a cannon blast rocked the air. People shouted, but, according to one spectator, "cheers and huzzahs conveyed but imperfectly the joy which enlivened every heart." The 115-foot-long vessel boasted eight compartments and twin engines supplying seven horsepower each. Three days later a large number of thrilled citizens crowded the boat's deck for a pleasure cruise on the river. A short distance from town passengers spied a group of Indians staring at them from the shore. One observer interpreted their scowling demeanor as a sign of comprehension that the *Kate Ward* signaled "the forerunner of their expulsion."[50] As the ship steamed back toward Austin, passengers could look up the Avenue and see the capitol building in the distance. And, although the building itself would prove temporary, the city's status as the capital of Texas would not. Mirabeau Lamar's dream of a permanent government seat at Austin was at last reality.

EPILOGUE

Austin survived two state-wide elections to finally gain official recognition as the permanent seat of government of Texas. The constitutionally mandated election of 1850, in which voters were to pick a capital for the next twenty years, resulted in an easy victory for the city. The pace of work involved in reorganizing the state after the Civil War delayed the 1870 vote by two years, but in 1872 Austin again won handily against its closest competitors, Houston and Waco. Thus, while the government of the Republic of Texas assembled at seven different locations in nine years, the state of Texas has had only one seat of government in its 161-year history.

Little of the Republic of Texas remains in Austin. Of the buildings mentioned in this book, only the French Legation survives. Dr. Joseph Robertson, one of the city's earliest residents, purchased the property from Mosely Baker in 1848. Ten years later his twelve-year-old daughter Julia painted a landscape of the house and grounds still on view inside the structure. In 1948 Dr. Robertson's descendents sold the complex to the state of Texas. It overlooks modern downtown Austin as a museum administered by the Daughters of the Republic of Texas.

Mirabeau Lamar's presidential mansion fell into such disrepair that the next president, Sam Houston, refused occupancy. Fire destroyed the building in 1847. A school for girls, St. Mary's Academy, built an impressive limestone structure on the site in 1885, which soon gained a reputation as an Austin landmark. Alas, when the school moved in 1947 the building was razed. Subsequent owners lowered the hill by several feet and built a large hotel and shopping complex covering the entire block.

Nor did "Lamar's folly" long survive the republic. The state erected a stone building in 1853 on the site chosen by Edwin Waller for the permanent capitol. Benjamin Noble's original wood edifice was torn down in 1857. The Texas government donated the land at Hickory (Eighth) and Colorado Streets to the city with the stipulation that it must use it for a city hall and market house. The resulting municipal building was torn down and rebuilt in 1905, then extensively remodeled in the 1930s. This building still stands, although municipal government has moved on. The 1853 capitol was lost to an 1881 fire. The state hastily constructed a temporary capitol on the southwest corner of Congress and Eleventh Street. This building housed the first classes of the University of Texas in 1883 before burning in 1899. The present pink limestone Texas capitol opened in 1888.

Richard and Mary Bullock's hotel lasted until 1875. Change in ownership prompted a name change to Swisher's in 1852 and Smith's in 1858. The hotel's demolition made way for an elaborate store building that was completed in 1876 on what came to be known as Cook's Corner. Long before then Abner Cook had graduated from constructing outhouses and one-room churches to become Austin's most prominent master builder. Although the buildings at Cook's Corner have disappeared, many other Cook creations, such as the governor's mansion and Woodlawn have not.

Austin's waterways yet flow but bear little resemblance to their ancestors. Colorado River floodwaters intermittently inundated the city throughout the nineteenth and early twentieth centuries. The first dam across the river failed with catastrophic results only five years after its completion in 1895. Its replacement did not prevent occasional disasters, the most recent of which occurred in 1935. Subsequent construction of a series of dams upriver created the "Chain of Lakes." This, plus an improved dam within the city, finally tamed the river. A dam downriver created Town Lake, recently renamed Lady Bird Lake in honor of Lady Bird Johnson. Canoes and kayaks now glide past cyclists, walkers, and runners on the trails following the shoreline.

No one swims in Shoal Creek any more. Dry for much of the year, the stream when flowing is usually filled with trash and debris. An ancient Indian trail leading from the creek mouth northward is now a hike-and-bike trail. Exercisers passing Gideon White's 1840s home site just north of Thirty-Fourth Street might relax under a grove of oak trees that shaded the ill-fated settler and his family.

Waller Creek has fared no better but faces a brighter future. The city recently found the necessary funding to begin construction of a tunnel near Fifteenth Street to divert floodwater to Lady Bird Lake. This is aimed at encouraging the development of an urban river walk lined with parkland, stores, and restaurants. Whether this dream becomes reality remains to be seen.

Just as they did in the 1840s, Austin visitors continue to flock to Billy Barton's springs. A tunnel diverts Barton Creek around the springs themselves, the flow of which is captured by a small dam to form an enormous and beautiful swimming pool. Bathers still marvel at fish darting around their feet and thrill at experiencing the cold shock of the chilly water on a hot summer day.

Austin's "mountains" west of town now lie well within the city limits. The tallest peak, Mount Bonnell, from which Sam Houston and Three-Legged Willie stared in awestruck wonder, is easily accessible by car. Those climbing the stairway from the parking lot at the crest of the hill enjoy a panoramic view of the Austin skyline and Colorado River (called Lake Austin at this point). To the north and west lies the country that previously served as a refuge for raiding parties of Comanches. Now houses, a country club, and office buildings compete with trees as occupants of the landscape.

Some of Austin's most prominent early residents ended up elsewhere, including the man who built the city, Edwin Waller. Not long after participating in the Battle of Plum Creek he moved to Austin County, which he represented at the Secession Convention in 1861. Because he was the only delegate in attendance who had signed the Texas Declaration of Independence, Waller was invited to be the first after the convention president to sign the secession ordinance. Edwin Waller died in 1881; his remains lie in the Texas State Cemetery in Austin.

Angelina Eberly, who may or may not have fired the cannon during the Archives War, moved to Lavaca in 1846 and Indianola in 1851. Indianola became a major nineteenth-century port but was destroyed beyond salvation by hurricanes in 1875 and 1886. The feisty Eberly did not witness those catastrophes, having passed away in 1860.

Francis Dieterich's second attempt at a career in Austin succeeded. His mercantile business supported his family until his death in 1860. Granddaughter Dora Dieterich Bonham gained prominence with her 1958 biography of Francis titled *Merchant to the Republic*.

After moving with his family to Austin in 1846, Frank Brown spent the rest of his long life as a city resident. Upon retirement in the 1890s he compiled the *Annals of Travis County and the City of Austin*, a valuable source of information on Austin life from its founding to the dawn of the twentieth century. Brown passed away at age seventy-nine in 1913.

Julia Lee Sinks eventually moved about forty-five miles east of Austin to Giddings. She became a frequent contributor of newspaper and journal articles about the lives of Texas's early Anglo settlers. In 1896 she wrote a series of articles about Austin's formative years, which appeared in the *Dallas Morning News* and the *Galveston News*. She died in 1904.

John Darlington, whose concern for the ancient oak trees under which Edwin Waller auctioned off the first city lots contributed to their preservation, was one of central Texas's oldest residents at his 1915 death at the age of ninety-four.

William Walsh, whose father Dennis helped construct the first buildings in Austin, died at the age of eighty-eight in 1924. He served on the board of public works during the construction of the city's first dam in 1895 and was also instrumental in the construction of the Confederate Veterans' Home on West Sixth Street. His series of articles in the *Austin Statesman* shortly before his death provides a fascinating look at early city history.

Edward Burleson served as a soldier and spy during the United States' War with Mexico. He and a business partner laid out the town of San Marcos in 1847. The following year he introduced a Senate resolution establishing Hays County on the southern border of Travis County, then donated land for the county courthouse. He died of pneumonia in 1851 while a member of the state Senate.

Anson Jones found little political success after his term as Texas president. Repeatedly passed over by the state legislature as a candidate for the US Senate, Jones became increasingly despondent until taking his own life in 1858. His plantation home is now a museum at Washington-on-the-Brazos State Historic Site.

Alphonse de Saligny's experience in Texas did not enhance his diplomatic career. He nevertheless remained in government service until being accused of shady financial dealings in Mexico in 1863. He never again worked for the French government and died in 1888 in Normandy.

Mirabeau Lamar never again directly challenged Sam Houston for political supremacy in Texas. With the death of daughter Rebecca in 1843, he temporarily withdrew from public life and turned his energies to poetry. Outbreak of war with Mexico in 1846 roused him from self-imposed exile; he joined the army as a lieutenant colonel under Zachary Taylor and fought at the Battle of Monterrey. Once a civilian again, Lamar represented San Patricio and Nueces Counties in the Texas legislature. In 1851 he married Henrietta Moffitt. Six years later he was appointed United States Minister to Nicaragua and Costa Rica. At about the same time he published a compilation of his poetry titled *Verse Memorials*. In 1859 Mirabeau Lamar completed his foreign service and returned to his plantation at Richmond. Two months later, on December 19, 1859, he died of a heart attack at the age of sixty-one.

Despite his repeated assertions of intentions to the contrary, Sam Houston never left the stage of Texas politics. Soon after annexation he accepted election by the Texas legislature to the US Senate, where he remained until 1859. His name often found itself on the short list of those bandied about for the presidency during the 1840s and 1850s. Support for the Kansas-Nebraska Act in 1855 earned him an official condemnation from the state legislature, which in turn voted him out of his Senate seat.

Houston ran unsuccessfully for governor in 1857. Two years later he found vindication by defeating the incumbent, Hardin Runnels, then missed by a whisker of receiving the National Union Party's presidential nomination in 1860. Houston's refusal to swear a loyalty oath to the Confederacy after secession proved the final straw for many Texans frustrated by his years of support for the union. After being evicted from the governor's chair, he moved with his wife and family to Huntsville, where he succumbed to pneumonia on July 26, 1863.

Mirabeau Lamar was never one to require affirmation of his righteousness. But if, while gazing into the distance from the porch of his presidential mansion in Austin, he could have received a glimpse of the future, any shred of self-doubt would likely have fled from his mind. In stark contrast to Lamar's Austin, today's city is a thriving metropolis in the heart of a prosperous state. While it never quite became "The Manufacturing Center of the South" envisioned by late-nineteenth century city leaders, Austin today attracts thousands of new residents annually with job opportunities, a relaxed atmosphere, and great natural beauty. A growing music industry validates the slogan "Live Music Capital of the World," while an intense local pride in individualism inspires residents to encourage each other to "Keep Austin Weird." But the heart of the city— in fact, its very reason for existence—shines every two years when the people's representatives gather from afar in the pink limestone edifice situated on the hill from which Mirabeau Lamar first imagined a glorious empire. And visitors to this place in Austin have a hard time imagining that it has ever been, or would ever be, anything but the permanent seat of government of the state of Texas.

NOTES

Chapter 1

1. As the crow flies, Hornsby's Bend lay about eight miles downriver, with the town of Bastrop another twenty-two miles downstream. A traveler following the river would have covered significantly greater distances.
2. Gammel, *The Laws of Texas 1822–1897*, 2:52; Barkley, *History of Travis County and Austin 1839–1899*, 13.
3. Gulick, *The Papers of Mirabeau Buonaparte Lamar,* item number 763, 183; *The Handbook of Texas Online,* s.v. "James Collinsworth."
4. Gulick, *The Papers of Mirabeau Buonaparte Lamar,* 161, item number 757.
5. Barkley, *History of Travis County and Austin,* 7; *The Handbook of Texas Online,* s.v. "Fort Colorado." The fort was also known as Fort Colorado. A historic marker on Highway 969 near Walnut Creek marks the fort's location. There are no visible ruins.
6. *The Handbook of Texas Online,* s.v. "Edward Burleson"; Barkley, *History of Travis County and Austin,* 12; *The Handbook of Texas Online,* s.v. "Waterloo"; *The Handbook of Texas Online,* s.v. "Jacob Harrell"; Barkley, *History of Travis County and Austin,* 31–32. The northbound portion of this trail now forms the Shoal Creek Hike and Bike Trail; the old trail turned west at modern Thirty-Fourth Street, which now approximates the old path. In Austin's early days this was still the westward route out of town.
7. *The Handbook of Texas Online,* s.v. "Waterloo." A document in the Austin City Lots file in the Texas State Archives lists the following as receiving compensation for land taken by the republic for the construction of Austin: James Baker, H. N. Baker, W. R. Baker, Joseph Barnhart, B. D. Bassford, Neri Chamberlain, R. T. Chandler, J. M. Harrell, Anderson Harrell, W. H. Miller, Joel Miner, B. B. Peck, and Samuel Fowler.
8. Terrell, *The City of Austin From 1839 to 1865.*
9. The *Northern Standard,* Sept 17, 1842, quoted in Sheppard, *An Editor's View of Early Texas.*
10. Terrell, *The City of Austin From 1839 to 1865.*
11. Lawrence, *Texas in 1840, Or the Emigrant's Guide to the New Republic,* 63; Roemer, *Texas,* 170; Settler George Flood to his mother in Ohio, November 27, 1840, George Flood biography file, Dolph Briscoe Center for American History, University of Texas at Austin; Thomas Bell Papers, Dolph Briscoe Center for American History, University of Texas at Austin; Gulick, *The Papers of Mirabeau Buonaparte Lamar,* item number 529.

12. Winkler, *The Seat of Government of Texas*; Brown, *Annals of Travis County and the City of Austin,* chap. 6; Gulick, *The Papers of Mirabeau Buonaparte Lamar,* item number 587. Edwin Waller used this phrase in a letter to Lamar written shortly after he arrived in the area for the first time.
13. Terrell, *The City of Austin From 1839 to 1865.*

Chapter 2

1. Fannin later achieved fame as the Texan commander captured with his army by the Mexicans at the Battle of Coleto Creek (near Goliad) in March 1836. Under orders from Santa Anna, and contrary to his own wishes, Mexican commander Jose de Urrea directed his soldiers to execute Fannin and his approximately four hundred men. The Goliad Massacre, as it quickly became known, together with Santa Anna's brutality at the Alamo, sparked the murderous fury displayed by the victorious Texans at the Battle of San Jacinto. For an excellent account of the incident see Brands, *Lone Star Nation,* 387–407.
2. Fontaine, *Mirabeau B. Lamar, Third President of the Republic of Texas,* 5; Gulick, *The Papers of Mirabeau Buonaparte Lamar,* item number 746, 166; *The Handbook of Texas Online,* s.v. "Mirabeau Buonaparte Lamar."
3. Gulick, *The Papers of Mirabeau Buonaparte Lamar,* item number 746, 167. Lamar wrote that he "received intelligence from Texas which induced me to abandon my private affairs to their fate, and hasten back to this country [Texas] with all possible speed."
4. Barker, *The San Jacinto Campaign*; David Burnet Papers, Dolph Briscoe Center For American History, University of Texas at Austin.
5. Bryant, *Texas Almanac 1872 ;* Fontaine, *Mirabeau B. Lamar,* 9 ; Moore, *Eighteen Minutes: The Battle of San Jacinto and the Texas Independence Campaign,* 278–79.
6. Fontaine, *Mirabeau B. Lamar,* 10; Moore, *Eighteen Minutes,* 290.
7. Moore, *Eighteen Minutes,* 350.
8. Ibid., 394; "The Reminiscences of Mrs. Dilue Harris, Part II."
9. Fontaine, *Mirabeau B. Lamar,* 14. "To Santa Anna," *Telegraph and Texas Register,* August 16, 1836.
10. In chronological order, these were Washington, Harrisburg, Galveston, the San Jacinto battlefield, Velasco, and Columbia.
11. Winkler, "The Seat of Government of Texas I"; *The Handbook of Texas Online,* s.v. "Washington."
12. The Barrington Living History Farm, one-time home of Anson Jones, the last president of the Republic of Texas, lies within the limits of modern Washington-on-the-Brazos State Historic Site, but is outside the original township.
13. Winkler, "The Seat of Government of Texas I"; *The Handbook of Texas Online,* s.v. "Washington."
14. Johnson, *A History of Texas and Texans,* 1:389.

15. *Laws of the Republic of Texas,* 1:18; Winkler, "The Seat of Government of Texas I"; Barker, "The San Jacinto Campaign"; Moore, *Eighteen Minutes,* 189.

16. Moore, *Eighteen Minutes,* 207; de la Pena, *With Santa Anna in Texas: A Personal Narrative of the Revolution,* 114.

17. Winkler, "The Seat of Government of Texas I"; Jackson, *Voyages of the Steamboat Yellow Stone,* xix, 134; *Telegraph and Texas Register,* September 6, 1836, September 13, 1836. The *Yellow Stone* required approximately ten cords of wood as fuel for a single day's travel. A cord consisted of a stack of four-foot lengths measuring eight feet wide and four feet high. Since there were no trees on Galveston Island, stocking the steamship relied on the time-consuming method of gathering driftwood.

18. Holley, *Texas,* 121–22; Fields, "David Gouverneur Burnet"; Winkler, "The Seat of Government of Texas I."

19. Description of people from Asa Brigham to his sister, March 8, 1835, Brigham Papers, Dolph Briscoe Center for American History, University of Texas at Austin; Winkler, "The Seat of Government of Texas I."

20. *Telegraph and Texas Register,* August 30, 1836. In a letter to a friend that was intended for publication, Houston wrote, "You will learn that I have yielded to the wishes of my friends in allowing my name to be run for President. The crisis required it or I would not have yielded. Duty, I hope, will not always require this sacrifice of my repose and quiet" (Ibid.) Throughout his lengthy career Houston repeatedly demonstrated his preference for the excitement of political office over the tranquility of private life.

21. *Senate Journal, Republic of Texas: First Congress, First Session,* 10, 27.

22. Thomas Lubbock survived the war. He participated in the siege at Bexar in December 1835 and then went to work on a steamboat in the upper Brazos River. He did not learn of Santa Anna's invasion of Texas until after the Battle of San Jacinto.

23. The newspaper followed the government during and after the revolution. Gail Borden founded the *Telegraph and Texas Register* at San Felipe de Austin in 1835. Borden fled with his equipment to Harrisburg in an unsuccessful attempt to escape Santa Anna's army, which ransacked the newspaper's office and threw the printing press into Buffalo Bayou. After receiving new machinery from Cincinnati, Borden resumed publication in Columbia August 2, 1836.

24. *The Handbook of Texas Online,* s.v. "Lubbock, Thomas Saltus"; Lubbock, *Six Decades in Texas,* 36, 48; *The Handbook of Texas Online,* s.v. "Telegraph and Texas Register"; Winkler, "The Seat of Government of Texas I."

25. *Senate Journal, Republic of Texas: First Congress, First Session,* 39; *The Handbook of Texas Online,* s.v. "Groce's Retreat"; *Senate Journal, Republic of Texas: First Congress, First Session,* 49; *Journals of the House of Representatives of the Republic of Texas: First Congress, First Session,* 146, 147. Groce's Retreat lay twelve miles south of present-day Navasota on the east bank of the Brazos River.

26. The details of the various proposals are from Winkler, "The Seat of Government of Texas I."

27. *Senate Journal, Republic of Texas: First Congress, First Session,* 67; Gammel, *The Laws of Texas 1822–1897,* 1:78.

28. This design was favored by early settlers throughout Texas. The dog run provided cooler quarters than the enclosed rooms during the stifling summer heat. Audubon referred to Sam Houston's house as being "after the Southern fashion" (Herrick, *Audubon the Naturalist,* 2:164).

29. Connor, et al., *Capitols of Texas,* 62–63.

30. Lubbock, *Six Decades in Texas or Memoirs of Francis Richard Lubbock,* 45–46; "The Reminiscences of Mrs. Dilue Harris, Part II." The Allens had first tried unsuccessfully to purchase the town of Harrisburg.

31. *Telegraph and Texas Register,* October 11, 1836. The Allen brothers placed an ad to publicize the new city of Houston.

32. Ibid.; Gammel, *The Laws of Texas 1822–1897,* 1:78; *The Handbook of Texas Online,* s.v. "Augustus Chapman Allen."

33. "The Reminiscences of Mrs. Dilue Harris, Part II."

34. Lubbock explained this by writing "the navigation after entering the bayou was good, with plenty of water and breadth" (Lubbock, *Six Decades in Texas,* 45, 46).

35. According to Lubbock, "no boat had ever been above this place" (Ibid).

36. Ibid.

37. *Houston and Galveston in the Years 1837–1838,* passim. A reprint of two articles from the *Hesperian, or Western Magazine,* Columbus, Ohio, 1838; Diary of John Winfield Scott Dancy, Dancy Papers, Dolph Briscoe Center for American History, University of Texas at Austin.

38. *Telegraph and Texas Register,* January 27, 1837; Morris, *Miscellany,* 343.

39. *The Handbook of Texas Online,* s.v. "Telegraph and Texas Register"; Winkler, "The Seat of Government of Texas I."

40. *Telegraph and Texas Register,* March 21, 1837, May 2, 1837; Lubbock, *Six Decades in Texas,* 53; *Journal of the House of Representatives of the Republic of Texas: First Congress, Second Session,* 20; *Journals of the Senate of the Republic of Texas: First Congress, Second Session,* 6; Winkler, "The Seat of Government of Texas I."

41. Lubbock, *Six Decades in Texas,* 54, 66, 67.

42. *Journal of the House of Representatives of the Republic of Texas, Second Congress 1837–1838.* The House then indefinitely tabled the proposal and did not address it again during that session.

43. "The Reminiscences of Mrs. Dilue Harris II."

44. *Telegraph and Texas Register,* May 16, 1837.

45. Ibid., October 11, 1837; *Alexandria Gazette,* as quoted in the *Telegraph and Texas Register,* January 20, 1838.

46. *Telegraph and Texas Register,* October 14, 1837.

47. Winkler, "The Seat of Government of Texas II"; Williams and Barker, *The*

Writings of Sam Houston, 1813–1863, 2:190. Houston wrote this February 1, 1838. In describing the house he lived in he wrote, "Four windows in it, and not one pane of glass nor shutter—three doors, and shutters to but two—no ceiling and the floor loose laid. Is not this a 'White House' with a plague to it?"

Chapter 3

1. Congressional journals of the Republic of Texas frequently employ this phrase.
2. *Telegraph and Texas Register,* October 14, 1837.
3. *Journals of the Senate of the Called Session of Congress Convened at the City of Houston, on the 25th Day of September, 1837; and of the Regular Session, on the Sixth Day of November, 1837,* 20; Gammel, *The Laws of Texas 1822–1897,* 1:1346–47.
4. *The Handbook of Texas Online,* s.v. "Old San Antonio Road."
5. *Journal of the House of Representatives of the Republic of Texas, Second Congress 1837–1838,* 62.
6. *Journals of the Senate of the Called Session of Congress Convened at the City of Houston, on the 25th Day of September, 1837; and of the Regular Session, on the Sixth Day of November, 1837,* 31, 38.
7. Winkler, "The Seat of Government of Texas II."
8. *The Handbook of Texas Online,* s.v. "Bastrop"; Winkler, "The Seat of Government of Texas II."
9. Winkler, "The Seat of Government of Texas II."
10. Ibid.
11. Jones of Brazoria, Burleson, Hill, Lumpkin, and Rowlett were chosen. Menifee was added as a sixth member after a motion by Sutherland.
12. Rusk, Sutherland, and Gant were given this task.
13. *Journal of the House of Representatives of the Republic of Texas, Second Congress 1837–1838,* 147; *Journals of the Senate of the Called Session of Congress Convened at the City of Houston, on the 25th Day of September, 1837; and of the Regular Session, on the Sixth Day of November, 1837,* 68, 75. The Senate selected Augustine, Barnett, Everitt, Rains, and Dana. When Augustine resigned November 25, Burton took his place.
14. *Journals of the Senate of the Called Session of Congress Convened at the City of Houston, on the 25th Day of September, 1837; and of the Regular Session, on the Sixth Day of November, 1837,* 87, 138. Winkler, "The Seat of Government of Texas II."
15. Dancy Papers, Dolph Briscoe Center for American History, University of Texas at Austin. On March 5, 1838, John Dancy wrote in his diary, "This was the day appointed for the commissioners, who were to select a suitable site for the location of the Seat of Government, to meet at La Grange. Two had already arrived, and one arrived afterwards making a majority of the five."
16. Ibid.

17. *Journals of the Senate of the Called Session of Congress Convened at the City of Houston, on the 25th Day of September, 1837; and of the Regular Session, on the Sixth Day of November, 1837,* 9–10.

18. *Journal of the House of Representatives of the Republic of Texas, Second Congress 1837–1838,* 43–44, 56–58; *Journals of the Senate of the Called Session of Congress Convened at the City of Houston, on the 25th Day of September, 1837; and of the Regular Session, on the Sixth Day of November, 1837,* 15, 33.

19. Winkler, "The Seat of Government of Texas II."

20. The House journal states that the Senate would appear at 3:30. The Senate journal states that the meeting began at 3:00 p.m.

21. *Journals of the Senate of the Called Session of Congress Convened at the City of Houston, on the 25th Day of September, 1837; and of the Regular Session, on the Sixth Day of November, 1837,* 52–53.

Here is the complete list of sponsors and nominees:

Sponsor	Location
Robertson	Nashville
Sutherland	Eblin's League on the Colorado
Burleson	Bastrop
Wilson	Black's Place in Montgomery County
Gazley	Houston
Jones of Austin County	San Felipe on the Brazos
Boyd	Nacogdoches
Wilson	Groce's Retreat in Montgomery County
Everitt	Comanche
Jones of Austin County	The Mound League in Washington County

22. Ibid.

Here is the complete balloting:

First vote:			
	Senate	House	Total
Nashville	1	2	3

Eblin's league	5	14	19
Black's place	1	4	5
Bastrop		4	4
San Felipe	1	1	2
Nacogdoches	3	2	5
Comanche	1	1	2
Mound league	1	1	2
Washington		1	1

Second vote:			
	Senate	**House**	**Total**
Nashville	1	1	
Eblin's league	7	20	27
Bastrop		1	1
Black's place	3	7	10
Mound league	1	1	2
Washington		1	1
San Antonio		1	1

23. *Journal of the House of Representatives of the Republic of Texas, Second Congress*, 108, 113; *Journals of the Senate of the Called Session of Congress Convened at the City of Houston, on the 25th Day of September, 1837; and of the Regular Session, on the Sixth Day of November, 1837*, 68–73. Burton also tried twice to table the bill until the next session of Congress. All of his proposals were defeated by the same 7-to-5 vote, with Senators Everitt, Robertson, Somerville, and Wilson consistently siding with Burton. These same five cast the only dissenting votes against the bill's final passage.

24. *Journal of the House of Representatives of the Republic of Texas, Second Congress*, 162–63.

25. The vote went against Rusk 16-to-7.

26. *Journal of the House of Representatives of the Republic of Texas, Second Congress*, 163, 166–68. The bill would have started the selection process over. Each house of Congress was to choose between two to four locations for consideration by the voters. At least one site had to be east of and one site west of the Brazos River. The commissions formed for the purpose would have until July 15, 1838, to announce their results. The president would then issue a proclamation calling for a general election at the next congressional elections in the fall.

27. Ibid., 97–98. Rusk voted for Black's league on both ballots.

28. Ibid., 169.

Chapter 4

1. Haley, *Sam Houston,* 9. Oolooteka was called John Jolly by local whites. The island lay in the Hiwassee upstream from its drainage into the Tennessee River.
2. Ibid., 12.
3. Also known as the Iroquois.
4. Houston received this promotion about four months after his enlistment.
5. This was Major Lemuel P. Montgomery, namesake of the Alabama city of Montgomery.
6. The barbed arrow remained fast after the man's first attempt. Houston then threatened the reluctant lieutenant with his sword, and a second effort proved successful.
7. Haley, *Sam Houston,* 14–15.
8. Present-day Oklahoma.
9. *The Handbook of Texas Online,* s.v. "Samuel Houston."
10. Christian, "Mirabeau Buonaparte Lamar." Christian, who wrote a brief biography of Lamar for the *Southwestern Historical Quarterly* in 1920, concluded that Lamar had only been a contributor to the newspaper, not its editor.
11. Lamar, Mirabeau, *Verse Memorials,* 109.
12. Ibid., 174.
13. Lubbock, *Six Decades in Texas,* 93.
14. Mary Austin Holley was a cousin of Stephen F. Austin. She was also an author who wrote a travelogue of Texas and several popular novels pertaining to Texas history.
15. Roberts, *The Personal Correspondence of Sam Houston,* 1:211; Holley, "The Texas Diary," 44; Ashbel Smith Papers, Dolph Briscoe Center for American History, University of Texas at Austin; Frederic Gaillardet, *Sketches of Early Texas and Louisiana,* 57.
16. Gulick, *The Papers of Mirabeau Buonaparte Lamar,* item number193; Moore, *Eighteen Minutes,* 290, 310.
17. Gulick, *The Papers of Mirabeau Buonaparte Lamar,* item number553, 561.
18. Armstrong is referring to Sam Houston.
19. At that time Houston was the congressman from San Augustine.
20. Gulick, *The Papers of Mirabeau Buonaparte Lamar,* item number 152, 537, 538. Secretary of the Navy Samuel Rhoades Fisher authored this phrase.
21. Roberts, *The Personal Correspondence of Sam Houston,* 1:135, 141, 148.
22. Gulick, *The Papers of Mirabeau Buonaparte Lamar,* item number 266, 267; Roberts, *The Personal Correspondence of Sam Houston, 1839–1845,* 1:125.

Chapter 5

1. "Allen's Reminiscences of Texas, 1838–1842," 287–304. Lamar's nervousness that day was noted by Senate chaplain William Y. Allen.
2. *Telegraph and Texas Register,* December 12, 1838; Haley, *Sam Houston,* 208.
3. *Journal of the House of Representatives, Third Congress,* 124. Lamar had 6,995

votes to Wilson's 252.

4. As related in the Introduction.

5. *Journal of the House of Representatives, Third Congress,* 124.

6. Anson Jones Papers, Dolph Briscoe Center for American History, University of Texas at Austin.

7. As quoted in *The Morning Star,* November 12, 1839.

8. *Telegraph and Texas Register,* December 12, 1838.

9. Ibid.; *Daily Picayune,* December 19, 1838, as found in the Bernard Bee Papers, Dolph Briscoe Center for American History, University of Texas at Austin; *Telegraph and Texas Register,* December 12, 1838.

10. "Allen's Reminiscences of Texas, 1838–1842."

11. To replace the deceased James Collinsworth, who had committed suicide July 11, 1838 during his campaign for the presidency.

12. *Journal of the House of Representatives, Third Congress,* 53.

13. *The Handbook of Texas Online,* s.v. "Moseley Baker." That Mosely Baker, who sustained a long-running feud with Sam Houston, would offer this proposal is surprising. During Houston's retreat after the fall of the Alamo, Baker, as captain of a volunteer company, refused an order from General Houston to abandon his position on the Brazos River. Before finally joining the march east several days later, he ordered his men to burn the town of San Felipe, which he afterwards defended by claiming that Houston had ordered the town's destruction. Houston denied this. Later, as a member of the First Congress, Baker authored articles of impeachment against President Houston.

14. *Journal of the House of Representatives, Third Congress,* 133.

15. Ibid., 196, 200–201. The committee was comprised of congressmen Bunton, Menifee, Hill, Butler, Jones, Roman, and Cullen. David Kaufman of Nacogdoches and Edward Holmes of Matagorda each offered unsuccessful amendments moving the eastern boundary from the Brazos River to the Trinity River.

16. Ibid., 202–3.

17. *Telegraph and Texas Register,* January 5, 1839.

18. When a bill is engrossed, it is prepared for its third and final reading, after which the vote for or against passage is taken.

19. The four dissenters were Lawrence, Joseph Bennett of Montgomery County, Hugh Johnston of Liberty County, and Isaac Parker of Houston County.

20. Lawrence did not follow through with this promise.

21. *Journal of the House of Representatives, Third Congress,* 223, 228, 229, 232. Nay votes came from Mosely Baker, William Lawrence, and Holland Coffee of Fannin County.

22. Representing Washington and Montgomery counties.

23. *Journal of the Senate of the Republic of Texas: First Session of the Third Congress 1838,* 6, 27, 65, 70, 100–101. Wilson was re-elected by his constituents in a special election January 11, 1839. While Wilson blew a trumpet, celebrants hoisted the victor onto their shoulders and carried him into the

Senate chamber, interrupting its deliberations. Wilson was later arrested and brought before the Senate, but two attempts at official reprimand failed.

24. Ibid., 82.

25. *Journal of the House of Representatives, Third Congress*, 267.

26. Ibid., 296, 297, 329–31. Ashbel Smith, a one-time roommate of Sam Houston, was in attendance that day at the Senate's request. The fight occurred during a brief recess of the Senate. A House investigating committee later advised that the House take no action, given that Smith was on Senate business at the time of the incident. House members rejected this advice and instead asked President Lamar to dismiss Dr. Smith from his position as army surgeon general.

27. Gammel, *The Laws of Texas, 1822–1897*, 2:161–65. The law also stipulated that no more than one league was to be purchased at the maximum price of three dollars per acre. The five commissioners would be paid eight dollars a day, with half given up front and the rest upon completion of their duties. Once the president had received the commission's report, he would appoint an agent to survey 640 acres upon which, under his supervision, the town would be constructed. Congress allotted one hundred thousand dollars to carry out the provisions of the law.

28. *Journal of the Senate of the Republic of Texas: First Session of the Third Congress 1838,* 108–9. Horton was a senator representing Matagorda, Jackson, and Victoria counties in the First and Second Congresses. He was one of the two vice presidential candidates defeated by David Burnet. At the time of his appointment, Burton represented two eastern counties, Nacogdoches and Houston.

29. *Journal of the House of Representatives, Third Congress,* 358.

30. *Matagorda Bulletin,* August 9, 1838, January 24, 1839; Winkler, "The Seat of Government of Texas II," 185–245. Lamar campaigned for president in favor of placing the seat of government west of the Brazos River.

31. *Journal of the House of Representatives, Third Congress,* 340, 362; *Journal of the Senate of the Republic of Texas: First Session of the Third Congress 1838,* 116.

32. Wallace, et al., *Documents of Texas History,* 132. Horton signed as chairman in the commission's report on April 13, 1839.

33. The information on the five commissioners was obtained from each man's biography in *The Handbook of Texas Online.*

34. Winkler, "The Seat of Government of Texas II," 185–245; Adair and Perry, *Austin and Commodore Perry,* 18; Bernard Bee Papers, Dolph Briscoe Center for American History, University of Texas at Austin. A March 19, 1839, article in the New Orleans *Daily Picayune* noted, "It is still the general impression that the next session of Congress will convene at Houston, as the commissioners appointed to locate the new seat of government have not yet fixed upon a place. The difficulty in erecting suitable buildings for the President, the Executive Departments, and Congress itself, in so short a time as intervenes before the next session, appear to us a very good reason why Congress should meet again at Houston."

35. Near present-day Marlin in Falls County.

36. Near present-day Marble Falls.

37. *Morning Star,* April 12, 1839; Stiff, *The Texan Emigrant,* 31. The commissioners placed a brief announcement of their decision in the April 15, 1839, edition of the *Morning Star.*

38. Wallace, *Documents of Texas History,* 131–32.

39. *Morning Star,* April 27, 1839.

Chapter 6

1. *The Handbook of Texas Online,* s.v. "Webberville, Texas." Early Austin residents referred to the area as Webber's Prairie. Later it became the town of Webberville.

2. Gulick, ed., *The Papers of Mirabeau Buonaparte Lamar,* item number 529.

3. Wallace, et al., *Documents of Texas History,* 132; Smither, 6–7.

4. *The Handbook of Texas Online, s.v.* "Houston Morning Star." Published in Houston, the *Morning Star* debuted April 8, 1839.

5. *Morning Star,* April 12, 1839, April 20, 1839, April 30, 1839.

6. *Telegraph and Texas Register,* April 17, 1839; *Morning Star,* April 17, 1839; Anson Jones journal, September 16, 1839, Anson Jones Papers, Dolph Briscoe Center for American History, University of Texas at Austin.

7. Gulick, *The Papers of Mirabeau Buonaparte Lamar,* item number 530; Lawrence, A. B., *Texas in 1840, Or the Emigrant's Guide to the New Republic,* 68–69; *Telegraph and Texas Register,* May 1, 1839.

8. Thomas Bell Papers, Dolph Briscoe Center for American History, University of Texas at Austin.

9. John Winfield Scott Dancy Papers, Dolph Briscoe Center for American History, University of Texas at Austin.

10. Wallace, et al., *Documents of Texas History,* 130–32.

11. *Telegraph and Texas Register,* April 21, 1839; *Morning Star,* May 31, 1839; June 19, 1839; June 12, 1839; June 29, 1839; July 1, 1839.

12. *Morning Star,* July 18, 1839.

13. *Telegraph and Texas Register,* July 31, 1839; *Matagorda Bulletin,* May 2, 1839; *Telegraph and Texas Register,* June 12, 1839.

14. *Telegraph and Texas Register,* May 1, 1839.

15. *The Handbook of Texas Online,* s.v. "Ayuntamiento." Under Mexican rule of Texas, the ayuntamiento was a local governing body whose members were elected by popular vote.

16. Fulton, ed., *Diary and Letters of Josiah Gregg: Southwestern Enterprises, 1840–1847,* 110.

17. A. S. Burleson to Professor Samuel Asbury, December 6, 1922, Edward Burleson, Sr., Papers, Dolph Briscoe Center for American History, University of Texas at Austin. A. S. Burleson is Edward Burleson's grandson.

18. Jenkins and Kesselus, *Edward Burleson, Texas Frontier Leader,* 159–60. This tract contained some of the most beautiful scenery in modern Austin,

including the grounds of Mayfield Park and the Austin Museum of Art at Laguna Gloria. Austin was never able to acquire clear title to the land.

19. *The Handbook of Texas Online,* s.v., "James Perry." James Perry married Stephen F. Austin's sister Emily in 1824. He moved his family to Texas in 1830 to settle on a land grant arranged by his empressario brother-in-law.

20. Edward Burleson, Sr., Papers, Dolph Briscoe Center for American History, University of Texas at Austin; Jenkins and Kesselus, *Edward Burleson, Texas Frontier Leader,* 160; *The Handbook of Texas Online,* s.v., "Jacob Harrell."

21. *Morning Star,* April 15, 1839; *Telegraph and Texas Register,* May 1, 1839.

22. *Telegraph and Texas Register,* May 1, 1839.

23. Mount Bonnell is now known to possess the highest natural elevation within the city of Austin.

24. *Telegraph and Texas Register,* May 1, 1839.

25. *The Handbook of Texas Online,* s.v., "Montopolis, Texas." Jesse Tannehill laid out the town of Montopolis four miles southeast of modern downtown Austin. Hampered in its growth by proximity to the new capital, Montopolis survived until 1951, when it was annexed by the city of Austin.

26. James F. and Stephen S. Perry Papers, Dolph Briscoe Center for American History, University of Texas at Austin, as quoted in Jenkins and Kesselus, *Edward Burleson, Texas Frontier Leader,* 162–63.

Chapter 7

1. A. B. Lawrence, *Texas in 1840,* 71–72; *A Visit Up the Colorado River: Extracts From an Anonymous Diary 17–25 July 1838,* 8. Lawrence heard this story from Barton in January 1840. Barton told him the incident had occurred "a few weeks since." Both the creek and the springs are now named for Barton. Barton Springs remains a popular swimming hole in Austin's Zilker Park and provides a view of the city's downtown skyline.

2. *The Handbook of Texas Online,* s.v., "William Barton"; *A Visit Up the Colorado River: Extracts From an Anonymous Diary 17–25 July 1838,* 8.

3. Wilbarger, *Indian Depredations in Texas,* 272; Lawrence, *Texas in 1840,* 71. Wilbarger claims that Barton wounded one of the party; Lawrence states that Barton's shot had no effect.

4. *The Handbook of Texas Online,* s.v., "Joseph Lee"; Wilbarger, *Indian Depredations in Texas,* 274. At the time of this incident, twenty-nine-year-old Joseph Lee was a new arrival in Texas. After Indians killed Travis County Chief Justice James W. Smith later that year, President Lamar appointed Lee to serve in Smith's place.

5. Peareson, *Sketch of the Life of Judge Edwin Waller,* 15; Gulick, ed., *The Papers of Mirabeau Buonaparte Lamar,* item number 244.

6. *The Handbook of Texas Online,* s.v., "Edwin Waller"; Peareson, *Sketch of the Life of Judge Edwin Waller,* 4, 7–8.

7. Under the Mexican government, the alcalde was a municipality's chief executive as well as the head of the regional ayuntamiento (*The Handbook of Texas*

Online, s.v. "Ayuntamiento" and "Alcalde").

8. Peareson, *Sketch of the Life of Judge Edwin Waller,* 9, 15; Ransom, box 2–9/25, folder 5, Texas State Archives.

9. *The Handbook of Texas Online,* s.v., "Francisco Xavier Mina"; *The Handbook of Texas Online,* s.v., "Bastrop County." The municipality was named for a Mexican rebel named Francisco Mina, who was executed by the Spanish colonial government in 1817.

10. *The Handbook of Texas Online,* s.v. "Travis County."

11. *The Handbook of Texas Online,* s.v. "Leander Calvin Cunningham." Cunningham, who moved to the area in 1833, was the first lawyer in Mina (Bastrop). He served in the Second Congress and was Bastrop County chief justice 1834–40.

12. *The Handbook of Texas Online,* s.v., "Logan Vandeveer ." Kentuckian Vandeveer suffered a serious injury at the Battle of San Jacinto. His name is inscribed on the battlefield monument. In 1853 he opened the first school in the town of Burnet, where a street still bears his name.

13. *The Handbook of Texas Online,* s.v. "Aaron Burleson." Youngest of the Burleson brothers, Aaron frequently served in expeditions commanded by Edward Burleson against Texas Indians. Aaron was among the party that captured Santa Anna after the Battle of San Jacinto.

14. *The Handbook of Texas Online,* s.v. "George Hancock." Hancock was one of the men assisting Deaf Smith in the destruction of Vince's Bridge at the Battle of San Jacinto. After moving to Austin in 1845, Hancock became one of the town's prominent citizens. He is buried in Oakwood Cemetery in Austin.

15. Austin File A8500 (2-a), Austin History Center. The commissioners reported the following land holdings:

George Neill	1/3 league or 1,476 acres
Logan Vandeveer	1/3 league or 1,476 acres
Aaron Burleson and George Hancock	1/3 league or 1,476 acres
Edward Burleson and J. Porter Brown	1/3 league or 1,476 acres
James Rodgers	1/3 league or 1,476 acres
Jacob Harrell	1 labor or 177 acres
Edward Burleson	1 labor or 177 acres

16. *The Handbook of Texas Online,* s.v. "William Pinkney Hill"; Austin File A8500 (2-a), Austin History Center. Jury members included Bartlett Sims, B. M. Clopton, John Brown, James Standiford, Jeptha Boyce, and James Linn; Seat of Government Papers, Texas State Archives. Hill served briefly as Bastrop mayor in 1839. He later became a prominent Texas judge both during and after the Civil War until his death in 1870.

17. Houstoun, *Texas and the Gulf of Mexico; or, Yachting in the New World,* 224, 230–31.

18. The modern driver follows Interstate 10 from Houston to Columbus, then takes Highway 71 to Austin. The other route involves Highway 290 leading from Houston to Brenham (near Washington-on-the-Brazos State Park), then on to Austin.

19. Lawrence, *Texas in 1840,* 28.

20. Ibid., 29–30.

21. Ibid., 31.

22. Ibid., 40

23. Ibid., 41–42.

24. Ibid., 46, 54.

25. Morris, *Miscellany,* 273–74.

26. Noah Smithwick, *The Evolution of a State,* 194; *Morning Star,* May 31, 1839, June 8, 1839.

27. Peareson, *Sketch of the Life of Judge Edwin Waller,* 11–12. The twelve were William T. Austin, Thomas G. Masterson, B. T. Archer, Thomas J. Green, William G. Hill, William Sims Hall, Samuel Whiting, John W. Hall, Louis P. Cooke, William Pettus, W. B. Aldridge, and Charles Donoho.

28. Box 2–10/945, Texas State Archives. These figures are from a memo written by Mirabeau Lamar October 6, 1839. Lamar added, "If this be deemed inadequate compensation he will have to apply to Congress for relief."

29. Brown, *Annals of Travis County and the City of Austin,* chap. 6.

30. Gammel, *The Laws of Texas 1822–1897,* 2:165. This was the amount appropriated by Congress in its act locating the seat of government.

31. *Morning Star,* June 8, 1839.

32. Republic Claims, Texas State Archives.

33. *Austin Statesman,* February 10, 1924; Gulick, *The Papers of Mirabeau Buonaparte Lamar,* item number 587. William C. Walsh, whose father, Dennis, was one of Waller's blacksmiths, recalled that the one-way trip in good weather took about three weeks. Waller wrote a letter to Mirabeau Lamar from Austin on May 23, twenty-one days after he and the wagons left Houston.

34. *Austin Statesman,* February 10, 1924; Brown, *Annals of Travis County and the City of Austin,* chap. 6. Brown claimed that "six, eight, or more cattle" pulled each wagon. The larger figure of six to eight yoke is from William Walsh.

35. *Austin Statesman,* February 10, 1924. The train evidently consisted almost exclusively of men. Walsh claimed that most of Waller's hands were single. Married men initially left their families at home as the trip was regarded as dangerous. Dennis Walsh accompanied the train from Houston to Austin but did not bring his family until January 1840.

36. Box 2–10/945, Texas State Archives. This information is from a bill of sale prepared by Forbes Brooks in Columbus.

37. Gulick, *The Papers of Mirabeau Buonaparte Lamar,* item number 568, 570.

38. Ibid., 587.

Chapter 8

1. Thomas Bell to his brother, August 7, 1839, Thomas Bell Papers, Dolph

Briscoe Center for American History, University of Texas at Austin.

2. Bell most likely was overly optimistic. The government paid between $3.00 and $3.50 per acre for the seat-of-government site.

3. Bell related these experiences in a letter to his brother, August 7, 1839, Thomas Bell Papers, Dolph Briscoe Center for American History, University of Texas at Austin; Austin; Galveston City Lots, Texas State Archives. Richard M. Spicer bought four lots in the first Austin sale. One he later forfeited for lack of payment. The three he kept were on block 69 and block 56. The block 69 property (lots 1 and 2) is located at modern East Sixth Street and Congress Avenue, now the site of the Littlefield Building. Spicer's other purchase, lot 7 of block 56, occupies the corner of East Sixth and Brazos Streets. Spicer presumably built his tavern on one of these lots.

4. Details of this encounter are from Moore, *Savage Frontier*, 2:202–8; Wilbarger, *Indian Depredations in Texas*, 157–65; and Report of Edward Burleson, May 22, 1839, Texas State Archives. The number of horses and mules captured is from Edward Burleson's official report of the encounter. Burleson received word of the chase May 17. He left Austin the next morning with about two hundred men to join the fight but encountered Rice's party on their return to Austin after the battle.

5. Edwin Waller to Mirabeau Lamar, May 23, 1839, in *The Papers of Mirabeau Buonaparte Lamar*, ed. Gulick, item number 587.

6. Gulick, ed., *The Papers of Mirabeau Buonaparte Lamar*, item number 587, 588.

7. Ibid.; *Morning Star*, May 10, 1839.

8. The creeks are so named on a map drawn in 1839 by L. J. Pilie from a survey by him and Charles Schoolfield.

9. Each block was marked out into twelve lots, with an alley separating two groups of six. Lots were twenty-three-by-forty-six feet. Waller selected this size in part because sawmills at the time typically cut logs into twelve-foot lengths. Thus, two logs overlapping by a foot would span a lot's width.

10. The 21.5 blocks break down as follows:

Public Square	4 separate blocks
Capitol Square	4 contiguous blocks
Courthouse	1/2 block
Jail	1/2 block
Armory	1 block
Penitentiary	4 contiguous blocks
University	1 block
Academy	1 block
Hospital	1 block
War Department	1/2 block
Navy	1/2 block

Postmaster	1/2 block
President's House	1/2 block
State Department	1/2 block
Treasury	1/2 block
Land Office	1/2 block
Attorney General	1/2 block
Market	1/2 block

11. Waller to Lamar, July 11, 1839, in *The Papers of Mirabeau Buonaparte Lamar,* ed. Gulick, item number 41.

12. Except for East Avenue, which was replaced by Interstate Highway 35, north-south streets retain their original names. From west to east these are West Avenue, Rio Grande Street, Nueces Street, San Antonio Street, Guadalupe Street, Lavaca Street, Colorado Street, Congress Avenue, Brazos Street, San Jacinto Boulevard, Trinity Street, Neches Street, Red River Street, Sabine Street, and IH35. Beginning at the river, cross streets and their modern names are as follows:

Original Name	Modern Name
Water Avenue	Cesar Chavez (First)
Live Oak Street	Second
Cypress Street	Third
Cedar Street	Fourth
Pine Street	Fifth
Pecan Street	Sixth
Bois d'Arc Street	Seventh
Hickory Street	Eighth
Ash Street	Ninth
Mulberry Street	Tenth
Mesquite Street	Eleventh
College Avenue	Twelfth
Peach Street	Thirteenth
Walnut Street	Fourteenth
North Avenue	Fifteenth

13. Seat of Government File, Texas State Archives. Waller agreed to pay the two men five thousand dollars for this work.

14. Waller to Lamar, May 30, 1839, in *The Papers of Mirabeau Buonaparte Lamar,* ed. Gulick, item number 1308.

15. *Austin Statesman,* January 27, 1924. This description is taken from the second installment of Captain W. C. Walsh's fourteen-part series on early Austin history, which appeared in the *Austin Statesman* between January 27, 1924 and April 27, 1924. Four-year-old William Walsh moved to Austin with his parents in 1840. Except for service during the Civil War, Walsh spent the rest of his life in Austin until his death August 30, 1924 (*The Handbook of Texas Online,* s.v. "William C. Walsh").

16. Republic Square is bounded by San Antonio, Guadalupe, Fourth, and Fifth Streets. The block is one of four set aside by Edwin Waller in 1839 for use as public squares. Only two of the four remain open, the other being Wooldridge Park on land bounded by Guadalupe, San Antonio, Ninth, and Tenth Streets.

17. This total is from Walsh's recollections in the *Austin Statesman,* January 27, 1924.

18. Created by Monroe Shipe in the 1890s, Hyde Park was Austin's first planned subdivision.

19. Terrell, "The City of Austin from 1839 to 1865," 113–28.

20. Wilbarger, *Indian Depredations in Texas,* 266–67; Barkley, *History of Travis County and Austin, 1839–1899,* 35. The corpse was the first buried in what is now Oakwood Cemetery.

21. *Austin Statesman,* January 27, 1924. The original Deep Eddy was a swimming hole in the Colorado River created by several underground springs emptying near a large rock protruding from the water. The rock caused local swirling currents, hence the area's name. Construction of Longhorn Dam formed Town Lake out of this section of river, and the rock is now under water. Modern Deep Eddy swimming pool, located in Eilers Park on the north bank above the original Deep Eddy rock, uses the same spring water that fed the old swimming hole. The park lies just west of Highway 1 (Mopac Expressway).

22. Edwin Waller to President Lamar, May 23, 1839, in *The Papers of Mirabeau Buonaparte Lamar,* ed. Gulick, item number 58; Barkley, *History of Travis County and Austin, 1839–1899,* 24–25, 37.

23. Barkley, *History of Travis County and Austin, 1839–1899,* 37. This spring was called Durham's Spring.

24. *Austin Statesman,* January 27, 1924; Moore, *Savage Frontier,* 2: 200–201; Republic Claims, Claim no. 125, ID no. 137165, http://www2.tsl.state.tx.us/trail/RepublicResults.jsp?page=9, Texas State Archives; Thomas Bell to his brother, November 18, 1839,Thomas Bell Papers, Dolph Briscoe Center for American History, University of Texas at Austin. Referring to his 1839 service for Waller, blacksmith Dennis Walsh noted in an 1858 petition that he "not only labored every day in behalf of the government and for the public alone, the length of time claimed by him, but he was also engaged the greater part of the time on Sunday, as the emergency of the times required."

25. Williamson, *Austin, Texas: An American Architectural History,* 9, 11; Gulick,

The Papers of Mirabeau Buonaparte Lamar, item number 11, 587. On May 23, 1839 Waller wrote Lamar, "The timber for your house is getting [*sic*] out; please inform me what position it would best please you to have it placed in; a central one or one more retired."

26. *Telegraph and Texas Register,* December 11, 1839; Julia Lee Sinks Vertical File, Dolph Briscoe Center for American History, University of Texas at Austin.

27. Lawrence, *Texas in 1840, Or The Emigrant's Guide to the New Republic,* 61; *The Handbook of Texas Online,* s.v. "Julia Lee Sinks"; Julia Lee Sinks Vertical File, Dolph Briscoe Center for American History, University of Texas at Austin; McCalla, *Adventures in Texas, Chiefly in the Spring and Summer of 1840,* 28–29. Julia Lee moved to Austin from Cincinnati with two brothers and a sister in the spring of 1840. Shortly thereafter she married George Sinks, at the time chief clerk of the post office of the republic.

28. An article in the December 11, 1839 *Telegraph and Texas Register* states that there was also a portico in the rear of the house.

29. *Telegraph and Texas Register,* December 11, 1839; Julie Lee Sinks, Dolph Briscoe Center for American History, University of Texas at Austin; Williamson, *Austin, Texas: An American Architectural History,* 12–13; Lubbock, *Six Decades in Texas,* 143; *Austin Statesman,* January 27, 1924. Lubbock first came to Austin as the republic's comptroller.

30. Williamson, *Austin, Texas: An American Architectural History,* 14; Brown, *Annals of Travis County and the City of Austin,* Chapter 7; Stiff, *The Texan Emigrant,* 33–34; Ferdinand Roemer, *Texas,* 170.

31. Brown, *Annals of Travis County and the City of Austin,* chap. 6; Williamson, *Austin, Texas: An American Architectural History,* 14.

32. In an article appearing December 11, 1839, the *Telegraph and Texas Register* described the capitol as 150-by-50 feet, with two 30-by-40 feet rooms separated by a twenty-foot hallway. Since the longer dimension consisted only of the two chambers and the dogtrot, the given room and hallway measurements are short by fifty to seventy feet. In addition, the capitol spanned only three lots measuring forty-six feet each, for a total of 138 feet. The 110 feet estimated by Williamson therefore seems more accurate.

33. *Austin Statesman,* January 27, 1924.

34. Unless otherwise noted, the details of the temporary capitol building are from Walsh's recollections in the January 27, 1924 *Austin Statesman.* Seymour Connor, one of the authors of *Capitols of Texas,* points out several discrepancies in Walsh's version. According to Connor, Edwin Waller's report to Congress in 1840 places the building on lots 9, 10, and 11 of block 98, while Walsh has it also covering the southwest corner lot, number 12. Walsh locates the chimneys several feet inside either end of the building, which to Connor seems an unlikely waste of space. Walsh also leaves out the central hallway, while other contemporary descriptions unanimously include it. Finally, Connor postulates the existence of columns in the main rooms to

support the heavy roof. Connor, et al., *Capitols of Texas,* 85.

35. *Austin Statesman,* January 27, 1924; Julia Lee Sinks Vertical File, Dolph Briscoe Center for American History, University of Texas at Austin; *Telegraph and Texas Register,* April 27, 1840; Gulick, *The Papers of Mirabeau Buonaparte Lamar,* item number 1738, 1743. H. Mollhausen had written to President Lamar in February 1840 offering to travel to Europe at his own expense and recommend Texas as suitable for emigration to Prussia, Russia, Austria, and "lesser powers." Lamar evidently did not take Mollhausen up on this offer, because the following month the Prussian, still in Austin, again wrote to the president with suggestions about artillery placement. Suggesting himself as commander of the cannon, Mollhausen signed the letter as "late Officer of Prussian Artillery."

36. *Austin City Gazette,* May 13, 1840, June 24, 1840.

37. George Grover to Charles Grover, June 17, 1840, Texas State Archives.

38. Gulick, *The Papers of Mirabeau Buonaparte Lamar,* item number 1329.

Chapter 9

1. Gulick, ed., *The Papers of Mirabeau Buonaparte Lamar,* item number 1430. This quote is from a letter written by W. H. Sandusky to H. J. Jewett in August 1839. William Sandusky assisted with the initial survey of Austin. He also made one of the earliest maps of the city.

2. Ibid., item number 1376. Mechanics were skilled craftsman. A letter from German immigrant William James to Mirabeau Lamar offering the services of himself and other "intelligent mechanics" mentions these specialties: painters and glaziers, carpenters, cabinet makers, brick makers, shoe and boot makers, tailors, Swiss straw hat manufacturers, butchers, and stonemasons.

3. Ibid., item number 1430.

4. *Austin Statesman,* January 27, 1924; Republic Claims Search, Claim no. 125, Texas State Archives. The details of Dennis Walsh's employment are from a petition he filed August 18, 1858. After the disagreement with Edwin Waller, Walsh's pride did not allow him to ask the agent for a certificate of service. His acquaintance Louis P. Cooke agreed to do so, but he delayed following through on his promise before fleeing the region around 1843 after killing a man. All of the documents proving Walsh's service went with Cooke. For several years, the blacksmith was prosperous enough that he forgot about his lost wages, but three years of financial misfortune led him to seek payment through his petition. Walsh eventually was awarded $312 for 156 days of service.

5. Bell, correspondence, August 7, 1839 and November 1, 1839. Thomas Bell Papers, Dolph Briscoe Center for American History, University of Texas at Austin.

6. Austin and Galveston City Lots File, Box 2–10/946, Texas State Archives. At the first public sale of lots August 1, 1839, Robert Spicer bought lots 1 and 2

on block 69 and lot 7 on block 56. His tavern was therefore presumably built either on the northeast corner of Brazos and Pecan Streets or the northwest corner of Congress Avenue and Pecan Street (now the site of the Littlefield Building); Bell, correspondence, November 18, 1839, Thomas Bell Papers, Dolph Briscoe Center for American History, University of Texas at Austin.

7. Seiders Family Papers, Austin History Center; Republic Claims Search, Un-numbered Claim 01, Texas State Archives. In 1839 Bastrop County included the city of Austin.

8. Republic Claims Search, Texas State Archives.

9. Republic Claims Search, Claim no. 3565, Texas State Archives.

10. Austin City Lots, Texas State Archives; Brown, *Annals of Travis County and the City of Austin,* chap. 7.

11. Waters, ed., *I Was Born in Slavery: Personal Accounts of Slavery in Texas,* 37–38.

12. Ibid., 119–20.

13. Ibid., 58.

14. *Texas Slave Narratives* website. Mary Ann is listed in the slave narratives by her married name of Patterson.

15. Hogan, *The Texas Republic: A Social and Economic History,* 23; Hollon, ed., *William Bollaert's Texas,* 272.

16. Hollon, ed., *William Bollaert's Texas,* 271, 293.

17. Ibid., Image 10900176; Lewis Porter's letter and the amounts paid by Waller are from documents in the Austin City Lots File in the Texas State Archives.

18. Hafertepe, *Abner Cook, Master Builder on the Texas Frontier,* 28. A nine-teenth-century master builder both designed and built his project. Cook arrived in Austin an unknown. By mid-century, he had become the premier master builder in the city. Extant Cook creations in modern Austin include Woodlawn (the one-time plantation home of Governor Marshall Pease), the Asylum for the Blind (now the Nowotny Building on the University of Texas campus), the Sampson-Henricks Building (today the oldest structure on Congress Avenue), and the Governor's Mansion.

19. *The Morning Star,* May 31, 1839, June 19, 1839; Gulick, ed., *The Papers of Mirabeau Buonaparte Lamar,* item number 1329. Burleson wrote his letter June 10, 1839; *The Morning Star,* June 8, 1839.

20. *The Morning Star,* July 18, 1839; *Telegraph and Texas Register,* July 31, 1839.

21. *Morning Star,* September 9, 1839; *Telegraph and Texas Register,* August 7, 1839.

22. *Morning Star,* April 30, 1839. Waller's newspaper advertisement contained sections 9 and 11 of the Seat of Government Act, which detailed the terms of the auction and the required payment schedule. Section 9 directed the agent to advertise: "For sale [the town's 640 acres], for ninety days, in all the public gazettes in the Republic, and also in the New Orleans Bulletin and Picayune."

23. *Morning Star,* June 29, 1839, June 19, 1839, August 12, 1839; Lamar, corre-spondence, August 19, 1839, in *The Papers of Mirabeau Buonaparte Lamar,*

ed. Gulick, item number 1413.

24. Ibid., item numbers 1363 and 1368. On July 15 Lamar approved a draft for the requested amount. Judge James Webb then took the cash to Waller in Austin.

25. Austin City Lots, Texas State Archives. These expenses are noted in an account submitted by Waller in 1840. The documents were printed by *The National Intelligencer* in Houston, whose editor was Samuel Whiting.

26. Gulick, ed., *The Papers of Mirabeau Buonaparte Lamar,* item number 1352. G. Everrette wrote to Lamar seeking the necessary approval June 24, 1839. He claimed that Waller's promise came in the presence of site selection commissioners Cooke and Campbell.

27. Ibid., item numbers 1390 and 1517. J. B. Ransom wrote to Lamar August 7, 1839 and reported, "Mr Henry a gentleman of veracity from Miss. has just arrived from Austin, & informs me that Doswell was the Auctioneer & that the first lot sold for $27,000." The auctioneer received a 5 percent commission, which amounted to the hefty sum of $9,129.25 for the first sale. Treasurer James Starr thought the compensation excessive for "a few days services in a capacity requiring the exercise of no rare latent or extraordinary prowess."

28. *Morning Star,* July 5, 1839. Eldredge also claimed that Congress had intentionally stricken the word "permanently" from the bill locating the seat of government.

29. Ibid. Eldredge reasoned that the law "interferes with a contract previously made . . . the law which removed the seat of government to the city of Houston." He also relied upon the claim that the post of commissioner constituted an office, meaning that serving members of Congress could not be commissioners July 27, 1839.

30. Ibid.

31. *The Handbook of Texas Online,* s.v. "John Washington Darlington"; *Austin Statesman,* April 16, 1911. Darlington added, "We laid off that public square for the benefit of those who might inhabit Austin. It is now diverted from its object, and I believe is leased out. It should be improved and beautified as a park for the people . . . I think some respect should be paid to the memory of the men who dedicated it as a public park." This city block is now Republic Square in downtown Austin. There is a historical marker near the live oak trees described by Darlington.

32. *Morning Star,* April 30, 1839. The Seat of Government Act stipulated that the auction would take place between 10:00 a.m. and 4:00 p.m. on the appointed day.

33. From a letter to the *Telegraph and Texas Register,* August 14, 1839.

34. Details of the purchases at the initial auction are from Austin and Galveston City Lots, Texas State Archives. Beatty's two lots are on the northwest corner of the intersection of Rio Grande and Mulberry (Tenth) Streets.

35. Austin City Lots, Texas State Archives; J. B. Ransom to Mirabeau Lamar, August 13, 1839, in *The Papers of Mirabeau Buonaparte Lamar,* ed. Gulick,

item number 1402.

36. Austin City Lots, Texas State Archives. The actual total was $182,585. Lot purchasers paid $47,935 in cash to Waller, the rest in promissory notes.

37. *Morning Star,* August 12, 1839; the *Picayune* editorial was reprinted in the *Telegraph and Texas Register* September 25, 1839. In those days almost all of the overland trade between Mexico and the United States passed through St. Louis. One of Mirabeau Lamar's main objectives in establishing Austin on the frontier was to divert this trade to Texas.

Chapter 10

1. Republic Claims Search, Texas State Archives. The actual contents of this particular iron chest are unknown. Other receipts describing wagons carrying Navy Department property list the items mentioned here.

2. *The Handbook of Texas Online,* s.v. "Samuel Alexander Roberts." Samuel Roberts had known Mirabeau Lamar when both lived in Georgia. Lamar briefly owned a store in Cahaba in partnership with Roberts's father. Samuel Roberts immigrated to Texas in 1837 on Lamar's advice and, in January 1839, was appointed notary public of Harrisburg County by President Lamar.

3. Gulick, ed., *The Papers of Mirabeau Buonaparte Lamar,* item number 1361; *The Morning Star,* August 12, 1839, September 10, 1839; Winkler, "The Seat of Government of Texas II," 185–245; *Telegraph and Texas Register,* October 9, 1839.

4. *The Handbook of Texas Online,* s.v. "John Pettit Borden"; Gammel, *The Laws of Texas 1822–1897,* 2:90–91; Gulick, ed., *The Papers of Mirabeau Buonaparte Lamar,* item number 1578. On January 23, 1839, President Lamar approved a supplemental bill to the Seat of Government Act which allocated "the sum of twenty thousand dollars, or so much thereof as may be necessary" for the transportation of the archives. The act also appears to call for constructing new government buildings from this same allocation. Borden later reported to Congress that he had spent $21,355 solely to move the archives.

5. Republic Claims Search, Texas State Archives. Another carpenter, William Rosenberry, received $160 for sixteen days labor in box construction.

6. Ibid. This dry goods store was owned by League, Andrews, and Company.

7. Ibid. Beatty earned ten dollars a day for this work.

8. Roemer, *Texas: With Particular Reference to German Immigration and the Physical Appearance of the Country,* 71. Roemer, writing of his Texas journey in 1845, states: "Many farmers occupy themselves with hauling goods during the winter months when work in the field does not require their presence at home."

9. Ibid. There are scores of receipts for wages paid to these laborers in the Texas State Archives. Some of these indicate as little as one dollar paid for carrying a single box to a wagon. This would seem to indicate that men loitered about Borden's crews in anticipation of picking up extra cash through the occasional odd job that might arise.

10. Ibid.

11. Ibid. Waples's pay receipt reads: "Recvd from John P. borden agent for removing the Archives of Government from Houston to Austin-ninety dollars. It being for 15 days services superintending the movement of the waggons on the road. Austin 7th Nov 1839 Joseph Waples."

12. Asa Brigham to Mirabeau Lamar, August 25, 1839, in *The Papers of Mirabeau Buonaparte Lamar*, ed. Gulick, item number 1420; Roemer, *Texas: With Particular Reference to German Immigration and the Physical Appearance of the Country*, 78–79.

13. Republic Claims Search, Texas State Archives. The load consisted of six hundred pounds of provisions, which were intended to supply twelve men for twenty days.

14. Ibid. John Borden kept a list of every voucher paid related to the move. With a single exception, all fall within the time period August 24, 1839, through October 3, 1839. Thomas William Ward did not receive his clerk's stipend of sixty-five dollars until October 28. Borden's term of employment stretched from August 26 until October 14.

15. *The Handbook of Texas Online*, s.v. "Reuben Hornsby"; Wilbarger, *Indian Depredations in Texas*, 8.

16. *Telegraph and Texas Register*, October 16, 1839. Reese was found with the smashed breech of his weapon still in his hands; Wilbarger, *Indian Depredations in Texas*, 19–20; *Telegraph and Texas Register*, October 16, 1839. Wilbarger gives Webster's first name as James and states that the fight occurred in 1838. Since he wrote his account many years later, I place more faith in the story appearing days after the incident in the *Telegraph and Texas Register*. The newspaper relates that the battle took place "about 10 days since." It lists the victims as two men named Reese of Brazoria, John Webster, John Stillwell, Willson Flesher of Virginia, Martin Watson of Scotland, Bazley, Nicholas Boyler, Milton Hicks of Kentucky, William Rice of Virginia, Albert Sillsbey of Kentucky, James Morton of Texas, a musician named Leusber, and a black slave belonging to Willson Flesher. Although the article claims that thirteen men were killed, it lists fourteen victims.

17. *Telegraph and Texas Register*, October 16, 1839; James Webb to Mirabeau Lamar, written from Bastrop, October 11, 1839, in *The Papers of Mirabeau Buonaparte Lamar*, ed. Gulick, item number 1368.

18. Webb served as acting Secretary of Treasury in March 1839 and as Secretary of State February 1839 through July 1839. Webb became Lamar's Attorney General on November 18, 1839.

19. James Webb to Mirabeau Lamar, October 11, 1839, in *The Papers of Mirabeau Buonaparte Lamar*, ed. Gulick, item number 1474.

20. Ibid., item number 1413.

21. *Morning Star*, September 27, 1839.

22. Ibid., October 7, 1839, as reprinted from *The Brazos Courier*.

23. Details of Mirabeau Lamar's entry into Austin and the reception dinner in

his honor are from an article in the *Austin City Gazette*, October 30, 1839. This was the first issue of Austin's first newspaper.

24. *Austin City Gazette*, October 30, 1839.

25. *Morning Star,* October 23, 1839. The *Morning Star* article is a fanciful, satiric account of Lamar's entry into Austin entitled "Grand Triumphal Entrée, of his Republican Highness Mirabeau I." The author has Lamar uttering these imaginary words:

> I cannot refrain from returning you my sincere thanks for the welcome, the cordial welcome I have this day received, and my joy at reaching a city where I shall be free from the persecutions of my enemies, or at least only hear them from afar, where I shall be among friends as well as subjects, who will
>
> 'Pass my imperfections by,
>
> Nor view them with a critic's eye.'
>
> Yes, my faithful subjects, here shall we be alone, and can manage the affairs of the nation at will—and in all my acts remember that I shall have an epecial eye to *your* and *my own* interest; as for the country and my enemies, they may all go the devil together.

26. Richard Bullock filed an undated petition to Congress, a transcript of which is in the Texas State Archives, in which he presents this history of the founding of his hotel. Edwin Waller, in a letter written December 13, 1839, verified his promise to withhold Bullock's lots from the first land sale. A transcript of Waller's letter is also found in the Texas State Archives.

27. This quote is from Bullock's petition.

28. *Austin Statesman,* April 6, 1924. Here is William Walsh's description of the hotel, written from memory in 1924:

> In describing the buildings in Austin, I neglected to mention one which, while not a public building, became by force of circumstances one of the most important in the city.
>
> This was Bullock's Hotel, or, as it came to be known, 'Bullock's fort.' It was situated at the northwest corner of the intersection of Congress Avenue and Sixth Street. The designers of the city had contemplated, when the sale of lots took place, that the choice properties would fall near and around Capitol Square. Much to their surprise, no bids were made for those lots but those at the crossing of Congress Avenue and Pecan (now Sixth Street) and the immediately continuous lots were bought at once. From that point two blocks south and three or four blocks east and one or two blocks west, the purchases were prompt and for several years, most of the building was in that section. Why this point should have such decided preference

was a mystery, and still greater mystery is found in the fact that, to this day, it has remained the business heart of the city. The hotel occupied a front of forty-six feet on the Avenue and ran back west on Sixth Street for some eighty feet. The architecture was in no sense original or imposing. The lower story was formed of the conventional double log cabin, with a twelve foot hall between. The logs here were hewn smooth and the corners carefully dove-tailed, so that but little 'chinking and dobbin' was needed. The second story, reached by a stairway in the hall, was of Bastrop pine. From the west end of the building proper, was a row of one story log cabins. From the end of this row, west to the alley, thence north forty-six feet, thence east to the northwest corner of the building, was a stockade of hewn logs of the same character as those surrounding the state building. The space enclosed was shaded with large oak and elms and was a pleasant resort in hot weather. In the center was a dug well furnishing abundance of water for all hands.

In our dark days it was arranged that, whenever Indians came, a kettle drum was beaten and all the women and children fled to the shelter of the fort. At the west end of the hall was placed our only piece of artillery, an eighteen pounder, which was kept loaded with grape-shot and so situated that one man could give it a start and it would roll through the hall and out into the street.

29. Unless noted otherwise, the information and quotes about Bullock's hotel in this paragraph are from "Early Days in Texas: Reminiscences of Julia Lee Sinks," which Sinks wrote for newspaper publication. There is a copy of her piece in the Julia Lee Sinks Vertical File, Dolph Briscoe Center for American History, University of Texas at Austin.
30. *Austin City Gazette,* October 30, 1839. Notable guests attending this dinner included Edward Burleson, Navy Secretary Louis P. Cooke, Secretary of War Albert Sydney Johnston, Treasury Secretary James Starr, Treasurer Asa Brigham, Army Paymaster Jacob Snively, Major Sturges, Thomas William Ward, and Quartermaster General of the Army William Gordon Cooke.
31. Jones was senator from Brazoria.
32. *Austin City Gazette*, November 12, 1839.
33. Republic Claims Search, Texas State Archives; Austin City Lots, Texas State Archives. I could find no record of the precise location of this dinner. A James Hall brought wagons 17 and 18 from Houston to Austin, but no one by that name purchased a lot in Austin at either the first or second offering. A man named John Hall bought lot 10 on block 54, which is on the south side of West Pecan Street between Lavaca and Colorado. If James and John

are the same man, then Houston's dinner would have occurred mere steps from Bullock's hotel.

34. Sam Houston to Anna Raguet, December 10, 1839, in *The Writings of Sam Houston 1813–1863,* ed. Williams and Barker, 2:322. Twenty-six years her elder, Sam Houston courted Anna Raguet for a time in the 1830s. After a final rift between the two, Houston's friend Robert Irion, who had served as a go-between for the pair, pushed his own suit and married Anna in the spring of 1840. For more on this threesome, see James Haley's biography of Houston, *Sam Houston.*

35. Details of the dinner for Sam Houston are from the *Austin City Gazette* of November 27, 1839, written by Samuel Whiting. A reprint of the article is found in Gulick, ed., *The Papers of Mirabeau Buonaparte Lamar,* item number 1544.

Chapter 11

1. *The Handbook of Texas Online,* s.v. "James Burke"; Austin and Galveston City Lots file, Texas State Archives.

2. The weekly *Austin City Gazette,* under editor Samuel Whiting, first appeared October 30, 1839.

3. *Texas Sentinel,* February 12, 1840. According to a newspaper notice advertising the sale of his Austin business, Burke owned lots 5, 6, and 7 of block 70, which included the southwest corner of Congress and Bois d'Arc and the southeast corner of Bois d'Arc and Colorado. His store and reading room faced Congress Avenue while a "comfortable Log House" sat to the rear facing Bois d'Arc Street.

4. *Austin City Gazette,* November 12, 1839.

5. Ibid., November 20, 1839, December 4, 1839.

6. *Austin City Gazette,* October 30, 1839, December 4, 1839; *Morning Star,* January 15, 1840. The *Star's* report noted that "the whole population, members of Congress, speculators, gamblers, loafers, and all, amounted to 856."

7. Contrary to what is seen in Hollywood westerns, faro and not poker was the most popular game of chance on the American frontier.

8. "Reminiscences of Julia Lee Sinks," Julia Lee Sinks Vertical File, Dolph Briscoe Center for American History, University of Texas at Austin. Building locations are from Williamson, *Austin, Texas: An American Architectural History,* 12.

9. Austin and Galveston City Lots, Texas State Archives; Terrell, "The City of Austin From 1839 to 1865." Alexander Russell purchased lots 6 and 7 on block 55 at the first auction in 1839. The $2,800 purchase price of lot 6 proved to be the largest of the day. Alex Terrell described the building as the first store in the city. Russell's store was a two-story frame house extending eighty feet back from its Congress Avenue front. The studding, sills, and joists were of mountain cedar; the planks for floors and weatherboarding were hand sawed.

10. Terrell, "The City of Austin From 1839 to 1865"; *The Handbook of Texas*

Online, s.v. "Hemphill, John"; Austin and Galveston City Lots, Texas State Archives. M. H. Beatty purchased this lot at the first auction in 1839. Alex Terrell recalled that John Hemphill and his slave Sabina lived in the cabin until 1853. Hemphill was an attorney practicing in Washington, Texas, when, in January 1840, Congress appointed him judge of the fourth judicial district. This appointment automatically placed Hemphill on the Supreme Court, meaning that the judge probably moved from Washington to Austin sometime after his January 20 confirmation.

11. "Reminiscences of Julia Lee Sinks," Julia Lee Sinks Vertical File, Dolph Briscoe Center for American History, University of Texas at Austin.

12. *Austin Statesman*, April 27, 1924; "Reminiscences of Julia Lee Sinks," Julia Lee Sinks Vertical File, Dolph Briscoe Center For American History, University of Texas at Austin. William Walsh, in the *Austin Statesman*, recalled that sometime between 1846 and 1852 Austin residents undertook the final clearing of Congress Avenue: "The first step was to grub up and remove the remaining stumps of trees [left] out at the laying out of the town." Citizens then hired Nelson Merrill to plough the entire avenue "to the proposed sidewalks." This job required six days, after which plans called for laying down green logs to form a roadway. Disaster struck in the form of ten straight days of heavy rains, leaving the avenue "impassable to man or beast."

13. Sam Houston to Anna Raguet, December 10, 1839, in *The Writings of Sam Houston 1813–1863*, eds. Williams and Barker, 2:322. Despite his illness, Houston may have written this letter from his seat in the House of Representatives. On December 18, 1840, he wrote to his wife Margaret, "My dear I always write in the Hall, for indeed I can not write in my room, as it is a thor'ofare [*sic*] when I am in it. . . . A constant prating is going on, and my ears are deafened by nonsense, and sound without reason" (Roberts, ed., *The Personal Correspondence of Sam Houston,* 1:50).

14. Smither, *Journals of the Fourth Congress of the Republic of Texas 1839–1840,* 1:2.

15. Ibid., 1:6–7. Advantages noted by Lamar included: "The centrality of its geographical position, the apparent healthfulness of its climate, the beauty of its scenery, the abundance and convenience of its material for constructing the most permanent edifices, its easy access to our maritime frontier, and its adaptation to protection against Indian depredation, thereby inviting settlements to one of the finest portions of our country."

16. Ibid., 2:27.

17. Winkler, "The Seat of Government of Texas," 185–245.

18. Ibid.; Smither, *Journals of the Fourth Congress of the Republic of Texas 1839–1840,* 2:93–94.

19. This withdrawal occurred in the context of Sam Houston and the army's eastward retreat leading up to the Battle of San Jacinto.

20. A paraphrased version of William Jack's entire speech is found in Smither,

Journals of the Fourth Congress of the Republic of Texas 1839–1840, 2:96–106.

21. Ibid., 107–12.
22. Ibid., 113–14.
23. Ibid., 115.
24. Ibid., 120.
25. *Austin City Gazette,* December 4, 1839.
26. Ibid. Menefee's motion and the subsequent House vote created excitement in the office of the *Austin City Gazette,* which reported, "We stop the press to say that the final vote has just been taken on the bill to submit the question on the removal of the Seat of Government, to the people—Thus—21 votes to reject the bill, and 16 in favor of submitting it to the people. Motion moved by the Hon. Wm. Menefee, of Colorado."
27. Ibid., December 25, 1839.
28. Jones represented Brazoria County.
29. Smither, *Journals of the Fourth Congress of the Republic of Texas 1839–1840,* 1:33, 35, 38, 169.
30. To read the entire act, see Gammel, *The Laws of Texas 1822–1897,* 2:386–91.
31. Jack made this statement in a letter to his Brazoria County constituents appearing in the *Brazos Courier,* December 3, 1839.

Chapter 12

1. *The Handbook of Texas Online,* s.v. "Robert McAlpirn Williamson." A San Jacinto veteran, Robert Williamson later served in the Fifth through Ninth Republic of Texas congresses. He is buried in the State Cemetery in Austin.
2. The modern name of this hill is Mount Bonnell. Much of the hill is now covered with expensive homes. There is a small park and observation post at the summit, which is reached from the parking area by climbing a stone stairway of about one hundred steps. The parking area is on Mount Bonnell Road, accessible from the south via West Thirty-Fifth Street and from the north via FM 2222. Mount Bonnell remains a popular tourist destination because of the excellent views of downtown Austin and Lake Austin (the dammed Colorado River) that it provides.
3. Brown, *Annals of Travis County and the City of Austin,* chap. 6.
4. Ibid.; Julia Lee Sinks Papers, Dolph Briscoe Center for American History, University of Texas. Frank Brown actually states that there was just one large log in front of the hotel. A sketch made by Julia Robertson to accompany Julia Lee Sinks's articles about early Austin, however, shows several.
5. Brown, *Annals of Travis County and the City of Austin,* chap. 6.
6. Terrell, "The City of Austin from 1839 to 1865."
7. *Austin City Gazette,* January 8, 1840.
8. Barkley, *History of Travis County and Austin 1839–1899,* 51; Brown, *Annals of Travis County and the City of Austin,* chap. 6; *Austin Statesman,* February 24, 1924. Walsh was only three years old when Waller became mayor. At the time of the election, his family had lived in Austin for only twelve days. His

opinion of Waller was obviously formed much later.

9. Brown, *Annals of Travis County and the City of Austin,* chap. 7; Barkley, *History of Travis County and Austin 1839–1899,* 54. The complete slate of elected officers is as follows:

Mayor	Edwin Waller
Aldermen	J. W. Garrity, Jacob M. Harrell, Moses Johnson, Nicholas McArthur, A. Savary, Charles Schoolfield, William Thompson, and Samuel Whiting
Treasurer	Francis Prentiss
Recorder	A. C. Hyde
Marshall	J. W. Hann.
Postmaster	A. C. Hyde
Sheriff	Wayne Barton (Wayne Barton's father was William "Uncle Billy" Barton)

10. *Austin City Gazette,* February 12, 1840.

11. McCalla, *Adventures in Texas,* 31; Joseph M. White to Mirabeau B. Lamar, June 1, 1839, in *The Papers of Mirabeau Buonaparte Lamar,* ed. Gulick, item number 1319. White wrote to Lamar in an attempt to persuade the president to grant five leagues of land to Italian exile Madame America Vespucci, a descendent of the explorer Amerigo Vespucci.

12. McDonnold, *History of the Cumberland Presbyterian Church,* 269; Brown, *Annals of Travis County and the City of Austin,* chap. 7.

13. Lawrence, *Texas in 1840, Or the Emigrant's Guide to the New Republic.,* 66–67.

14. Brown, *Annals of Travis County and the City of Austin,* chap. 7. As noted by Amos Roark in his January 1840 census.

15. Julia Lee Sinks Vertical File, Dolph Briscoe Center for American History, University of Texas at Austin. Julia Lee Sinks recalled that any public gathering requiring a meeting hall took place in the Senate chamber: "The senate chamber was the only public hall in the place. Why it was always chosen instead of congress hall I don't know, but it was the forum of the people for the public expression of all feelings. It was where they went to enjoy themselves by any manner or means; if it was preaching they went to the senate chamber; if it was the ministration of the ordinance of baptism or the Lord's Supper, they went to the senate chamber . . . So if a man deserved honor at the hands of the public . . . The people, young and old, met and decorated the senate chamber and tendered him the honor of a ball. If any military feat had been performed they decorated the senate chamber and made bravery feel by kindly smiles and congratulations their laurels as a benediction. If any envoy came from another nation . . The old senate chamber was made glorious with garlands."

16. George Bonnell, in his 1840 book *Topographical Descriptions of Texas,*

wrote, "A Presbyterian church has been commenced, and I understand the Methodists have one under contract" (as quoted in Kennedy, *Texas: The Rise, Progress, and Prospects of the Republic of Texas,* 785). The *Austin City Gazette* reported March 4, 1840, "The Presbyterians have already completed the frame of their new church."

17. Hafertepe, *Abner Cook, Master Builder on the Texas Frontier,* 28–30.

18. Ibid., 31; Brown, *Annals of Travis County and the City of Austin,* chap. 7. Cook owned lot 8 in block 71, which is on the south side of Bois d'Arc Street between Lavaca and Colorado Streets. The church lay just west of this. Frank Brown states that it was on the corner, which would be lot 12 of block 71.

19. *The Morning Star* of December 13, 1839 reported: "Two thousand dollars have already been subscribed for the erection of a church in the city of Austin, to be under the charge of the Presbyterians, but free to all other denominations."

20. Hafertepe, *Abner Cook, Master Builder on the Texas Frontier,* 30; *Texas Centinel,* October 7, 1841, as quoted in the Austin File Chronological 1841, Austin History Center; Hafertepe, 33. The *Texas Sentinel*'s name was changed to *Texas Centinel* on April 22, 1841. For further information on the history of the paper, see "Austin *Texas Sentinel* [1840–1841]," *Handbook of Texas Online* (http://www.tshaonline.org/handbook/online/articles/eeayz), accessed February 28, 2013. Published by the Texas State Historical Association.

21. Brown, *Annals of Travis County and the City of Austin,* chap. 7.

22. *Morning Star,* June 8, 1839.

23. A letter in the August 14, 1839, *Telegraph and Texas Register* claimed, "Crops in spite of all that has been said to the contrary, are quite abundant, and there is nothing to prevent a large emigration this fall. The people of the Colorado, anticipating a heavy demand for corn, commenced planting very early, and continued it late. Up to the middle of June, they were preparing ground and planting corn. Some of the late corn has been injured very much by the drought. This has been seized on by the enemies of Austin, and short crops and want of provisions has been wrung from one end of the republic to the other. People wishing to visit that place need have no fears of a famine."

24. *Morning Star,* October 21, 1839; Brown, *Annals of Travis County and the City of Austin,* chap. 7; *Texas Sentinel,* October 17, 1840.

25. Jenkins, ed., *Recollections of Early Texas, The Memoirs of John Holland Jenkins,* 202–4; *Austin Statesman,* February 17, 1924; Thomas William Ward Papers, Dolph Briscoe Center for American History, University of Texas at Austin. In a letter dated November 24, 1845, Jonathan Hull wrote from Houston to Ward, "I have sent you a box of Lemons which will arrive in Austin with his goods. I have been expecting to hear from you every mail for the last three or four weeks but as yet have not received anything from you since the order for the Potatoes onions beans etc."

26. Williams, *Travis County Residents Biographical Notes,* vol. 3, Austin History Center; *Austin Statesman,* February 17, 1924; Brewster Jayne Papers, Dolph

Bricoe Center for American History, University of Texas at Austin.

27. *Austin Statesman,* February 17, 1924.

28. *Daily Bulletin,* December 24, 1841, December 27, 1841; Brown, *Annals of Travis County and the City of Austin,* chap. 8.

29. Brown, *Annals of Travis County and the City of Austin,* chap. 6.

30. Thomas Ward to Sam Houston, February 23, 1842, Madge W. Hearn Papers, Dolph Briscoe Center For American History, University of Texas at Austin; *Austin Statesman,* February 10, 1924. On one such 1842 expedition with his friends, Walsh witnessed a group of Indians kill and scalp a man named William Fox as he worked in his corn field. The boys sprinted naked back to their homes near Congress Avenue and escaped. The relieved mothers at first hugged their children gratefully, but then, as Walsh reports, "our naked bodies were temptations too strong to be resisted [and] each mother, with tear-stained cheeks, was spanking her darling boy." In wonderment Walsh wrote, "Never having been a mother this proceeding is still a mystery to me." Thomas Ward wrote of this incident to Sam Houston: "Fox was shot through the breast, cut in the abdomen with a knife and scalped. A negro boy that was with him escaped."

31. Brown, *Annals of Travis County and the City of Austin,* chap. 11; George Grover to Charles Grover, June 16, 1840, Texas State Archives. Twenty-year-old George Grover moved with his father to Texas in 1839. They settled on a riverside plot of land about eight miles downriver from Austin and two miles east of Walnut Creek.

32. Brown, *Annals of Travis County and the City of Austin,* chap. 6. According to Brown, the race track was in the area of modern East Fifth and Comal Streets in east Austin. It was used until 1850, when a track was built in what is now the Hyde Park neighborhood.

33. *Morning Star,* February 11, 1840. At the time of this incident Everitt was the representative from Jasper County in the Fourth Congress.

34. George Grover to Charles Grover, June 17, 1840, Texas State Archives. In the 1920s a dam was placed on the creek below the springs to form a large swimming area. The creek is diverted around the pool, which therefore contains only spring water. The main springs are now under water beneath the diving board across from the bath house.

35. Brown, *Annals of Travis County and the City of Austin,* chap. 6 and 11.

36. *Austin City Gazette,* March 3, 1841. The ball took place February 26, 1841. Secretary of War Albert Sydney Johnston introduced Cooke to the assembly by remarking, "Ladies and gentlemen, permit me to introduce to you Col Wm. G. Cooke; a gallant soldier, who supported the cause of Texas in her darkest hour; the man we delight to honor." Cooke, a veteran of the Siege of Bexar, San Jacinto, and the Santa Fe Expedition, is interred in the State Cemetery in Austin.

37. Ibid., July 14, 1840.

38. *Morning Star,* March 10, 1840.

39. *Texas Sentinel*, April 15, 1840.

40. Lawrence, *Texas in 1840, Or the Emigrant's Guide to the New Republic,* 71. After meeting Barton, Lawrence wrote, "Before returning to town, we paid a visit to an aged man, the only resident we believe in the neighborhood on the southern side of the river."

Chapter 13

1. Lamar's essay is item number 13 in Gulick's *The Papers of Mirabeau Buonaparte Lamar.* Gulick, however, only includes a brief description of the piece. The complete essay is in the Mirabeau Lamar Papers, Texas State Archives.

2. Gulick, ed., *The Papers of Mirabeau Buonaparte Lamar,* item number 948. Lamar made these remarks in his first message to Congress as president December 21, 1838.

3. Wallace, et al., *Documents of Texas History,* 125, 128.

4. Anderson, *The Conquest of Texas: Ethnic Cleansing in the Promised Land, 1820–1875,* 177–78.

5. See chapter 7.

6. Edward Burleson to Mirabeau Lamar, May 22, 1839, Texas State Archives. Burleson wrote, "With much pleasure and satisfaction I transmit to you many (I consider important) documents that were a few days since taken from a party of Mexicans and Indians, that, you will find from the papers, were making their way to the northern Indians."

7. Reagan, "The Expulsion of the Cherokees from East Texas," 38–46. The elderly Bowles was, according to Reagan, the last of the defeated and retreating Cherokees to attempt to leave the battlefield. His horse disabled, Bowles dismounted and started to walk away from the Texans when Major Henry Connor shot him in the back. Still alive, Bowles attained a sitting position facing the Texans. As Reagan ran toward the wounded man "wishing to save his life," Captain Robert Smith walked up and shot the chief through the head.

8. John Welsh to Sam Houston, January 7, 1842, R. Niles Graham-Pease Collection (1840–1890), Austin History Center. Welsh, who lived near Austin in Webber's Prairie, sent Houston a mocking letter after Houston's failed attempt to remove the government archives from Austin. Welsh dared Houston to "try Ned Burleson's spunk-just try to move these papers, and old Ned will serve you just as he did your Cherokee brother when he took that Hat what you give to your Daddy Bowles."

9. Sibley, *Travelers in Texas 1761–1860,* 121.

10. *Morning Star,* February 28, 1840.

11. For more on the Comanche rise to prominence at the expense of other indigenous peoples see Hämäläinen, *The Comanche Empire,* and DeLay, *War of a Thousand Deserts: Indian Raids and the U. S.-Mexican War.*

12. Details of this incident are from Wilbarger, *Indian Depredations in Texas,* 145–48, and Jenkins, ed., *Recollections of Early Texas,* 56–57. Jenkins's account differs from Wilbarger's in stating that Mrs. Coleman died without a

word. Both agree that five-year-old Tommy was captured by the raiders. The Indians also carried off seven of Joel Robertson's slaves.

13. Lawrence, *Texas in 1840, Or the Emigrant's Guide to the New Republic,* 41, 46–47.

14. Barkley, *The History of Travis County and Austin 1839–1899,* 35. Development over the years has taken significant bites out of Sabine Street, which no longer exists between Seventh and Eleventh streets.

15. *Austin City Gazette,* January 20, 1841.

16. Brown, *Annals of Travis County and the City of Austin,* chap. 7. This chapter in Brown contains excerpts from Anson Jones's 1840 diary.

17. *Morning Star,* March 21, 1840. The Indians shot James Headley several times through the heart, slit his throat, and scalped him. Ward's body was found pierced with ten arrows and two bullet wounds.

18. *Austin City Gazette,* March 25, 1840; H. Mollhausen to Mirabeau Lamar, March 13, 1840, in *The Papers of Mirabeau Buonaparte Lamar,* ed. Gulick, item number 1743; *Austin City Gazette,* June 24, 1840.

19. *Austin City Gazette,* April 1, 1840.

20. Julia Lee Sinks Vertical File, Dolph Briscoe Center for American History, University of Texas at Austin.

21. Ibid.

22. *Austin City Gazette,* July 8, 1840. The community of Gilleland Creek no longer exists. It was on what is now Farm Road 969 about twelve miles east of downtown Austin. Gilleland Creek itself originates near Pflugerville and flows through the site of the old town of that name before meeting the Colorado River.

23. *San Augustine Journal and Advertiser,* undated, as quoted in the *Austin City Gazette,* December 16, 1840.

24. *Austin City Gazette,* December 16, 1840.

25. Details are from Linn, *Reminiscences of Fifty Years in Texas,* as quoted in the *Sons of DeWitt Colony Texas* website.

26. The details in this paragraph are from Wilbarger, *Indian Depredations in Texas,* 28–29.

27. Brazos, *Life of Robert Hall,* as quoted in the *Sons of DeWitt Colony Texas* website; conversation between Ezekiel Smith and his son French after the Battle of Plum Creek, from Nichols, *Now You Hear My Horn*; Huston's report to War Secretary T. B. Archer, August 12, 1840, as quoted in the *Sons of DeWitt Colony Texas* website.

Chapter 14

1. Julia Lee Sinks stated that de Saligny was one of her neighbors on West Pecan Street. Frank Brown recalled that de Saligny lived on the corner that in Brown's time was the home of a Dr. Swearingen. The Austin City Directory of 1887 lists Dr. Richard M. Swearingen's residence at 313 West Sixth, or the southeast corner of West Sixth and Guadalupe.

2. De Saligny to M. le Comte, March 16, 1839, 7–9; de Saligny to M. le Comte, April 17, 1839, in *Alphonse in Austin*, ed. Hart, 13.

3. De Saligny to M. le Marechal, January 30, 1840, in *Alphonse in Austin*, ed. Hart, 19.

4. Ibid., 31.

5. *Austin City Gazette,* November 18, 1840; Barker, ed., *The French Legation in Texas,* 170.

6. Hart, ed., *Alphonse in Austin* , 42, 44; Roberts, *The Personal Correspondence of Sam Houston,* 1:85; *Texas Centinel,* July 1, 1841. On January 31, 1841, Houston wrote to his wife, "My dear, I have just returned to the hall at 7 oclk. from dining with Mr. Saligny, and all that I drank was a thimble glass of 'absinth.'" Margaret Houston proved to be an effective reformer of her husband, as de Saligny noted in a letter written February 19, 1841, "General Houston's happy reformation of habits since his marriage, and the dignity with which he was able to conduct himself, despite several mistakes, during the last session, have made him regain all his popularity."

7. Denton, "Count Alphonse de Saligny and the Franco-Texienne Bill"; *Texas Centinel,* May 27, 1841.

8. De Saligny, official dispatch, February 19, 1841, in *Alphonse in Austin*, ed. Hart, 44.

9. *Texas Centinel,* July 1, 1841.

10. Ibid.

11. De Saligny to James Mayfield, February 19, 1841, in *Alphonse in Austin* , ed. Hart, 49.

12. This observation is from William Walsh, *Austin Statesman,* March 30, 1924.

13. De Saligny to Secretary of State Mayfield, March 21, 1840, in *Alphonse in Austin*, ed. Hart, 53.

14. *Austin Statesman,* March 30, 1924.

15. The details in this paragraph and those that follow are from de Saligny's correspondence with James Mayfield and Richard Bullock's petition to Acting President David Burnet, as they appear in Hart, ed., *Alphonse in Austin*, 49–56.

16. *Austin City Gazette,* March 31, 1841, May 5, 1841.

17. De Saligny, correspondence, June 23, 1842, June 29, 1842, in *The French Legation in Texas*, ed. Barker, 340–41.

18. Ibid., April 11, 1842, 301.

19. De Saligny's house and grounds remain in modern Austin as the French Legation Museum at 802 San Marcos Street.

Chapter 15

1. C. J. Berger to M. B. Lamar, undated, in *The Papers of Mirabeau Buonaparte Lamar,* ed. Gulick, item number 2410.

2. Gulick, ed., *The Papers of Mirabeau Buonaparte Lamar,* item number 2077.

3. Wallace, et al., *Documents of Texas History,* 131; *Austin City Gazette,* August 26, 1840, November 20, 1839.

4. Austin File Chronological, 1841, Austin History Center.

5. Gulick, ed., *The Papers of Mirabeau Buonaparte Lamar*, item number 913; William Jefferson Jones to Mirabeau Lamar, February 8, 1839, in *The Papers of Mirabeau Buonaparte Lamar*, ed. Gulick, item number 1049.

6. *New Orleans Bulletin*, January 3, 1842, as quoted in the *Austin City Gazette*, January 19, 1842.

7. Ibid.

8. *Journals of the House of Representatives of the Republic of Texas, Fifth Congress First Session*, 45; Fontaine, *Mirabeau Lamar, Third President of the Republic of Texas*, 19.

9. *Austin City Gazette*, April 28, 1841; Reuben M. Potter to Mirabeau Lamar, June 5, 1841, in *The Papers of Mirabeau Buonaparte Lamar*, ed. Gulick, item number 2040.

10. The town of Angelina was eight miles north of present-day Lufkin.

11. James Durst to Mirabeau Lamar, April 24, 1841, in *The Papers of Mirabeau Buonaparte Lamar*, ed. Gulick, item number 2010.

12. Spellman, *Forgotten Texas Leader*, 60; *Austin City Gazette*, June 9, 1841.

13. Spellman, *Forgotten Texas Leader*, 58; Edward Burleson to Mirabeau Lamar, June 4, 1841, in *The Papers of Mirabeau Buonaparte Lamar*, ed. Gulick, item number 2038.

14. Kendall, *Narrative of the Texan Santa Fe Expedition*, 1:20. George Kendall, who accompanied the expedition as an unofficial chronicler, noted this widespread sentiment in May 1841, shortly after arriving in Galveston on his way to Austin.

15. Ibid., 71–72. This was George Kendall's estimate. Contemporary writers often used the euphemism "servant" instead of the more accurate word "slave," but I have found no proof that Kendall did so in this instance.

16. This rendezvous occurred at Kenney's Fort near present-day Round Rock. There is now an historic marker identifying the spot on US Highway 79 about 2.5 miles east of Interstate Highway 35.

17. *Texas Sentinel*, June 10, 1841; *Austin City Gazette*, June 9, 1841.

18. McLeod to Lamar, June 10, 1841, in *The Papers of Mirabeau Buonaparte Lamar*, ed. Gulick, item number 2049.

19. Kendall, *Narrative of the Texan Santa Fe Expedition*, 69–70.

20. Samuel Roberts to Mirabeau Lamar, July 14, 1841, in *The Papers of Mirabeau Buonaparte Lamar*, ed. Gulick, item number 2063; Thomas Blackwell to Mirabeau Lamar, July 23, 1841, "Santa Fe Expedition 1841–1842," *Sons of DeWitt Colony Texas*, Wallace L. McKeehan, accessed March 5, 2013, http://www.tamu.edu/faculty/ccbn/dewitt/santafeexped.htm#blackwelllamar.

21. *Austin City Gazette*, August 25, 1841.

22. *Colorado Gazette and Advertiser*, December 13, 1841.

23. *Austin City Gazette*, January 5, 1842.

24. Spellman, *Forgotten Texas Leader*, 83–84.

25. *Austin City Gazette*, March 2, 1842.

26. Spellman, *Forgotten Texas Leader*, 114.

Chapter 16

1. Haley, *Sam Houston,* 221.
2. David Burnet Papers, Dolph Briscoe Center for American History, University of Texas at Austin.
3. Sam Houston to Margaret Houston, January 23, 1841, in *The Personal Correspondence of Sam Houston,* ed. Roberts, 1:76.
4. Ibid., January 25, 1841, 79.
5. Ibid., February 2, 1841, 95.
6. Haley, *Sam Houston,* 222; Sam Houston to William Wallach, May 31, 1841, in *The Writings of Sam Houston, 1813–1863,* eds. Williams and Barker, 2:368.
7. *Texas Centinel,* August 5, 1841; *Austin City Gazette,* August 25, 1841; *Texas Centinel,* August 26, 1841, as quoted in the Austin File Chronological, 1841, Austin History Center; *Texas Centinel,* July 29, 1841.
8. Haley, *Sam Houston,* 224.
9. Williams and Barker, eds., *The Writings of Sam Houston, 1813–1863,* 2:376–86. The two surviving "Truth" letters are dated August 16 and 18, 1841.
10. De Saligny, August 14, 1841, in *Alphonse in Austin,* ed. Hart, 45.
11. Haley, *Sam Houston,* 227; *Austin City Gazette,* September 8, 1841.
12. Sam Houston to Margaret Houston, December 2, 1841, in *The Personal Correspondence of Sam Houston,* ed. Roberts, 1:116.
13. Ibid., December 9, 1841, 123.
14. Haley, *Sam Houston,* 227; Sam Houston to Margaret Houston, December 13, 1841, in *The Personal Correspondence of Sam Houston,* ed. Roberts, 1:134. Writing about the inaugural ball in his honor, Houston reported that he had not danced: "I had a thousand reasons for declining, but I will only cite one, and that is simply that you wou'd prefer that I wou'd not."
15. At Water (First) Street and East Avenue.
16. Sam Houston to Margaret Houston, December 13, 1841, in *The Personal Correspondence of Sam Houston,* ed. Roberts, 1:135. Details of the inauguration ceremony are from the *Daily Bulletin,* December 13, 1841, as quoted in the Austin File Chronological, item 2, 1841, Austin History Center.
17. Sam Houston to Margaret Houston, December 9, 1841, in *The Personal Correspondence of Sam Houston,* ed. Roberts, 1:125; Ibid., December 13, 1841, 135–36.
18. Report to Congress Concerning the Condition of the President's Residence, December 23, 1841, in *The Writings of Sam Houston, 1813–1863,* eds. Williams and Barker, 2:409–10.
19. *The Daily Bulletin,* January 8, 1842.

Chapter 17

1. Josiah Whipple diary, January 22, 1842, in Brown, *Annals of Travis County and the City of Austin,* chap. 9; Wilbarger, *Indian Depredations in Texas,* 271; Jake Snively to James H. Starr, February 23, 1841, Austin File Chronological, 1841, Section 5, Austin History Center.

2. Sam Houston to Margaret Houston, December 26, 1841, in *The Personal Correspondence of Sam Houston,* ed. Roberts, 1:148; *The Daily Bulletin,* December 27, 1841.

3. John Welsh to Sam Houston, January 7, 1842, R. Niles Graham-Pease Collection, AF A8500 (1840s-1890s), Austin History Center.

4. *Daily Bulletin,* January 18, 1842, as quoted in Austin File Chronological, 1842, Section 1, Austin History Center.

5. Sam Houston to the Texas Congress, February 5, 1842, *The Writings of Sam Houston, 1813–1863,* eds. Williams and Barker, 2:481–82.

6. *Austin City Gazette,* February 23, 1842, as quoted in Austin File Chronological, 1842, Section 2, Austin History Center.

7. Josiah Whipple diary, July 10, 1842, in Brown, *Annals of Travis County and the City of Austin,* chap. 9.

8. Sam Houston Unpublished Correspondence, Dolph Briscoe Center for American History, University of Texas at Austin.

9. Thomas William Ward Papers, Austin History Center; Austin File Chronological, 1842, Section 7, Austin History Center.

10. To William H. Abell of Fredonia, New York, April 11, 1843, Austin File Chronological, 1843, Section 3, Austin History Center. The letter writer's name does not appear in the citation.

11. Josiah Whipple diary, March 7, 1842, in Brown, *Annals of Travis County and the City of Austin,* chap. 9; Sam Houston to George Hockley, March 10, 1842,.., *The Writings of Sam Houston, 1813–1863,* eds. Williams and Barker, 2:495; George Hockley to Sam Houston, March 16, 1842, Sam Houston Unpublished Correspondence, Dolph Briscoe Center for American History, University of Texas at Austin..

12. Sam Houston Unpublished Correspondence, Dolph Briscoe Center for American History, University of Texas at Austin. Samuel Whiting, James Mayfield, and ninety-eight others signed a letter to Hockley requesting that the archives stay put until they could communicate with the president. They believed that once Sam Houston fully understood the situation at Austin, he would realize that there was no emergency requiring removal. They pledged to protect the archives with their lives if threatened but added that, in the event of removal, they would forcibly return them. Hockley enclosed the committee's letter, along with his refusal to delay, in his March 17 correspondence to President Houston.

13. Austin File Chronological, 1842, Section 10, Austin History Center. This fact was provided by Joseph Lee in a newspaper article titled "Reminiscences of the Archives War and Other Incidents: How Austin Was Finally Selected as the State Capital," which appeared in the *Austin Statesman,* February 12, 1888.

14. Sam Houston to Henry Jones, April 4, 1842, Thomas William Ward Papers, Austin History Center. Houston wrote, "You are hereby specially enjoined and COMMANDED in no wise to interfere with, or obstruct the fulfilment of

the executive order . . . Directing the removal of the Government archives from the City of Austin. . . . Any such interferences, either directly or indirectly by yourself or through any agent or agents acting under your orders, or Countenance, will be promptly met with that disgrace and punishment due to the CRIMES OF TREASON AND 'INSURRECTION'"; Henry Jones to Thomas William Ward, April 15, 1842, Thomas William Ward Papers, Austin History Center.

15. Sam Houston Unpublished Correspondence, Dolph Briscoe Center for American History, University of Texas at Austin. On March 17, the same day he refused the Austin committee's request to delay removal, Hockley sent this dispatch to William Pettus, who was en route with the wagons necessary for moving the archives: "In consequence of the excitement and state of public feeling at this place, together with the fact that the Department has no military force to carry out its measure, it becomes expedient to direct you to halt at some convenient place, with the transportation you may have for the removal of the archives of Government until further orders."

16. Austin File Chronological, 1842, Section 7, Austin History Center; Joseph Waples to Anson Jones, April 9, 1842, in Jones, *Memoranda and Official Correspondence Relating to the Republic of Texas,* 171.

17. *Austin City Gazette,* March 30, 1842.

18. Smither, ed., *Journals of the Sixth Congress of the Republic of Texas, 1841–1842, to which Are Added the Special Laws,* 44–45; George W. Terrell to Sam Houston, March 18, 1842 and March 25, 1842, Sam Houston Correspondence, Catholic Archives of Texas, Austin; Sam Houston to George Hockley, March 22, 1842, in *The Writings of Sam Houston, 1813–1863,* eds. Williams and Barker, 2:529–30.

19. *Austin City Gazette,* April 12, 1842, as quoted in Barkley, *History of Travis County and Austin, 1839–1899,* 62; Sam Houston Unpublished Correspondence, Dolph Briscoe Center for American History, University of Texas at Austin.

20. Washington Miller to William Daingerfield, April 13, 1842, Sam Houston Unpublished Correspondence, Dolph Briscoe Center for American History, University of Texas at Austin; Madge Hearn Papers, Dolph Briscoe Center for American History, University of Texas at Austin; James, *The Raven,* 325–26. Houston issued a proclamation calling the special session on May 24, 1842

21. Jenkins ed., *Recollections of Early Texas: The Memoirs of John Holland Jenkins,* 166n; Brown, *Annals of Travis County and the City of Austin,* chap. 9. Black and Dolson were killed August 1, 1842. Frank Brown gives the location as a quarter mile from the creek mouth. Since he also stated that Black and Dolson had crossed the river this would mean the attack occurred near the southern end of the modern Lamar Boulevard Bridge across the Colorado. In 1843 Captain Jack Hays and his men captured three Mexican bandits who reportedly confessed to the killings. Hays had the men executed.

22. *Austin City Gazette,* August 17, 1842.

23. General Adrian Woll to Secretary of War and the Navy Isidro Reyes, September 20, 1842, in *Sons of DeWitt Colony, Texas* website.

24. *The Handbook of Texas Online,* s.v. "Battle of Salado Creek."

25. Richardson Scurry to Sam Houston, September 7, 1842, Sam Houston Unpublished Correspondence, Dolph Briscoe Center for American History, University of Texas at Austin; Sam Houston to the Texas Senate, January 13, 1843, in *The Writings of Sam Houston, 1813–1863,* eds. Williams and Barker, 3:291–92; Williams and Barker, eds., *The Writings of Sam Houston, 1813–1863,* 3:200. Houston issued a presidential proclamation November 21, 1842, in which he stated that "from reasons unknown to him, a quorum has not been formed in Congress."

26. Sam Houston to Thomas William Ward, October 8, 1842, in *The Writings of Sam Houston, 1813–1863,* eds. Williams and Barker, 4:149; Samuel Whiting to Thomas William Ward, September 23, 1842, Austin File Chronological, 1842, Section 7, Austin History Center; President's Message to the Seventh Congress, December 1, 1842, as reported in the *Northern Standard,* December 24, 1842, Austin File Chronological, 1842, Austin History Center. When reporting this act of Houston's, the *Northern Standard* complained that, of twenty thousand dollars appropriated by Congress for frontier defense, the president had used only a small portion to relocate the government to Houston: "The much more *symphonious* sound of that name, has apparently a wondrous charm to the ear of his Excellency."

27. Washington Miller to Ashbel Smith, December 8, 1842, Ashbel Smith Papers, Dolph Briscoe Center for American History, The University of Texas at Austin. Miller cited William Cazneau of Travis, John Caldwell of Bastrop, Smallwood Fields of Fayette, James Dennison of Matagorda, Thomas Haynes of Victoria, William Hunter of Goliad, Lindsay Hagler of San Patricio, and Rafael de la Garza of Bexar as the truant congressmen.

28. Haley, *Sam Houston,* 252; the *Southern Intelligencer,* March 22, 1866, as quoted in Austin File Chronological, 1842, Section 8, Austin History Center; Sam Houston to Thomas I. Smith and Eli Chandler, December 10, 1842, in *The Writings of Sam Houston, 1813–1863,* eds. Williams and Barker, 3:226–27; Ibid., Sam Houston to Thomas William Ward, December 10, 1842, 229–30.

29. Latham, *Travels in the Republic of Texas, 1842,* 25. A visitor in May 1842 estimated a population of about two hundred people.

30. *Cincinnati Gazette,* November 2, 1844, City of Austin Collection, Texas State Archives.

31. Details of the attempt by Chandler and Smith to spirit the archives out of Austin and Mark Lewis's successful move to stop them are from the twelfth installment of William Walsh's recollections in the *Austin Statesman,* April 13, 1924; Brown, *Annals of Travis County and the City of Austin,* chap 9; and Austin File Chronological, 1842, Sections 7 and 9, Austin History Center. In

1901 and 1902 Frank Brown interviewed several Austinites who had lived in the city at the time of the incident and named the following men who had participated: Mark B. Lewis, John Nelson, George Barrett, W. Seiders, Edward Seiders, Alfred Smith, Jacob M. Harrell, John Harrell, Anderson J. Harrell, William Hornsby, Joseph Hornsby, James Edminston, Aleck Peyton, Thomas P. Wooldridge, A. C. Coleman, C. C. Browning, Thomas Glasscock, and William Allen.

32. Thomas Ward to Sam Houston, January 8, 1843, in *The Writings of Sam Houston, 1813–1863*, eds. Williams and Barker, 3:230–31.

33. Samuel Whiting to Anson Jones, December 10, 1842, in Brown, *Annals of Travis County and the City of Austin*, chap. 9.

Chapter 18

1. Brown, *Annals of Travis County and the City of Austin*, chap. 9; *Telegraph and Texas Register*, May 8, 1844.

2. Jenkins and Kesselus, *Edward Burleson, Texas Frontier Leader*, 324–26.

3. Hollon and Butler, eds., *William Bollaert's Texas*, 141–42, 183.

4. Ibid., 195, 198.

5. Austin File Chronological, 1843, Section 3, Austin History Center.

6. *Cincinnati Gazette*, November 2, 1844; Smithwick, Noah, *The Evolution of a State* or *Recollections of Old Texas Days*, 206.

7. Lewis P. Cooke served in the Third and Sixth Congresses and was also Secretary of the Navy under President Lamar. He was one of the five commissioners selecting Waterloo as the seat-of-government site in 1839. Details of the encounter resulting in the deaths of Noland, Lewis, and Peyton are from the *Cincinnati Gazette*, November 2, 1844; Smithwick, *The Evolution of a State* or *Recollections of Old Texas* Days, 206–7; and Brown, *Annals of Travis County and the City of Austin*, chap. 9.

8. *Morning Star*, January 26, 1843.

9. Ibid., February 16, 1843.

10. Ibid., February 3, 1844, April 11, 1844.

11. Ibid., April 26, 1845.

12. The public printer received all government printing orders, which included publishing the House and Senate journals. Assuming that the government paid its bills, this was an envied and profitable position.

13. Jones, *Memoranda and Official Correspondence Relating to the Republic of Texas, its History and Annexation*, 181–82.

14. Ibid., 259, 304.

15. Wilbarger, *Indian Depredations in Texas*, 274.

16. According to J. W. Wilbarger, Davis was riding "in the valley east of College Hill." This would place him somewhere between present-day Fifteenth and Twenty-Sixth Streets on or near Interstate 35. Most of this area is now part of the University of Texas campus and includes the football stadium, basketball arena, and LBJ Presidential Library.

17. This would put Lee in the heart of the present University of Texas campus not far from the UT Tower.

18. Wilbarger, *Indian Depredations in Texas,* 141–42.

19. White's cabin sat in an oak grove now known as Seider's Oaks, across Shoal Creek from Seider's Springs. These trees may still be seen on the western creek bank below Shoal Creek Hospital between Thirty-Fourth and Thirty-Eighth Streets. Thirty-Fourth Street, once called State Street, was originally part of an Indian trail leading from the river along Shoal Creek before turning west. In Austin's early days, State Street provided the main western route toward the hills west of town.

20. These two incidents from Wilbarger, *Indian Depredations in Texas,* 275.

21. "Early Days in Texas: Reminiscences of Julia Lee Sinks," Julia Lee Sinks Vertical File, Dolph Briscoe Center for American History, University of Texas at Austin.

22. Built by Abner Cook, Governor Marshall Pease's one-time antebellum plantation home still stands at 6 Niles Road amid the extravagant homes of old west Austin.

23. This area is now a northwestern suburb of Austin straddling Spicewood Springs Road.

24. Wilbarger, *Indian Depredations in Texas,* 139–40. Tommie Simpson was returned to his mother eighteen months later by Indians who traded with the kidnappers for the boy.

25. Ibid., 260; *Morning Star,* June 28, 1845. Anson Jones described the murders as "the result of a personal hatred and vow of revenge on the part of a Comanche Indian." Nevertheless, Hornsby's friends and family were ready to kill six hundred Comanches in an effort to capture the one man responsible (Jones, *Memoranda and Official Correspondence Relating to the Republic of Texas, Its History and Annexation,* 473).

26. *Morning Star,* August 3, 1843, April 11, 1844; Latham, *Travels in the Republic of Texas,* 18, 21; Brown, *Annals of Travis County and the City of Austin,* chap. 9.

27. James Webb to Mirabeau B. Lamar, May 4, 1843, in *The Papers of Mirabeau Buonaparte Lamar,* ed. Gulick, item number 2151; Latham, *Travels in the Republic of Texas,* 16–25.

28. Hollon and Butler, eds., *William Bollaert's Texas,* 193–98.

29. William Abell, correspondence, April 11, 1843, Austin File Chronological, 1843, Section 3, Austin History Center.

Chapter 19

1. Jones, correspondence, December 31, 1843, in *Memoranda and Official Correspondence Relating to the Republic of Texas,* 39.

2. *Texas National Register,* April 24, 1845. When his business dried up after 1842, Cazneau, a Travis County representative in the Seventh, Eighth, and Ninth Congresses, temporarily left Austin for Galveston.

3. Jones, *Memoranda and Official Correspondence Relating to the Republic of Texas,* 26.

4. Ibid., 37, 41.

5. Ibid., E. Morehouse to Anson Jones, January 27, 1844, 304.

6. A. S. Burleson to Samuel Asbury, December 6, 1922, Edward Burleson, Sr., Papers, Dolph Briscoe Center for American History, University of Texas at Austin. A. S. Burleson was Edward Burleson's grandson.

7. Jenkins and Kesselus, *Edward Burleson, Texas Frontier Leader,* 333; Peter McGreal to Anson Jones, December 1843, in Jones, *Memoranda and Official Correspondence Relating to the Republic of Texas,* 275. One Jones supporter wrote, "Although Gen. Burleson may, for aught I know, be a good, honest man; yet, from his ignorance and want of capacity, he would be but an automaton in the hands of designing, unprincipled, and dishonest politicians of the country" (*La Grange Intelligencer,* March 28, 1844).

8. Committee of Citizens of Independence to Anson Jones, November 10, 1843, in Jones, *Memoranda and Official Correspondence Relating to the Republic of Texas,* 265, 301. Jones wrote this in a January 1844 note to himself that he attached to a letter from George Hockley supporting his candidacy.

9. *Morning Star,* July 13, 1844, August 24, 1844.

10. *The Telegraph,* September 4, 1844.

11. Jones, unsent letter to M. P. Morton, June 6, 1844, in *Memoranda and Official Correspondence Relating to the Republic of Texas,* 361, 366.

12. Jones, *Memoranda and Official Correspondence Relating to the Republic of Texas,* 353. Jones wrote this in response to a letter of denial from Sam Houston.

13. Williams and Barker, eds., *The Writings of Sam Houston, 1813–1863,* 4:354–57, as quoted in Jenkins and Kesselus, *Edward Burleson, Texas Frontier Leader,* 349.

14. William Ochiltree to Anson Jones, September 24, 1844, in Jones, *Memoranda and Official Correspondence Relating to the Republic of Texas,* 385.

15. James Morgan to Samuel Swartout, September 28, 1844, as quoted in Jenkins and Kesselus, *Edward Burleson, Texas Frontier Leader,* 351.

16. Asa Lewis to Mrs. Lewis, December 25, 1842, Austin History Center.

17. Brown, "Old Washington" (unpublished), 14–20, Frank Brown Papers, Dolph Briscoe Center for American History, University of Texas at Austin.

18. Ibid., 22–24.

19. Ibid., 21.

20. Details of the inauguration, including the quotes from the speeches made by Sam Houston and Anson Jones, are from the December 14, 1844 issue of *The Texas National Register.*

21. Bonham, *Merchant to the Republic,* 95, 140–44.

22. *The Telegraph,* November 13, 1844.

23. *The Morning Star,* December 19, 1844.

24. *Texas National Register,* December 28, 1844.

25. Ibid., January 4, 1845. The protesters were John Ford, William Richardson Scurry, James Truit, William Sadler, Robert Williamson, Gustavus Parker, Stephen Johns, John Lewis, and Benjamin Hardin.

26. Jones, *Memoranda and Official Correspondence Relating to the Republic of*

Texas, 34–35. In September 1839, Jones wrote "No policy could possibly have been more unwise than the removal of the seat of government to Austin, and corrupt means were used to place it there; but now that so much money has been expended, I shall be for its remaining at that place. . . . 'Two removes are as bad as a fire,' says poor Richard, and so I say about the seat of government, for *one* has been about equal to a moderate conflagration."

27. *Texas National Register*, January 11, 1845.

28. Ibid., January 25, 1845, February 8, 1845.

29. This summary of the history of Texas annexation to the United States is from *The Handbook of Texas Online*, s.v. "Annexation."

30. *Texas National Register*, April 17, 1845.

31. Ibid., May 8, 1845.

32. Ibid., March 8, 1845.

33. Andrew Donelson to Ebenezer Allen, March 31, 1845, in *Journals of the Extra Session, Ninth Congress of the Republic of Texas* [*1845*], 12.

34. Ibid., 43, 93.

35. *The Handbook of Texas Online*, s.v. "Anderson, Kenneth Lewis." Anderson's law partner, James Pinckney Henderson, eventually became the first Texas governor. In 1846 the town of Fanthorp was renamed Anderson in the late vice president's honor.

36. James L. Haley, *Sam Houston*, 290.

37. *Journals of the Convention*, 58–59.

38. *Texas National Register*, July 24, 1845.

39. William Ochiltree to Anson Jones, July 8, 1845, in Jones, *Memoranda and Official Correspondence Relating to the Republic of Texas*, 477–78.

40. Ibid., James Farquhar to Anson Jones, July 25, 1845, 479–80.

41. Ibid., William Ochiltree to Anson Jones, August 8, 1845, 483.

42. Ibid., 170. Jones' use of the term "hegira" (an Arabic word meaning "migration") refers to Muhammed's flight from Mecca in AD 622.

43. *Texas National Register*, August 21, 1845.

44. Ibid., October 2, 1845.

45. *Morning Star*, February 1, 1845.

46. *Texas National Register*, January 3, 1846. Rip Ford and his partner M. Cronican published their first Austin edition November 15, 1845 but did not change the name of the newspaper to *Texas Democrat* until early in 1846.

47. Bonham, *Merchant to the Republic*, 160. Russell erected this building on the southwest corner of Pecan and Congress in 1839. This was the first store building in Austin. The site is now occupied by the Scarbrough Building (1910), which was the first skyscraper built in Austin.

48. *Texas National Register*, December 17, 1845; *Texas Democrat*, March 20, 1847. Thompson's hotel building, on the northeast corner of Hickory (Eighth) and Neches Streets, was one of the largest in Austin when it opened in 1840. It burned to the ground March 1, 1847, costing Francis Dieterich $3,500.

49. Smithwick, Noah, *The Evolution of a State*, 211–12.

50. *Texas Democrat*, March 11, 1846, March 18, 1846.

BIBLIOGRAPHY

Adair, A. Garland, and E. H. Perry. *Austin and Commodore Perry.* Austin: The Steck Company, 1956.

"Allen's Reminiscences of Texas, 1838–1842, I." *Southwestern Historical Quarterly Online* 17, no. 3 (1914): 283–305. http://www.tsha.utexas.edu/publications/journals/shq/online/v017/n3/article_3_.

Anderson, Gary Clayton. *The Conquest of Texas: Ethnic Cleansing in the Promised Land, 1820–1875.* Norman: University of Oklahoma Press, 2005.

Anderson, John Q., ed. *Tales of Frontier Texas 1830–1860.* Dallas: Southern Methodist University Press, 1966.

Austin File Chronological. Austin History Center. Austin, Texas.

Barker, Eugene C. "The San Jacinto Campaign." *Southwestern Historical Quarterly Online* 4, no. 4 (1901): 237–345. http://www.tsha.utexas.edu/publications/journals/shq/online/v004/n4/article_4.html.

Barker, Nancy Nichols, ed. *The French Legation in Texas.* Austin: Texas Historical Association, 1971.

Barkley, Mary Starr. *History of Travis County and Austin 1839–1899.* Austin: Austin Printing Company, 1981.

Bell (Thomas William) Family Papers. Dolph Briscoe Center for American History. University of Texas at Austin. Austin, Texas.

Bell, Thomas William. *A Narrative of the Capture and Subsequent Sufferings of the Mier Prisoners in Mexico.* 1845. Reprint, Waco: Texian Press, 1964.

Bracht, Viktor. *Texas in 1848.* San Marcos: German-Texan Heritage Society, 1991.

Brands, H. W. *Lone Star Nation: How a Ragged Army of Volunteers Won the Battle For Texas Independence—and Changed America.* New York: Doubleday, 2004.

Brigham (Asa) Papers. Dolph Briscoe Center for American History. University of Texas at Austin. Austin, Texas.

Brown, Frank. *Annals of Travis County and the City of Austin.* Compiled between 1892 and 1913. Austin History Center. Austin, Texas.

Christian, A. K. "Mirabeau Buonaparte Lamar." *Southwestern Historical Quarterly Online* 23, no. 3 (1920): 231–70. http://www.tsha.utexas.edu/publications/journals/shq/online/v023/n3/contrib_DIVL1752_print.ht.

Connor, Seymour V., James M. Day, Billy Mac Jones, Dayton Kelley, W. C. Nunn, Ben Procter, and Dorman H. Winfrey. *Capitols of Texas.* 4th ed. Waco: Texian Press, 2001.

Dancy (John Winfield Scott) Papers. Dolph Briscoe Center for American History. University of Texas at Austin. Austin, Texas.

De la Pena, Jose Enrique. *With Santa Anna in Texas: A Personal Narrative of the Revolution*. Edited by Carmen Perry. College Station: Texas A&M University Press, 1997.

DeLay, Brian. *War of a Thousand Deserts: Indian Raids and the U. S.-Mexican War*. New Haven: Yale University Press, 2008.

Denton, Bernice Barnett. "Count Alphonso de Saligny and the Franco-Texienne Bill." *Southwestern Historical Quarterly Online* 45, no. 2 (1941): 136–146. http://www.tsha.utexas.edu/publications/journals/shq/online/v045/n2/contrib_DIVL2493.html.

Dienst, Alex. "Contemporary Poetry of the Texan Revolution." *Southwestern Historical Quarterly Online* 21, no. 2, (1917):156–84. http://www.tsha.utexas.edu/publications/journals/shq/online/v021/n2/article_4_print.html.

Fields, Dorothy Louise. "David Gouverneur Burnet." *Southwestern Historical Quarterly Online,* 49, no. 2 (1945):215–232. http://www.tsha.utexas.edu/publications/journals/shq/online/v049/n2/contrib_DIVL3043.html.

Fontaine, Edward. *Mirabeau B. Lamar: Third President of the Republic of Texas*. Olma Verde, 1857.

Ford, John Salmon. *Rip Ford's Texas*. Edited by Stephen B. Oates. Austin: University of Texas Press, 2004.

Fulton, Maurice Garland, ed. *Diary and Letters of Josiah Gregg: Southwestern Enterprises, 1840–1847*. Norman: University of Oklahoma Press, 1941.

Gammel, H. P. N. *The Laws of Texas 1822–1897*. Austin: The Gammel Book Company, 1898.

Gaillardet, Frederic. *Sketches of Early Texas and Louisiana*. Translated with an introduction and notes by James L. Shepherd III. Austin: University of Texas Press, 1966.

Graham, Philip. *The Life and Poems of Mirabeau B. Lamar*. Chapel Hill: University of North Carolina Press, 1938.

Gulick, Charles Adams, Jr., ed. *The Papers of Mirabeau Buonaparte Lamar*. 6 vols. Austin: Texas State Library, 1922.

Hafertepe, Kenneth. *Abner Cook: Master Builder on the Texas Frontier*. Austin: Texas State Historical Association, 1992.

Haley, James L. *Sam Houston*. Norman: University of Oklahoma Press, 2004.

Hämäläinen, Pekka. *The Comanche Empire*. New Haven: Yale University Press, 2008.

Hamilton, Jeff. *My Master: The Inside Story of Sam Houston and His Times, as told to Lenoir Hunt*. Austin: State House Press, 1992.

The Handbook of Texas Online, s.v. "Alcalde." Accessed September 30, 2006. http://www.tsha.utexas.edu/handbook/online/articles/AA/nfa1.html.

The Handbook of Texas Online, s.v. "Allen, Augustus Chapman." Accessed June 5, 2006. http://www.tsha.utexas.edu/handbook/online/articles/AA/fal17.html.

The Handbook of Texas Online, s.v. "Anderson, Kenneth Lewis." Accessed November 10, 2007. http://www.tsha.utexas.edu/handbook/online/articles/AA/fan8.html.

The Handbook of Texas Online, s.v. "Annexation." Accessed November 8, 2007. http://www.tsha.utexas.edu/handbook/online/articles/AA/mga2.html.

The Handbook of Texas Online, s.v. "Ayuntamiento." Accessed September 28, 2006. http://www.tsha.utexas.edu/handbook/online/articles/AA/nfa3.html.

The Handbook of Texas Online, s.v. "Baker, Mosely." Accessed September 16, 2006. http://www.tsha.utexas.edu/handbook/online/articles/BB/fba37.html.

The Handbook of Texas Online, s.v. "Barton, William." Accessed May 26, 2006. http://www.tsha.utexas.edu/handbook/online/articles/BB/fba97.html.

The Handbook of Texas Online, s.v., "Bastrop County." Accessed February 8, 2011. http://www.tshaonline.org/handbook/online/articles/hcb03.

The Handbook of Texas Online, s.v. "Bastrop, Texas." Accessed July 29, 2006. http://www.tsha.utexas.edu/handbook/online/articles/BB/hgb4.html.

The Handbook of Texas Online, s.v. "Battle of Salado Creek." Accessed March 24, 2007. http://www.tsha.utexas.edu/handbook/online/articles/SS/qfs1.html.

The Handbook of Texas Online, s.v. "Borden, John Pettit." Accessed December 5, 2006. http://www.tsha.utexas.edu/handbook/online/articles/BB/fbo25.html.

The Handbook of Texas Online, s.v. "Burke, James." Accessed December 26, 2006. http://www.tsha.utexas.edu/handbook/online/articles/BB/fbu32.html.

The Handbook of Texas Online, s.v. "Burleson, Aaron." Accessed October 1, 2006. http://www.tsha.utexas.edu/handbook/online/articles/BB/fbu37.html.

The Handbook of Texas Online, s.v. "Burleson, Edward." Accessed May 29, 2006. http://www.tsha.utexas.edu/handbook/online/articles/BB/fbu40.html.

The Handbook of Texas Online, s.v. "Collinsworth, James." Accessed May 28, 2006. http://www.tsha.utexas.edu/handbook/online/articles/CC/fco97.html.

The Handbook of Texas Online, s.v. "Cunningham, Leander Calvin." Accessed October 1, 2006. http://www.tsha.utexas.edu/handbook/online/articles/CC/fcu23.html.

The Handbook of Texas Online, s.v. "Darlington, John Washington." Accessed November 26, 2006. http://www.tsha.utexas.edu/handbook/online/articles/DD/fda14.html.

The Handbook of Texas Online, s.v. "Fort Colorado." Accessed May 28, 2006. http://www.tsha.utexas.edu/handbook/online/articles/FF/qcf1.html.

The Handbook of Texas Online, s.v. "Grayson, Peter Wagener." Accessed May 28, 2006. http://www.tsha.utexas.edu/handbook/online/articles/GG/fgr29.html.

The Handbook of Texas Online, s.v. "Hancock, George Duncan." Accessed October 1, 2006. http://www.tsha.utexas.edu/handbook/online/articles/HH/fha45.html.

The Handbook of Texas Online, s.v. "Harrell, Jacob M." Accessed May 29, 2006. http://www.tsha.utexas.edu/handbook/online/articles/HH/fha77.html.

The Handbook of Texas Online, s.v. "Hemphill, John." Accessed December 28, 2006. http://www.tsha.utexas.edu/handbook/online/articles/HH/fhe13.html.

The Handbook of Texas Online, s.v. "Hill, William Pinkney." Accessed October 1, 2006. http://www.tsha.utexas.edu/handbook/online/articles/HH/fhi28.html.

The Handbook of Texas Online, s.v. "Hornsby, Reuben." Accessed December 10, 2006. http://www.tsha.utexas.edu/handbook/online/articles/HH/fho60.html.

The Handbook of Texas Online, s.v. "Houston *Morning Star*." Accessed September 25, 2006. http://www.tsha.utexas.edu/handbook/online/articles/HH/eeh3.html.

The Handbook of Texas Online, s.v. "Houston, Samuel." Accessed August 29, 2006. http://www.tsha.utexas.edu/handbook/online/articles/HH/fho73.html.

The Handbook of Texas Online, s.v. "Jones, William Jefferson." Accessed September 24, 2006. http://www.tsha.utexas.edu/handbook/online/articles/JJ/fjo68.html.

The Handbook of Texas Online, s.v. "Lamar, Mirabeau Buonaparte." Accessed May 27, 2006. http://www.tsha.utexas.edu/handbook/online/articles/LL/fla15.html.

The Handbook of Texas Online, s.v. "Lee, Joseph." Accessed September 30, 2006. http://www.tsha.utexas.edu/handbook/online/articles/LL/fle15.html.

The Handbook of Texas Online, s.v. "Lubbock, Thomas Saltus." Accessed September 10, 2006. http://www.tsha.utexas.edu/handbook/online/articles/LL/flu2.html.

The Handbook of Texas Online, s.v., "Mina, Francisco Xavier." Accessed February 8, 2011. http://www.tshaonline.org/handbook/online/articles/fmi46.

The Handbook of Texas Online, s.v. "Montopolis, Texas." Accessed September 30, 2006. http://www.tsha.utexas.edu/handbook/online/articles/MM/hvmac.html.

The Handbook of Texas Online, s.v. "Old San Antonio." Accessed August 11, 2006. http://www.tsha.utexas.edu/handbook/online/articles/OO/exo4.html.

The Handbook of Texas Online, s.v. "Perry, James." Accessed October 1, 2006. http://www.tsha.utexas.edu/handbook/online/articles/PP/fpe44.html.

The Handbook of Texas Online, s.v. "Roberts, Samuel Alexander." Accessed December 3, 2006. http://www.tsha.utexas.edu/handbook/online/articles/RR/fro19.html.

The Handbook of Texas Online, s.v. "Sinks, Julia Lee." Accessed November 5, 2006. http://www.tsha.utexas.edu/handbook/online/articles/SS/fsi31.html.

The Handbook of Texas Online, s.v. "*Telegraph and Texas Register.*"
Accessed June 14, 2006. http://www.tsha.utexas.edu/handbook/online/
articles/TT/eet2.html.

The Handbook of Texas Online , s.v., "Travis County." Accessed February 8, 2011.
http://www.tshaonline.org/handbook/online/articles/hct08.

The Handbook of Texas Online, s.v. "Vandeveer, Logan." Accessed October 1,
2006. http://www.tsha.utexas.edu/handbook/online/articles/VV/fva18.
html.

The Handbook of Texas Online, s.v. "Walsh, Wiliam C." Accessed November 13,
2005. http://www.tsha.utexas.edu/handbook/online/articles/WW/fwa44.
html.

The Handbook of Texas Online, s.v. "Washington-On-The-Brazos, TX." Accessed
June 3, 2006. http://www.tsha.utexas.edu/handbook/online/articles/WW/
hvw10.html.

The Handbook of Texas Online, s.v. "Waterloo, TX." Accessed May 29, 2006.
http://www.tsha.utexas.edu/handbook/online/articles/WW/hvw13.html.

The Handbook of Texas Online, s.v. "Webberville, Texas." Accessed September
25, 2006. http://www.tsha.utexas.edu/handbook/online/articles/WW/
hnw30.html.

The Handbook of Texas Online, s.v. "Williamson, Robert Mcalpirn." Accessed December 28, 2006. http://www.tsha.utexas.edu/handbook/online/articles/
WW/fwi42.html.

Hart, Katherine, ed. *Alphonse in Austin*. Austin: The Encino Press, 1972.

Hearne (Madge) Papers. Dolph Briscoe Center for American History. University
of Texas at Austin.

Herrick, Francis Hobart. *Audubon the Naturalist: A History of His Life and Times*. 2
vols. New York: D. Appleton and Company, 1917.

Hogan, William Ransom. *The Texas Republic: A Social and Economic History*.
Austin: Texas State Historical Association, 2006. First published 1946 by
University of Oklahoma Press.

Hollan, W. Eugene, and R. L. Butler, eds. *William Bollaert's Texas*. Norman: University of Oklahoma Press, 1956.

Holland, J. K. "Reminiscences of Austin and Old Washington." *Southwestern Historical Quarterly Online* 1, no. 2 (1897): 92–95. http://www.tsha.utexas.edu/
publications/journals/shq/online/v001/n2/article_5_

Holley, Mary Austin. *Texas*. 1836. Reprint of the first edition published by J.
Clarke. Austin: Texas State Historical Association, 1985.

———. "The Texas Diary." *The Texas Quarterly* 8, no. 2 (1958):12–72.

Houstoun, Matilda Charlotte. *Texas and the Gulf of Mexico; or, Yachting in the New
World*. 1845.

Irion (Robert) Papers. Dolph Briscoe Center for American History. University of
Texas at Austin.

Jackson, Donald. *Voyages of the Steamboat Yellow Stone*. New York: Ticknor and
Fields, 1985.

James, Marquis. *The Raven: A Biography of Sam Houston*. 1929. Reprint of original edition published by Bobbs-Merrill. Austin: University of Texas Press, 2004.

Jenkins, John H., ed. *Patriotic Songs and Poems of Early Texas*. Austin: Pemberton Press, 1966.

———. *Recollections of Early Texas: The Memoirs of John Holland Jenkins*. Austin: University of Texas Press, 2003.

Jenkins, John H., and Kenneth Kesselus. *Edward Burleson, Texas Frontier Leader*. Austin: Jenkins Publishing Company, 1990.

Johnson, Frank W. *A History of Texas and Texans, Volume I*. Chicago: The American Historical Society, 1914.

Jones, Anson. *Memoranda and Official Correspondence Relating to the Republic of Texas, Its History and Annexation*. Chicago: Rio Grande Press, 1966.

Journal of the Senate of the Republic of Texas, First Session of the Third Congress 1838. Houston: National Intelligencer Office, 1839.

Journal of the House of Representatives of the Republic of Texas: First Congress, Second Session. Houston: Office of the *Telegraph*, 1838.

Journal of the House of Representatives of the Republic of Texas: Regular Session of Third Congress, Nov. 5, 1838. Houston: National Intelligencer Office, 1839.

Journal of the House of Representatives of the Republic of Texas, Second Congress 1837–1838. Houston: National Banner Office, 1838.

Journals of the Convention Assembled at the City of Austin on the Fourth of July, 1845, For the Purpose of Framing a Constitution For the State of Texas. Austin: Miner & Cruger, 1845.

Journals of the House of Representatives of the Extra Session, Ninth Congress of the Republic of Texas. Washington: Miller & Cushney, 1845.

Journals of the House of Representatives of the Republic of Texas Fifth Congress First Session, 1840–1841. Austin: Cruger and Wing, 1841.

Journals of the House of Representatives of the Republic of Texas: First Congress, First Session. Houston: Office of the *Telegraph*, 1838.

Journals of the Senate of the Called Session of Congress Convened at the City of Houston, on the 25th Day of September, 1837; and of the Regular Session, on the Sixth Day of November, 1837. Houston: National Banner Office, 1838.

Journals of the Senate of the Republic of Texas: First Congress, Second Session. Houston: Telegraph Office, 1838.

Kendall, George Wilkins. *Narrative of the Texan Santa Fe Expedition*. 2 vols. London: Wiley and Putnam, 1844.

Kennedy, William. *The Rise, Progress, and Prospects of the Republic of Texas*. 2nd ed. 1841. Reprint, Fort Worth: The Molyneaux Craftsmen, 1925.

Lamar, Mirabeau B. *Verse Memorials*. New York: W. P. Fetridge & Co., 1857.

Latham, Francis S. *Travels in the Republic of Texas, 1842*. Edited by Gerald S. Pierce. Austin: Encino Press, 1971.

La Vere, David. *Life Among the Texas Indians: The WPA Narratives*. College Station: Texas A&M University Press, 1998.

Lawrence, A. B. *Texas in 1840, Or the Emigrant's Guide to the New Republic*. 1840.

Reprint, Austin: W. M. Morrison Books, 1987.

Laws of the Republic of Texas. Vol. 1. Houston: Office of the *Telegraph*, 1838.

Leach, Joseph. *The Typical Texan: Biography of an American Myth.* Dallas: Southern Methodist University Press, 1952.

Lester, C. Edwards. *Life and Achievements of Sam Houston, Hero and Statesman.* New York: Hurst and Company, 1883.

Lubbock, Francis Richard. *Six Decades in Texas or Memoirs of Francis Richard Lubbock.* Edited by C. W. Raines. Austin: Ben C. Jones & Company, 1900.

McCalla, William L. *Adventures in Texas, Chiefly in the Spring and Summer of 1840.* Philadelphia: printed by the Author, 1841.

McDonnold, B. W. *History of the Cumberland Presbyterian Church.* Nashville: Cumberland Presbyterian Church, 1899.

McDowell, Catherine W., ed. *Now You Hear My Horn: The Journal of James Wilson Nichols 1820–1887.* Austin: University of Texas Press, 1967.

Moore, Stephen L. *Eighteen Minutes, The Battle of San Jacinto and the Texas Independence Campaign.* Dallas: Republic of Texas Press, 2004.

———. *Savage Frontier.* Vol. 2, *1838–1839.* Denton: University of North Texas Press, 2006.

Morris, T. A. *Miscellany: Consisting of Essays, Biographical Sketches, and Notes of Travel.* Cincinnati: L. Swormstedt & H. G. Power, 1852.

Olmsted, Frederick Law. *A Journey through Texas or, a Saddle-Trip on the Southwestern Frontier.* 1857. Reprint, Austin: University of Texas Press, 1978.

Peareson, P. E. "Reminiscences of Judge Edwin Waller." *Southwestern Historical Quarterly* 4, no. 1 (1900): 33–53. http://www.tsha.utexas.edu/publications/journals/shq/online/v004/n1/article_6.html.

———. *Sketch of the Life of Judge Edwin Waller.* 1874. Reprint, Austin and New York: Jenkins Publishing/Pemberton Press, 1970.

Raines, C. W. "Enduring Laws of the Republic of Texas. II." *Southwestern Historical Quarterly Online* 2, no. 2 (1898):152–61. http://www.tsha.utexas.edu/publications/journals/shq/online/v002/n2/article_4_.

Ramsay, Jack C., Jr. *Thunder Beyond the Brazos.* Austin: Eakin Press, 1985.

Reagan, John H. "The Expulsion of the Cherokees from East Texas." *Southwestern Historical Quarterly Online* 1, no. 1 (1897): 38–46. http://www.tsha.utexas.edu/publications/journals/shq/online/v001/n1/article_9.html.

"The Reminiscences of Mrs. Dilue Harris II." *Southwestern Historical Quarterly Online* 4, no. 3 (1901):155–89. http://www.tsha.utexas.edu/publications/journals/shq/online/v004/n3/article_3.html.

"Reminiscences of Mrs. Dilue Harris. III." *Southwestern Historical Quarterly Online* 7, no. 3 (1904): 214–22. http://www.tsha.utexas.edu/publications/journals/shq/online/v007/n3/article_3_.

Republic Claims Search. Texas State Archives. http://www.tsl.state.tx.us/arc/repclaims/index.html.

Roberts, Madge Thornall, ed. *The Personal Correspondence of Sam Houston.* Vol.

1, *1839–1845*. Denton: University of North Texas Press, 1996.

———. *The Personal Correspondence of Sam Houston*. Vol. 2, *1846–1848*. Denton: University of North Texas Press, 1998.

Roemer, Ferdinand. *Texas: With Particular Reference to German Immigration and the Physical Appearance of the Country*. 1849. Reprint, Austin: Eakin Press, 1995.

Senate Journal, Republic of Texas: First Congress, First Session. Columbia: G. & T. H. Borden, 1837.

Sheppard, Lorna Geer. *An Editor's View of Early Texas: Texas in the Days of the Republic as Depicted in the* Northern Standard *(1842–1846)*. Austin: Eakin Press, 1998.

Sibley, Marilyn McAdams. *Lone Stars and State Gazettes: Texas Newspapers before the Civil War*. College Station: Texas A&M University Press, 1983.

Siegel, Stanley. *The Poet President of Texas: The Life of Mirabeau B. Lamar, President of the Republic of Texas*. Austin: Jenkins Publishing/Pemberton Press, 1977.

———. *A Political History of the Texas Republic 1836–1845*. Austin: University of Texas Press, 1956.

Sinks (Julia Lee) Papers. Dolph Briscoe Center for American History. University of Texas at Austin.

"Sinks, Julia Lee," Vertical File. Dolph Briscoe Center for American History. University of Texas at Austin.

Smith (Ashbel) Papers. Dolph Briscoe Center for American History. University of Texas at Austin.

Smither, Harriet, ed. "Diary of Adolphus Sterne." *Southwestern Historical Quarterly Online* 31, no. 1(1927): 63–83. http://www.tsha.utexas.edu/publications/journals/shq/online/v031/n1/article_8_.

———. *Journals of the Fourth Congress of the Republic of Texas 1839–1840*. 3 vols. Austin: Texas Library and Historical Commission, State Library, 1930.

———. *Journals of the Sixth Congress of the Republic of Texas, 1841–1842, to Which Are Added the Special Laws*. 3 vols. Austin: Von Boeckmann-Jones, 1940–1945.

Smithwick, Noah. *The Evolution of a State or Recollections of Old Texas Days*. Austin: University of Texas Press, 1984.

Sons of DeWitt Colony Texas website. http://www.tamu.edu/ccbn/dewitt/dewitt.htm.

Sowell, A. J. *Life of "Big Foot" Wallace*. Austin: State House Press, 1989.

Spellman, Paul N. *Forgotten Texas Leader: Hugh McLeod and the Texan Santa Fe Expedition*. College Station: Texas A&M University Press, 1999.

Stiff, Edward. *The Texan Emigrant: Being a Narration of the Adventures of the Author in Texas and a Description of the Soil, Climate, Productions, Minerals, Towns, Bays, Harbors, Rivers, Institutions, and Manners and Customs of the Inhabitants of That Country*. 1840. Reprint, Waco: Texian Press, 1968.

Terrell, Alex W. "The City of Austin from 1839 to 1865." *Southwestern Historical*

Quarterly Online 14, no. 2 (1910): 113–28. http://www.tsha.utexas.edu/publi-catons/journals/shq/online/v014/n2/article_2.html.

———. "Recollections of General Sam Houston." *Southwestern Historical Quarterly Online* 16, no. 2 (1912): 113–36. http://www.tsha.utexas.edu/publica-tions/journals/shq/online/v016/n2/article_1_print.html.

Texas Slave Narratives website. freepages.genealogy.rootsweb.com/~ewyatt/_borders/Texas%20Slave%20Narratives/Texas%20Index.html.

Thrall, Homer S. *A Pictorial History of Texas, from the Earliest Visits of European Adventurers, to A.D. 1879*. St. Louis: N.D. Thompson and Company, 1879.

Tyler, Ron and Lawrence R. Murphy. *The Slave Narratives of Texas*. Austin: State House Press, 1997.

"A Visit Up the Colorado River: Extracts From an Anonymous Diary 17–25 July 1838." *Telegraph and Texas Register*. May 1, 1839.

Wallace, Ernest, David M. Vigness, and George B. Ward. *Documents of Texas History*. Austin: Texas State Historical Association, 2002.

Ward (Thomas William) Papers. Austin History Center. Austin, TX.

Waters, Andrew, ed. *I Was Born in Slavery: Personal Accounts of Slavery in Texas*. Winston-Salem: John F. Blair, 2003.

Weems, John Edward. *Dream of Empire: A Human History of the Republic of Texas 1836–1846*. New York: Simon and Schuster, 1971.

Wilbarger, J. W. *Indian Depredations in Texas*. 1889. Reprint, Austin: Eakin Press, 1985. Williams, Amelia W., and Eugene C. Barker, eds. *The Writings of Sam Houston, 1813–1863*. Vol. 2. Austin: University of Texas Press, 1939.

Williams, J. R. *Travis County Residents Biographical Notes*. Vol. 3. Austin History Center. Austin, TX.

Williamson, Roxanne Kuter. *Austin, Texas: An American Architectural History*. San Antonio, Trinity University Press, 1973.

Winkler, Ernest William. "Destruction of Historical Archives of Texas." *Southwestern Historical Quarterly Online* 15, no. 2 (1911): 148–55. http://www.tsha.utexas.edu/publications/journals/shq/online/v015/n2/article_2_.

———. "The Seat of Government of Texas I." *Southwestern Historical Quarterly Online* 10, no. 2 (1906): 140–71. http://www.tsha.utexas.edu/publications/journals/shq/online/v010/n2/article_2_print.html.

———. "The Seat of Government of Texas II." *Southwestern Historical Quarterly Online* 10, no. 3 (1907): 185–245. http://www.tsha.utexas.edu/publications/journals/shq/online/v010/n3/article_1_print.html.

INDEX

Sims, Bartlett, 235
Sims, Captain, 90
Sinks, George, *133*, 240
Sinks, Julia Lee, 87, 113–14, *119*, 120, *122, 133*, 189, 219, 250, 251, 255
    Austin, arrival in, 85–86
    Indian attack, fear of, 144–45, 195
site selection commission,
    Second Congress, 29–30, 32
    Third Congress, 51, 54–58, 60, 62, 70, 125, 243
Sixth Street. *See* Pecan Street
slaves, 7, 10, 56, 72, 92, 151–52, 245, 248, 254, 257
    Austin, city ordinances regarding, 130
    Austin, construction of, 94–95, 97
    Austin, experiences in, 82, 95–97, 145
    Austin, population in, 131
    treatment of, 95–97
Sloat, Mr., 196
Smith, Alfred, 261
Smith, Ashbel (Dr.), 34, 43, 53, 182, 232
Smith, Deaf, 235
Smith, Ezekial, 147, 255
Smith, French, 147, 255
Smith, George (senator), 53
Smith, Henry, 25
Smith, Jackson, 68
Smith, James W. (chief justice), 234
Smith, Mrs. James, 205
Smith, Robert, 254
Smith, Thomas (Major), 184–87, 261
Smith's Hotel, 218
Smithwick, Noah, 191, *214*, 215
Snively, Jacob, 107, 247
Souls, 195
South San Gabriel River, 77
Spicer, Richard M., 237
Spicer, Robert, 93, 241
Spicer's Tavern, 77, 130
Spicewood Springs, 196
Spicewood Springs Road, 263
Spring Creek, 62

St. David's Episcopal Church, 85
St. Louis, 104, 130, 161, 244
St. Mary's Academy, 217
Stafford, William, 15
Stanbery, William, 40
Standiford, James, 235
Stark, Mrs. William, 94
Stark, William, 94
Starr, James (treasury secretary), 243, 247
State Department, 84, 107, 120, 178, 184, 238
Stiff, Edward, 88
Stillwell, John, 245
Stone, Samuel, 213
streets (Austin). *See individual street names*
Sturges, Benjamin (Major), 112
Sulphur Springs, 31
Sutherland, George, 30–33, 227, 228
Swearingen, Richard M. (Dr.), 255
Swisher's Hotel, 218

Tallapoosa River, 36
Tannehill, Jesse, 234
Taylor, Zachary, 220
Tecumseh, 36
Telegraph and Texas Register, 13, 16, 18, 21, 22, 24–27, 30, 48–49, 51, 61–64, 84, 86, 89, 99, 102, 104, 106, 110
Tenoxticlan, 28
Tenth Street. *See* Mulberry Street
Terrell, Alexander, 248
Terrell, George (attorney general), 179–80
Teulon, George, 193–94
Texas Centinel, 132, 152, 154, 158, 170, 252
Texas Declaration of Independence, 14, 18, 56, 69–70, 86, 167, 207, 219
Texas Democrat, 214, 265
Texas National Register, 206, 212–13, 265
Texas Revolution, 3
Texas Sentinel. See Texas Centinel